THE ENCYCLOPÆDIA *of* CURTAINS

THE ENCYCLOPÆDIA *of* CURTAINS

The Complete Curtain Maker

Catherine Merrick and Rebecca Day

Edited by Phoebe Phillips

MERRICK & DAY

THE ENCYCLOPÆDIA *of*
CURTAINS

For the boys:
NWTW NASM ROD CJD

First published 1996
Second impression 1998
Third impression 2000

ISBN 0 9516841 4 0

Production consultant: Kenneth Cowan
Reproduction by Daylight Colour Singapore
Printed and bound in Great Britain by
Butler & Tanner Ltd, Frome and London

FOR MERRICK & DAY:

Photographic and Pictorial Acknowledgements
Diagrams, pp 100-231: Suzanne Kettle
Watercolours, pp8-17: Tom Robb
Photographs, pp2, 18-22, 24, 25(top), 30, 33(top), 36-7, 44-5, 48-50, 54-5, 60-1, 92-4; Brian Harrison

Designer, pp17, 28-9, 31, 40-43, 56-9, 62-9, 74(top) Carolyn Holmes of Carolyn Holmes Interiors
(Photographer: Brian Harrison)

Stylist, Kate Hardy and Photographs, Tony Hopewell pp34, 38-39

Merrick & Day
Redbourne Hall, Redbourne, Gainsborough, Lincolnshire DN21 4JG England

Telephone +44 (0)1652 648814 Facsimile +44 (0)1652 648104
e-mail sales@merrick-day.com Web site: http://www.merrick-day.com

FOREWORD

CURTAINS IN ALL the designs and styles you can imagine are enjoying a revival, but it could be argued that traditional curtain making skills are a forgotten art.

For the past seven years we have been working towards the publication of this book, learning every moment of every working day, trying out ideas, finding the best methods for us and for the best results.

Each design has been a challenge and an opportunity to create something different.

Life and curtains are never dull – there is always something unusual to explore and exciting to discover.

The methods we outline here have been adapted from those developed in our own workroom but there is no reason why you shouldn't in turn adapt them to your own situation and expertise, benefitting from our hard-earned knowledge, eliminating guesswork and enjoying timesaving shortcuts and professional techniques.

These are the tips which, at the beginning, we would have given a fortune to know.

Curtain making encompasses many different skills beyond the sewing machine, from using rubber bands, to pattern cutting, to a little carpentry and a lot of enthusiasm.

Rather than limit the instructions to a few projects, which may or may not suit your needs, we have given careful outlines of techniques which can be applied to an infinite number of styles and designs.

Treat the book like a pick and mix counter; take what you want, and come back for more when you've found out how satisfying it can be to look out at the world through a well dressed window.

Throughout the book, no matter what your experience or skill, we hope you will find what you need, whether it's the simplest seam or the most elaborate swags and tails.

Because we have included a great deal of detailed information, the make-up instructions are coded with a series of needle and thread icons, from one to four.

They indicate the level of skill needed, from very easy to expert. But be encouraged; almost all the techniques, even the four needle ones, depend more on your patience and time than on years of experience.

Getting started is all that it takes to begin.

During the making of this book, we have been given great cause to be thankful to the following friends, colleagues and clients:

Enormous and continuing thanks to Carolyn Holmes of Carolyn Holmes Interiors

also to

Mr & Mrs D Goose

Mr & Mrs G Maitland Smith

Mr & Mrs J Milligan-Manby

Mr G Meace

Mr N Rhodes & Mr R Burgess

Mr & Mrs G Rowles Nicholson

Mrs B Sheldon

Mr & Mrs J Walton

Thanks to Sarah Corney for her editorial assistance and, for their ever present support, to our colleagues at Merrick & Day: Anne, Betty, Brenda, Glynnis and Pauline.

MERRICK & DAY BOOKS AND PATTERNS

THE CURTAIN DESIGN DIRECTORY   THIRD EDITION

A manual of black and white illustrations, with over 300 design ideas for curtains and soft furnishings.
Complete with an exciting new easy to use style guide to enable you to quickly identify
the appropriate window treatment for any situation.
The twelve sections include Design Details, Poles, Valances, Bay Windows, Tall and Narrow Windows,
Problem Windows, Beds and Accessories.
The ultimate guide to the creative world of choosing and designing window treatments.

THE SWAG AND TAIL DESIGN AND PATTERN BOOK

Everything you need to make beautiful swags and tails in one book.
Over 70 swag designs to choose from, supported by make-up notes and full sized swag and tail patterns.
Complete with tracing paper to copy patterns from the Master Pattern Sheet.

SUPPLEMENTARY SWAG PATTERNS

To complement The Swag and Tail Design and Pattern Book, this Master Pattern Sheet contains a further
eight swag patterns graded in size up to 170 cm (67in) wide.
The pattern sheet and tracing paper are presented in a wallet.

PROFESSIONAL PATTERNS FOR TIE-BACKS

Patterns for plain, banana and scalloped shaped tie-backs each in eight sizes.
Each style has clear step-by-step instructions on the pattern sheets; presented in a wallet with tracing paper.

THE FABRIC QUANTITY HAND BOOK

An essential tool for anyone involved in curtain making and design.
Accurate and easy to use – for fabric, fringe and trim quantities.
Includes quantity tables for curtains, valances, pelmets, swags, blinds, bed valances, covers, tablecloths etc

Mail order service available from

Merrick & Day Orders Department
Redbourne Hall, Redbourne, Gainsborough, Lincolnshire DN21 4JG England

Credit card orders
Telephone +44 (0)1652 648814 Facsimile +44 (0)1652 648104
e-mail sales@merrick-day.com Web site: http://www.merrick-day.com

All books are subject to availability.

CREATIVE CURTAIN COURSES

MERRICK & DAY run a range of curtain making courses in their Lincolnshire workroom.
They are based on practical tuition and offer a wealth of professional hints and tips.

CONTENTS

LOOKING BACK: Glimpses of the Past

Curtains are relatively new in history, yet there is no doubt that they are one of the major influences in modern interior decoration. While some of the ideas of the past are perhaps too dramatic and too complicated for contemporary taste, we can learn a great deal by seeing just how our ancestors dealt with the same problems facing us today - a practical need whose solution should also be satisfying to the eye.

Until this century the only records we have came from paintings and drawings. Yet with the exception of a few specialised print-makers, curtains or window treatments of any kind were very much literally and figuratively in the background, obscured by the portraits or genre scenes which were the real subject of the artist's work.

Because of this, in a short visual trip through some of the more recent period influences we have chosen to bring curtains out of their background into fresh, new watercolours which let the windows take centre stage, so to speak, so we can look at the styles in a clear setting. We hope you enjoy the result as much as we did in compiling the sources.

Until recently, windows were the front line in the battle between letting in light and keeping out the enemy, be that marauding soldiers or wind, snow and rain.

At first, protection won, all the time. Windows were small and easily barred at night by loose boards, whilst work stopped when the sun went down. Over many centuries, as fighting waned the area of open windows and doors increased. Larger and better-made shutters were hinged onto the frames, and hooked on the wall. But that still created a dark interior. Oiled paper was put up in the manor houses but it was not very strong. The first glass panes were tiny squares, set into wood with heavy leading, but nonetheless glazed windows were a great advance.

Gradually as glass became clearer and thinner, the panes grew larger, and the frames narrower. In 1597 when Bess of Hardwick finished building her famous Hall, its enormous windows set a style which has never gone out of fashion.

Left
A late medieval hall. With its vaulted ceiling and stone floor, it must have been quite cold. One answer was to hang the walls with some sort of covering. This acted as an insulator and as visual warmth, helping to raise the temperature.

This illustration from an illuminated manuscript shows thick wool or leather wall hangings, which could be easily taken down and sent with the owner to make his travels more comfortable.

Later the effect of pleated folds of cloth was repeated in wood linenfold panelling.

Hangings were always set on the wall and over doorways - they never appear at windows, which were still being left open during the day and shuttered tightly at night or during extremes of weather.

Right
During the 17th and early 18th centuries curtains were still seldom seen at windows which were too new and far too important a status symbol to be covered in any way. Some builders did introduce the decorative effect of stained glass but mostly they were left plain and unadorned.

Curtains were used to enclose much smaller areas where their insulating qualities could be better appreciated. Bed hangings were always present both for warmth and privacy; in homes where rooms were used by everyone in the family the only place to be alone was inside your bed, the curtains drawn tightly closed.

Although we associate images of stately homes with magnificent four-posters, even the humblest housewife used bed curtains, as this sketch of a clock-maker's home shows. The room is almost a carbon copy of one in a Hogarth painting of the 1730s, so we can assume it is typical of working artisan conditions; the bed is carefully divided off by the dormer wall and the long curtain. The window is shuttered with open trellis; the temperature of the room was obviously cold, because the wife is working with her cloak wrapped right around her body and her head.

Above
Later in the century, one of a series of etchings shows a curtain over a window, drawn back to show the winter moon.

Right
In a more prosperous home of the same period, the big window at the back of the room is still uncovered, although a length of fabric has been drawn to one side. But the curtain has come in from the bedroom and is acting as a protector to keep books from collecting too much dirt and soot from open fires. There must have been a ladder to reach the top. Books and papers were still precious commodities.

The draped table makes a little extra warmth for knees and toes.

Right
Huge, swagged curtains were essential as stage sets for paintings, and especially amongst late 17th and early 18th century portrait artists.

A bare window would be shown quite happily at the back of a scene, but the foreground would be framed handsomely with an elaborate bravura of rich fabric.

Many early historians thought these curtains were in the sitter's room but we know now they were part and parcel of any artist's studio, such as the detail of one sketched here. Both chair, curtain and even the same doorway would appear in various paintings and drawings, as the artist would have only limited sittings with his subjects, and the background was probably painted in the studio.

However, happily for us, some clients were proud of their homes and intended the painting to be a record of the family mansion as well as the people. Such paintings give us a real glimpse of everyday life, with tables, objects and so on, but..... few curtains!

Right
By the late 1700s, curtains were used to decorate around the frame, although they were seldom functional. That was left to the shutters, still a fine feature of Georgian homes. This grand reception room c. 1785 is typical of the period, with its clerestory arches left bare, the windows swagged and tailed with slender fringed falls of rich silk.

In fact, compared to the Regency curtains only a few years later (see overleaf) these are simple and elegant, with relatively little trimming.

By the second half of the 18th century, domestic architecture had settled into a period of such style and grace that we are still trying to copy its best attributes today.

Rooms were carefully planned to follow classical proportions, detailed plaster mouldings painted in pinks, blues and greens gave quiet elegance to every corner.

Most period homes of today reflect our own preferences for clutter and comfort - clusters of tables, chairs, lamps, and so on, but in the 18th century rooms were bare. Furniture was scarce, especially in the summer. It was moved from room to room as required, for entertaining or just relaxing. An outdoor life and continual visiting for long periods meant relatively little time spent at home.

Below

This room was crowded in the original painting with friends and family, but without the occupants, we can see how it looked when there was no entertaining. The curtains have been left one rolled up, valance and all, and the other let down, a sheer blue silk.

Below

Not all rooms were as grand. This little study is delightfully simple, with nothing to keep the 18th century writer from staring out at the street except a bit of muslin.

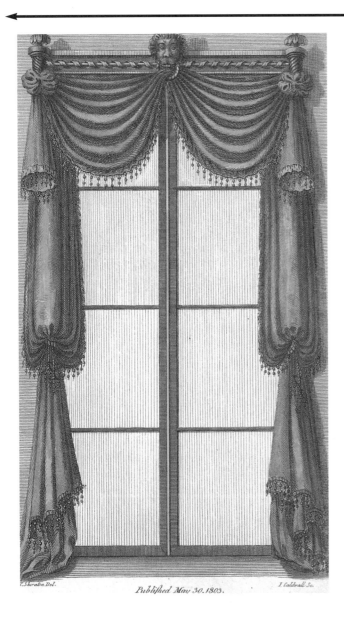

C. Sheraton Del.   Published May 30. 1803.   J. Caldwall Sc.

choux puffs at the top. The dress curtains at the sides are taken up into Bishop's sleeves with tassels. The fringe shows that these are made of two pieces, the sleeve and the descending tail falling on the floor.

Right
A similar design, also from 1803; swathes of fabric hang from classical masks, in front of a box pleated valance trimmed with fringe. The side curtains are caught up in Bishop's sleeves with tassels. This design could be made in one piece, with the side hangings tacked up in the middle and then allowed to fall to the floor; a braided hem completed the elaborate decoration.

Designs in books and catalogues were popular in all the great houses and rapidly growing cities of fashionable Europe. Greek and Roman influences were very strong during this period of exploration and excavation of ancient towns and civilizations.

Every owner of a fine mansion house wanted to show off his taste and hospitality. Interior decorations were usually designed by the architect or the furniture maker to create a sympathetic ambiance for the rest of his work.

At the height of the Regency period, furniture and interior craftsmen published catalogues of their designs, offered to the genteel public for their enjoyment and to collect orders.

Thomas Sheraton's firm created these two designs; as advertisements for the company the curtains were more fanciful than could be realised in gilt wood and fabric, and anyone seeking to copy them today would be hard pressed to make them accurately.

Above
This lovely plate from Ackerman's magazine shows a pair of swags taken through a central lion's head ring, mounted on a shallow carved gilt cornice box. At each side there are bell-shaped trumpets with

←

Above
We are not the first to recommend simple white muslin swags for the summer - this Scandinavian room of the 1880s could be a model for any of our no-sew projects.

Left
An American home overlooking the Hudson river shows a restraint not usually associated with the height of the Victorian period, 1862.

The very grand arched bay window has been leaded to provide some pattern in an enormous expanse of glass. Inside the room a narrow shaped pelmet holds only the lightest of fixed sheer curtains. Today we can still admire the clean yet entirely fresh effect of the deep red walls and sheer white printed muslin curtains.

Unhappily we may not have such a fabulous window to show off, but it shows how effective simple sheers can be even in the most formal room schemes.

Left
Another example of less being more. This simple net valance of the same 1860s period would look just as delightful now, although in a modern home we might appreciate blinds underneath which could be pulled up during the day to give some privacy. You could achieve the same effect with lace panels dyed in rich colours, then-hemmed into points and fringed and tasselled. Or you could use a coarse net frill instead of the fringe.

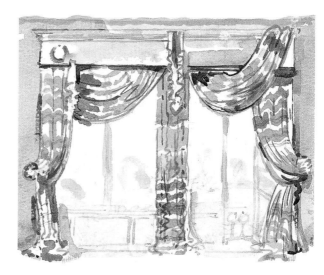

Above left
In Scotland in the 1900s the remarkable Charles Rennie MacIntosh was designing bold, ebonised furniture and interiors. This four poster could only be from that period. The bed hangings are appropriate in their design and construction, falling from a built-in rail, and featuring the famous tulip pattern, its colours picked up in the striped built-in settee.

Above
In spite of all the modern movements the lust for the theatrical continued; these truly swaggering swags were copied in 1910 for an opera house.

Left
In France the sinuous Art Nouveau style was sweeping all before it. A gathered portiére of green velvet hangs from an embroidered yoke, with flanking cabinets in the same style.

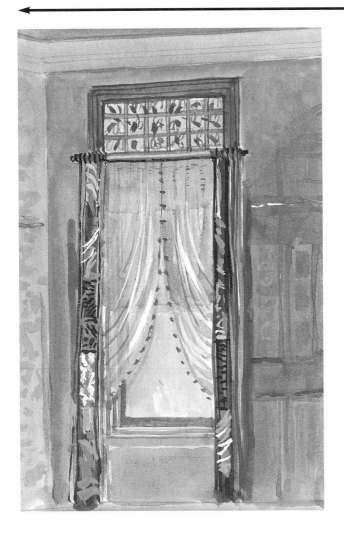

Above
The extent of oriental influence is seen in this simple panelled fall of patchwork brocade hung on a wooden pole below the fanlight. An Aesthetic dandy of the 1890s would have been at home in this Tiffany room.

Above right
The Egyptian influence on the 1920s-1930s is evident in this Art Deco treatment, the curved pelmet echoing the shape of one of Nefertiti's collars, the wall behind stencilled in simplified geometric style.

Right
With this 1950s New York apartment, the wheel of classical influence has come full circle. Starting from a look at a Danish painting of 1870, then married to the delicate furniture of Sheraton and modern iridescent silk, here is a curtain treatment worthy of the name. Not for shy or retiring owners, deep blue rep has been used in huge quantities, then bordered with white and blue fringe which has been hand-sewn with crystals for extra glitter.

Today our homes are more diverse and more individual than ever before. Even the word contemporary is hard to define - does it mean the quiet neutrality of an elegant glass town house like the one above?

Is it the traditional combination of comfort and warmth we see in the homes of our clients like the study on the right? A dramatic fling of satin or the country charm of chicks in the nursery (top right)?

None of us are sure what will be defined a hundred years from now as <u>the</u> room of the 90s, but as we learn more about making curtains every day, we are fascinated by ideas from the past, and enthused by the concepts of the future. We hope these portfolios of sketches and pictures will give you the incentive to get started. We intend to be around photographing our work (right) and perhaps yours, for a very long time to come.......

STYLE AND DESIGN PORTFOLIO

This section is a look at the range of designs we have worked with during the past few years. The majority of the projects have been made in our workshop, a few have come from friends and family. We've tried to include as many styles as possible, so that it becomes a portfolio for you to browse through, a gateway to inspiration.

Planning for new situations and working with interior designers is a constant pleasure to us; every home is unique, and every one has their own ideas about what he or she needs and wants. The most successful designs combine both requirements to create something special and appropriate.

Whether you are making your own, or choosing a style for someone else to make, spend as much time as you need in looking through the these pictures, and as many other sources you can find - there are some suggestions at the back of the book. Imagine the possible variations which will take an appealing detail and adapt it to your own situation. It's those little touches which give an enormous fillip; a lovely finial, an extra-long tail, an antique fabric pelmet used to blend new and old together.......the potential is unlimited.

The best ideas can temper your dreams with reality. It's surely a mistake to settle for dirt-concealing grey when your heart is crying out for magnificent red, but having the courage of your convictions should be tempered with considerations of other options; a blast of red top to bottom is not the only answer - a generous topping of crimson silk over soft print curtains might give you the zing without making everyone dizzy. Think about proportions, too. Throughout our step-by-step instructions in the second half of the book, we've included advice about changing depth, height widths and lengths to suit individual rooms.

Above all, remember that when you furnish a home you are creating a setting for your life; curtains are one of the most important elements in a room.

Left and detail, right
This country hallway welcomes you to a casual but very comfortable life. Burnt gold velvet was chosen to reflect all the warm ruddy colours of ancient leather and faded upholstery. A velvet brown braid finishes off the edges.

Sill length curtains would have looked a little skimpy - these go right down to the old chest beneath, and really make an enormous difference to the design .

The curtains are quite full so they can be pulled close on cold winter evenings, but the pelmet is fairly flat, with only a little extra width to allow the fabric to hang from the old iron butcher's hooks set directly into the beam. Many cottage windows have old beams above them, and this is a brilliant solution.

Look for unusual accessories like the hooks; attractive, functional, adding that touch of wit.

Left
The colours in the antique tapestry pelmet dictated the soft green of the new curtains, with tassels and fringe blended in green and gold.

The pelmet makes use of an old piece which might otherwise have to be cut up into cushions. The door curtain is quite a different colour; it was made in really thick heavy velvet to keep out any stray draughts. A tassel braid is used down both sides.

The pole is a lot wider than the door so the curtain can be pushed to the side when the door is in use. A portière rod would be an alternative; attaching directly onto the door.

The curtains also frame ceramics and plants on the window sill, and make a background for the lovely old wooden, iron-bound box on the table in front.

Comforts have been allowed for in the cushioned chairs, the soft wall lights, and pictures hang low enough to enjoy while waiting for the post.

Above
Another unusual pelmet which makes use of antique materials. A landing window with little room for manoeuvre was too deep to make a blind feasible. The solution; a lightly-stiffened fixed pelmet over some simple scoops of muslin, edged to match.

21

Left
The formal elegance of a lovely arched fanlight above a Georgian door.

The natural balance of this classic doorway blends with the portiére which keeps out the also classic draughts. The curtain is richly detailed in damask silk, lined and interlined, the tie-back and leading edge fringed to match. The brass portiére rod is heavy enough to take the weight.

Right
A cottage back door with another portiére, hung on a plastic track which goes round the left-hand corner so that the curtain can be pulled back when the door is in use. The fabric is a quiet print, and the smocked tie-back suits this informal interior. Like any effective door curtain it has been lined and interlined to keep out draughts.

Both portiéres have hand sewn French headings; this is the best choice when you have to stack back the curtain.

Old-fashioned Edwardian door curtains in chenille, a pleasant alternative, are usually fairly narrow, so we recommend buying a pair and seaming them together for the best result. Take off one side fringe from each pair and use for tie-backs.

Left

On a much more formal landing, far from casual but without the cold grandeur of perfect reproduction; the gilt cornice box came from a demolished castle, the tapestries falling below came from France, and new gold silk curtains with antique braid on the leading edges tie everything together.

Silk in plain colours can be bought today at very low cost, and it makes sense to use it in generous quantities to create this magnificent effect, while the more valuable antique tapestry swathes used up a panel too small to be well displayed on a wall.

The curtains are scooped up permanently so the only functional items are the soft, unlined Roman blinds in matching silk. These protect the silk and the antique fabrics, bathing the entire staircase hall in a golden light which creates a perpetual summer throughout the year.

The blinds are fitted within the recess.

Surprisingly the curtains and blinds were up already before the owner found the cornice box and tapestries, but what a magnificent ensemble it all makes now!

Above
A detail of another carved cornice box, with a quilted valance.

Try architectural salvage companies for similar boxes, or elaborate door frames or carvings which can be re-built.

Right, below
A common problem when curtaining stairs without landings are the uneven lengths of fabric on one or the other side of the window.

Here it has been cleverly solved by letting one side of the heavy red velvet curtains drift onto the stairs in a rich puddle of crimson.

That may take up too much space on a narrower staircase but here the side is held back by

brass bands. If you have young children or family members who are careless or might be likely to trip, then try another solution, perhaps just one curtain swept across onto the longest side - something like a door curtain. Fix it permanently to the pelmet or track and use a blind underneath to control the light.

The smallest room is usually just off the hall or landing, and its decoration can be left to chance. But knowing it will be used generally for only minutes at a time, why not make it into a tour-de-force.

Most cloakrooms share the same problems; a narrow space, a small window and too high a ceiling.

Right
A modern version of the 18th century print room, with plenty to look at on the walls, and a neat, elegant Roman blind with black and cream edging. Classic.

Far right
Some kind of blind is a good solution; this is in fact an upstairs dressing room but it shares the same difficulties. Here a flowered Austrian blind with uneven stringing can be left permanently tied up in pretty scallops; it is backed by a plain Roman blind for privacy.

Below right
Another unlined blind, this time a fantailed design which is extremely decorative.

Below far right
An even simpler Roman blind, the base cut in jester points underneath the batten.

Above
These rich red felt curtains were the perfect solution to a double view - they had to be equally attractive from both sides of the arch. This pair were made up in the usual way, but it would have been perfectly possible to make them into a no-sew project. The interlined double layers of felt hang from a pole set inside the arch on the door side. They do close for cold and stormy winter evenings, but most of the time they are held back by a tassel. One of the great advantages when you use felt to make up large curtains like these is that the fabric comes in extra-wide sizes.

Left
This lovely living room is one of our favourites, with its tranquil atmosphere. The curtains also deal with the need to accommodate two French doors and windows in the same room; their tops are at uneven heights.

If the poles had been fixed at the usual height above their frames, the effect would have been jarring, calling attention to the difference.

The poles were both placed at the height of the taller door, and that created a wonderful sweep right across the room.

The curtains are vanilla silk taffeta, goblet headed with an attached valance, hanging from painted cream poles.

Hand sewn goblets on the heading are only three inches deep - they can be up to 6 inches but then they will look much more prominent; here the aim was to blend the curtaining into the room leaving just enough detail in the frilled valance to create texture and interest.

Attached valances are the best way of using a valance without losing any light.

Below
Ombras are usually in metal; here wooden ones-been painted in vanilla and gilt to blend in with the curtain fabric and the matching poles. Most hardware can be painted.

Left
In a very masculine room owned by a bachelor farmer, the effect is achieved by using tartan as the main pattern. The curtains are nonetheless made with considerable fine detail in the hand-sewn heading.

The red of the tartan is reflected in almost every object in the room and in all the soft furnishings except for one or two cushions in green and brown.

Below
To appreciate the difference curtains can create, look again at this detail of the room on the previous page and the other pictures of the living room on this and the subsequent pages. In both the walls and ceiling are light cream, with neutral carpets; there are traditional portraits on the walls, comfortable chairs and fresh flowers; but with light upholstery and especially the long run of light curtains, the room below is all freshness and elegance, while the room on the left and overleaf reflects a more casual, country farmhouse life, perfectly suited to the the owner's interests and hobbies.

Remember curtains usually cover a large area and they become an important focal point in the room.

Left

The pole is old, and had been found in the attic when the owner moved in. It was brushed with dark woodstain to blend with the antiques.

The curtains are goblet pleated, to create good, heavy folds of cloth without feminine frills or flounces. The goblets are longer than the ones on the vanilla curtains on the previous page, and you can see that these are more substantial and like tubes rather than the traditional wineglass effect.

Right

The other side of the living room, with its huge Jacobean fireplace. There are no windows here but the tartan continues in a sofa throw on the arm just out of the picture, and on backs of the cushions scattered all around.

A huge fringed shawl in blending colours covers the big armchair, adding extra texture and repeating the fringe on the tartan tablecloth.

Left

Detail of the tie-backs. There are two sets of tie-backs which are used at various times; the tasselled ones are in the big picture on the previous page, and these, more tailored, are wide bands which create the effect of a kilt. Tie-backs can often be used to add a touch of contrast, but here they are in place not just to keep the curtains open but also to let your eye sweep over the matching fabric, in an unobstructed line to the floor. With the tassels or these wide bands, the lined and interlined curtains can be carefully dressed to create an almost kilt-like effect of deep, swinging pleats.

Right
Even the tablecloth gets the tartan top treatment. The table isn't used too often for drinks or food, so the wool makes a satisfactory throw, and it's been fringed along all the sides to add the finishing touch.

However, where the table is used for dining, or young children might be a problem you can add a glass top or choose a blending, washable cotton instead.

Left
A window looking down onto a peaceful scene, with an antique folding chair and table creating a little corner to relax while reading a book or sipping a cup of coffee.
The wallpaper is a traditional architectural pattern in green and wine, and the interlined taffeta curtains pick up the colour, adding a little extra sparkle with a double-coloured block fringe which defines the edges in green and red.

This is a formal swag and tail treatment,

although the swags are detailed with three deep scoops, and the centre swag is slightly shallower to allow more light into the room.

To avoid having the window frame show where the swags intersected, two small underswags were added, marked with a bolster tassel.

The cone-shaped tails are quite long, narrow at the top and wider at the bottom to give the whole effect substance and elegance. The swags are interlined with domette

for firmness, the curtains have a heavier interlining to allow them to hang softly but firmly.

The block fringing makes a strong statement with its two colours in distinct strands.

A twisted fringe of two or three colours usually blends into the curtain because none of the colours stand out.

Below
The top of the pelmet board is edged with rope to define the shape and add an extra touch.

Left

A good example of how simple fabric can be enhanced with careful detail and a substantial pole. These plain, even austere pole-hung curtains in natural hessian, with almost no trimming except for an inset braid on the leading edges and above the hem.

The heavy black pole with matching rings speak the same quiet language of a cool, almost architectural treatment; only brass finials and bracket ends add a bit of glitter.

The hessian is lined and interlined so that it hangs in perfect, heavy pleats. The rings are hand sewn directly onto the curtain, and they will have to be unpicked whenever the curtains are cleaned. Only the natural coloured tassels hung from the edges of the pole contribute a touch of frivolity.

When you inset braid in this way, the margin of plain curtain on the leading edge should always be less than the margin of curtain at the hem; this gives an extra bit of depth to the base.

Severe styles like this should never be puddled on the floor - they should just clear the boards or carpet so that the folds hang perfectly straight.

Below

A detail of the top. In spite of the deep pleats this is quite an economical design - it uses only twice the width of the window and yet looks handsome and beautifully tailored.

Left
A magnificent French window which brought out the best in our designer - the result brings an incredible feeling of light and freshness into this spacious living room.

We had the advantage of not worrying about access - the French doors are kept closed all the time - and so we could let the airy swathes of fabric fall in the most graceful swags and billows, without having to be too practical!

A table in the front was chosen because its light lines echoed the feeling of the delicate print of the sheer fabric.

The curtains are made of a generous amount of unlined cotton lawn, showing off the hand-blocked pattern in gold and black, based on a Saxon medallion.

The swags have been lined in plain cream so that they have a little weight and body; the tails have been lined and interlined in order to hang properly in front of the pole without blowing out or moving too much in the summer air.

We made the tails first without the interlining, but they looked too limp; re-thinking the make up, persuaded us to add the extra stiffening of domette, and now it always looks just right.

The curtains themselves are hung on a track behind and below the pole, which has been left for the swags and tails.

Even though it need not carry much weight, the pole has to be heavy enough to make a clear statement and it's been painted black to emphasise this. Cream would have been too light, but

it might have also looked well with gilt.

The swags and tails are actually made of five different pieces of material, although the end result looks like a bravura draping of a single thrown length!

An important part of the effect is the light filtering through the fabric. A dark fabric would have ruined this.

The design could be easily copied for a no-sew project using yards of light muslin or even silk organza, stapled to the underside of the pole, with swags tacked on in the same way.

But we wouldn't try to make the same crisp tails. It would be better to let them fall naturally in more billows.

Left
A quietly elegant living room with a scallop-shape pelmet board and curtains, in a gently softly-coloured printed linen.

Inside it is all comfort and tradition, with beautiful antique pieces set against fabric battened against the walls, and shown off by stripped pine doors.

The fabric is a pretty rosy print; all the lengths used here were the same, but prints often come in two weights, one for upholstery and a lighter weight for the curtains. The handsewn pencil pleated valance has a

contrast top, and a hand-sewn knotted rope below shows off two tassels hanging down at either end.

Pencil pleating tape is available which will make the job easier for beginners. We hand sew most headings because you can control each inch so much more carefully, pulling in or sideways, or up or down in tiny amounts. Nonetheless, you can achieve very good results if you use tape wisely, choosing a good make, and follow instructions.

The same two soft colours make up the fan-

topped block fringe, hand sewn along the lower edge of the pretty valance.

The curtains are held back by rope ties to display a most vital part of the ensemble, an unusual blind with calligraphic decoration.

The central blind makes an immediate impact no matter who comes into the room, and so the curtains are seldom drawn except in the coldest of winter evenings.

Below
Detail of valance.

Left
 One of the details in this room which gave us the greatest pleasure to make are the little rosettes at the top of each tail, the stripes circling around to create a subtle point.

Below
The colour of this particular silk taffeta was so rich and glorious that the designer decided to use the most elegant of tassel tie-backs in order to let the taffeta and the colour show to best advantage.

The rope and tassels were custom made in gold, green and purple.

Today there are quite a few combinations kept in stock at major suppliers or at the better department stores.

Left
A stunning dining room, with dramatic intensity in the colours and choice of curtain style.

Dark green silk taffeta is made up so generously that every fold seems to gleam in the light; the swagged top is thrown over a pole, edged in purple fringe. The tails hang fairly loosely fixed to the pole.

Because the swags allow most of the pole to show, it was reeded in burnished gold.

Striped fabric swags work remarkably well, even in much simpler fabrics than this silk. Combining two brilliant fabrics like this brings a real sense of the theatre.

Tails are lined in the curtain fabric so that they show both surfaces as they fall.

Left
Simple yet luxuriouxly rich and warm, with its plain colourings and polished formal and country furniture, this dining room creates the most comfortable atmosphere for any dinner party.

The curtains are in red damask, with no decoration except the antique braid on the valance.

The slight variations in colour and tone which patterns the silk damask is reflected from the window onto the table, and emphasizes the ruddy glow of mahogany and oak, which will look just as relaxing in candle-light.

Below
The valance is unusual; it hasn't been stiffened, and it lies almost flat, with just a few tucks to give the braid and fabric a little extra sparkle.

The fringe is applied right to the edge of the valance so the light filters through it. There are always debates about this - many curtain makers prefer to put the fringe higher up so that it looks more substantial, but here the filtered light seems to add to the general effect of comfortable formality.

The braid is handsewn, its curves echoing the gently-scalloped and fringed edge. The braid and fringe are probably genuine gold thread, so old that they look burnished rather than glittery, adding the final touch to the window.

Above
Against the current trend for pastel prints in country kitchens, this is a magnificent treatment with a bold, unusual fabric which would also be suitable for any formal living room.

The cabinets are natural wood, the baskets and copper samovar with the black iron chandelier are set off by the gold leaf motif on green, divided by vertical red and gold stripes.

Two completely different treatments are quite near each other. There is an Austrian blind over the sink, quite practical where anything else might be splashed, and a single tassel-tied curtain over a small awkwardly-placed window.

Although the styles are quite different, the fabric and the matching goblet headings keep them visually harmonised. The goblets on both blind and curtain have been carefully hand-pleated so that the motif is shown off beautifully between the stripes. The motifs could have been reversed, with only the terracotta stripes showing.

Right, below
At the top, underneath the goblets, a sewn rope with knotted motifs marks the start of the full pleats. This is repeated on both the blind and the curtain, which you can see in the picture above.

Far right
The curtain is held back by a tassel which has been looped over a painted ombra. Because of the way the heading has been designed, the stripes have almost disappeared into the folds and only the green and gold motif is visible.

Right
The detail on the curtain
adds a final flourish with
its decorative bracket,
the heavy ribbed pole
painted black, and the
pineapple gilded finial.

All kitchens share one problem; grease, dirt and steam play havoc with many fabrics unless they can be easily washed. You can of course ignore all such practicalities in favour of impact and style, but we do have to warn clients of the risks.

Above
The corner of a garden-utility room might have become just a space where everything is dumped on the way in and out of the house. Instead, with an imaginative cornice box made from an old door frame, and a simple Austrian blind of unlined fabric, the maximum light is achieved with style and charm.
Blinds are the best solution for most kitchens, although if you have deep sills you can set curtains into the recess.

Above and right
Small goblet pleated curtains with a bright red band along the top. Hung from a thin wrought iron pole and held back by wrought iron curtain hooks, simple, effective, and cheerful. A few loose red ties are the only extra decoration. Iron is a good choice in kitchens, but make sure it has a lacquered finish to make it rust-free.

Right
Another pull up blind, in a traditional kitchen, cornered with a dresser of blue and white china.

The owner chose a bouquet print over a blue and white delft chintz, which might have looked too contrived with her collection of china on the dresser. A connecting cornice does repeat the pine moulding of the dresser, set around the pelmet board to make a narrow cornice box.

This sets off the soft-pleated London blind, which hangs in front of the window frame.

Although it can drop down, the blind is usually left up to allow space and air around the herbs and flowerpots growing happily on the window sill.

Left

Fabric runs the same risks in bathrooms as in kitchens, especially when they are as near to the water as this curtain, used instead of a tile splashback. It adds a touch of softness to a large old-fashioned room which can look cold because of its white walls and fittings; a dark wood chair adds another comfortable note.

The pretty unglazed cotton fabric is unlined so it can be washed regularly. Both splashback and matching curtains are slotted through thin brass poles. Curtains at the window are hung from a dormer rod - the fabric is similar but not exactly the same. Matching everything can look too contrived. It's also a way of using short lengths of old prints which are too small to curtain a whole room.

Right

The sharp contrast of an abstract black background with a brilliant printed fabric on a pure white wall.

The no-sew blind lets the fabric speak for itself - the ties are plain white ribbon and there is no braiding or edging.

Right

Here the sparkle of pure white is emphasised by the pristine billows of a white muslin curtain.

An extravagant use of the no-sew techniques is perfect for bathrooms, cloakrooms and nurseries, where you might want to change your curtains a little more often than in the rest of the house.

Left
Simple sheer and washable fabric with gold-printed fleur-de-lis makes the perfect bathroom curtain. The top of the curtain is fixed so that it can be swept up in a dramatic scoop to fall informally onto one side and puddle on the floor.

The fabric is transparent so a blind would be necessary for privacy.

Below left and right
Details of the simple puff heading and the thin brass ombra which holds the scooped folds.

Right
No one ever does the practical thing all of the time. In this lovely bathroom-dressingroom in a traditional Georgian house, we were asked to provide a blind made from a few yards of antique green silk, it's damask trellis pattern still glittering in the light. It was so fragile that it had to be stiffened with Vilene before it could even be laid out.

The design had to be appropriately simple; a central scoop and drop down sides, finished with fringe. Fullness comes from just two pleats.

Left

A guest bedroom with extremely difficult windows, small and high up on the wall on either side of an old chimney stack. This is not unusual in a converted attic which was intended as a floor of small rooms for children and servants.

There were two choices; to fit them with individual blinds, which would have left them looking quite mean and might have shut out the much-needed light, or to treat the two as if they were one ordinary window.

The valance was set right at the ceiling to lose as little of the light as possible. Each window has only one curtain, set under the valance in front of the frame to take advantage of the small amount of wall as a stackback.

The valance is trimmed with a frill of the same fabric, a flowered chintz Twin beds on either side in openwork iron are tucked into the corners, leaving the centre space free and making the room look far more spacious than it is.

If the windows had been different sizes, the same design could have evened them out - the valance would be cut to the longest measurement from ceiling to reveal.

Left
A bouquet of a bedroom, dominated by a lovely tulip chintz, its colours picked up in a dark blue and white checked gingham used to contrast and show off the print.

This shows how successful such a combination can be, and it offers inspiration for choosing to use various patterns together. In the past this would have been considered far too busy, now we can see how perfectly the fabrics set each other off.

The gentle curve of the serpentine valance is echoed in the curved headboard, emphasised by the shirred border of gingham, which reappears as a blind behind the curtains, and on the lampshade.

Above
The curtains are edged with a gingham knife-pleated frill, picked up in the ruffled bed valance, and in the dressing room blind shown on the next page. This kind of repetition in details can bring together all the elements of a room, even when the furniture and ornaments may be very varied in style and colour.

Above right
The blind in the connecting bathroom was made from the tulip chintz rather than the gingham check to bring a touch of bright colour to the small room.

It was made up as a very simple Roman blind pattern with only a little contrast binding on the edges.

Left
This detail of the lamp-shade shows off the attention to detail which characterises the best interior decorators.

The shirred gingham is lined with white, bound top and bottom and edged with a matching tiny frill.

Below
Sometimes smocking can be sewn in a blending thread, but here it was a navy blue, picking up the outline colour in the tulip print and the main colour of the gingham.

To show it off even more, the top stiches were added in a heavier white and blue twisted thread.

Right
An Austrian blind in the dressing room adds a few scallops of its own to the original scheme.

The tulip chintz is bordered by the same gingham frill that was used to edge the curtains in the bedroom.

The smocked heading is also the same, with a contrast band of the chintz at the top, and the check was also used to cover the easy chair between built in cupboards. A dark blue cushion reinforces the colour scheme. The cat was not made in our workroom.

Left
A stately blue and gold
bedroom, the rich classic
damask fabric teamed
with a broad band of
antique gold border, so
completely suited to the
four poster bed, its regal
hangings and the elabo-
rate gilded cornice box
over the curtains.

Because it was such a
marvellous object, the
curtains were designed
around the cornice box,
with a shallow box-
pleated valance tucked
into the bottom, empha-
sised by the gold border,
which also edges the
sides and the hem of the
curtains puddling with
casual luxury on the
floor. You can see that
the border is set inside
the edge to allow a mar-
gin of the blue to show -
this makes the border
seem even larger.

Everything else in the
room uses the same com-
bination of deep smokey
blue damask and gold,
like the footstool, and the
tablecloths, and of course
the bedhangings. A case
of when you have a room
as spectacular as this, let
it speak for itself.

61

Left
Another glamourous bedroom, with a simple corona.

Coronas have become increasingly popular over the past decade, as they provide an easy way of making a focal point for the bedroom which no longer has a fireplace.

They can be surprisingly simple to create, quite easy to sew, and once in place can usually be left for quite a while before they need be taken down for cleaning.

Here a pretty chintz bouquet print has been used for the quilted bedspread and headboard, itself with a shirred plain colour edge and a piped seam for contrast.

The corona is lined in a jade green fabric, its valance fringed in pink and green. Angled lamps are attached to the wall and the corona draped over their stems.

Right
Across the room, the curtains hang from a scalloped shaped pelmet board. The fringe is set below the edge, so the light comes through.

The gathered top is contrast bound in green, and the tie-backs are nicely scalloped to match the pelmet.

Left
Twin bedded room featuring green ivy with dark blue berries on a trellis glazed chintz.

A tiny green and white stripe was chosen as its companion with royal blue as a contrast binding. The high headboards were covered in the chintz with no contrast or edging - the designer felt that their shape was attractive enough to be left to shine in simplicity.

The equally simple Roman blind and the quilted bedcovers are pure white, the spreads just edged in blue and green stripes, with the striped chintz as a knife-pleated valance below.

Right, above
A detail of the curtain valance frill, the blue binding at top and bottom of the narrow knife pleats.

Right below
The tie-backs are particularly pretty, their bound contrast top made as a yoke for the knife-pleated frill.

Somewhere the owner found ivy-patterned china to put on the sill for emphasis!

Above
An unusual four- poster painted bed, romantically frilled and flounced in the gentlest way. The attractive feature was that it's the painted bed-frame which is curved and the valance which is straight.

The choice of fabric and wallpaper was dictated by the painting on the bed - a very soft leaf print and a matching mini-print were the perfect answer. The bed-head is quite plain, the miniprint makes a tailored spread, and ropes were twisted to outline the splits for the bed-posts. A simple cream fringe completed the hangings.

Right
The leaf print was used to make matching blinds and curtains at the window. Only the puff heading below the cream-painted pole interrupts the classic elegance.

Below
The bed canopy is lined with the solid colour chintz, gathered in the middle and centred with a circle of choux in matching fabric.

The bed hangings are also lined in the same fabric, and because the hangings enclose the bed at the sides, the lamps are set inside them, their bases hidden in the folds of fabric. This is one of the best solutions to a common problem - look for lamps which have an angled stem so that they can be moved to accommodate the readers.

In spite of appearances, coronas and four-poster hangings are not that difficult to make. You will need patience, that's all.

Two children's bedrooms of very different style. These are both made to last, but children's rooms can also benefit from a fairly robust no-sew construction.

If you choose that route, use more or less temporary designs with washable fabric, until the children learn to stop swinging on the tassels and crayoning on the walls and fabrics.

Left
For an older child, elegantly strung curtains on a curved pelmet board are light and pretty without being too childish. With smocked and fixed headings, the Roman blind made in blue and white printed fabric is used every day.

At the centre of the gently rising heading is a Maltese cross; contrast binding on the top and on the leading edges of the curtains are the only other decoration.

Right above
Curtains, especially in children's rooms, need not be elaborate. It's true that these are made from silk gingham, but cotton would look just as fresh and appealing.

The box pleated pelmet is set on a yoke, and yellow contrast binding adds a zinging note. The roller blind in gingham is set behind the curtain.

Right
A good solution when you don't have built-in cupboards, especially for a child or guest room, is a simple white curtain set around a small deep pelmet board to make a temporary wardrobe.

The curtain hangs from a net (expanding) wire underneath the board, and a piece of lace edging is tacked around the top to finish it off.

Left
A no-sew design cut and put up in an afternoon.

A new baby, a new nursery, and neither time nor money to convert a room quickly. The perfect solution, this no-sew curtain is held by ribbons looking so fresh and pretty that no baby could be anything but good. A good addition would be to add a white, black-out roller blind to cut out unwanted light, and to make it possible to leave the bows tied up.

Everything can be taken down in a few minutes and put through the washing machine - be sure and choose a muslin or sheer washable fabric that is pre-shrunk.

Although only curtains are shown here, you could make crib hangings and a changing table frill to match, keeping them as simple and reasonably full. But once the child reaches the crawling stage, it might be an idea to re-make the hems to lift them clear of the floor.

The curtains are hung from tie-back hooks to keep it even more simple. If you have another colour on the walls, you can pick it up by changing the white ribbons to match your own scheme.

Right
A detail of the tie-back, showing the wide satin ribbon used instead of ombras or hooks. A little tack at the back holds the curtain itself tight against the frame, so that the ribbon has all the support it needs.

Keep the bows as big and floppy as possible to show off the gleam of the satin.

Below
Another bow is centred at the top to hide the edges of the curtains where they meet. You can see the faint teddy-bear pattern on the sheer, but clipspot or plain muslin would be just as nice for adult rooms.

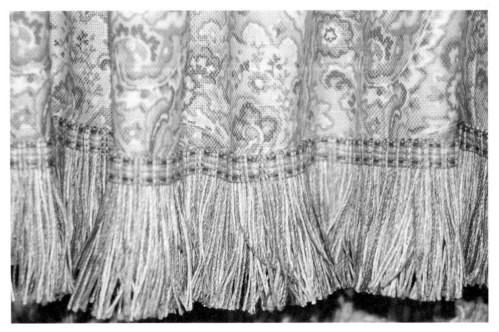

Above, left
A goblet heading, edged with a fringe and with a contrast bound top. The plain fabric is given a little extra punch.

Above
A gathered valance set underneath a deep yoke. The fringe picks up the colour of the piping.

Left
A fringe repeats the same soft pink and cream threads in the woven linen print. This added texture without being too strong a contrast.

Above
The edge of a no-sew pelmet in generous swags of toile de jouy which matches the wallpaper. A big bow finishes off the top.

Above, right
A tassel showing how much richness you can achieve in a small accessory like this.

Right
A smocked tie-back coordinating with a similar valance top.

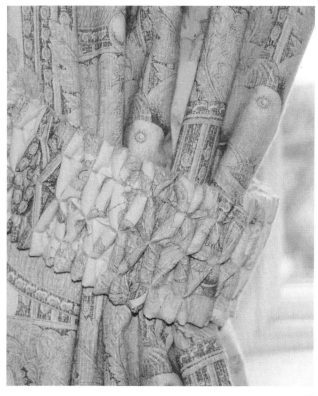

Left
An attached valance, in goblet headed pleats. The shimmering silk is quietly luxurious and needs no contrast, so the self-coloured knife-pleated frill is the only elegant decoration.

Below left
Solving the problem of an awkward angled corner in a bay. The flat pelmet has double pleated trumpets with rope trim.

Below
Cushion edged with a fan braid to finish it off in style.

Right
Braid finishes off a cornered settee. It needs to be tacked on fairly firmly or clothes may catch on the edges.

Below
A tablecloth with a thick, rich fringe.

Below right
Cushion with tasselled and piped edges.

FABRIC GLOSSARY

Fabrics are first referred to either by the name of the fibre, or by the loom on which they are woven or by the name given to the weave construction used in their manufacture. Then they are defined by type - heavy or light, thick or thin, glossy or matt, rough or smooth. And finally they are grouped into plain patterned, and printed. Plain means one colour, although some may have textured surfaces; patterned designs use woven components to create texture and usually colour, while prints have a design only on the surface of a generally smooth fabric.

Within these categories there are many subtle variations - today there is such an amazing choice that the problem is an embarrassment of riches. But do take time and thought to make your decision; fabric is the single most substantial cost in all soft furnishings, and curtains offer a major opportunity to set the style and atmosphere of a room which will be an important part of your life.

In deciding what fabric to buy these are some considerations;

There are variations in handling - wool and most man-made fibres are easy to drape into soft folds while cotton and silk need to be tweaked into shape for the best effect, and linen will crease badly unless you handle it with care.

Fibre content also affects the permanency of the colours - if the fabric has to withstand constant strong sunlight it increases the chance of fading.

The visual effect of a fabric will change dramatically with the weave. A plain weave can hold a crisp design, a deep texture blurs it.

Weight is a factor, too; full length curtains which must keep out cold air, noise and light will have to be fairly heavy, with lining and interlining for the best result.

A light, unlined fabric floats out and adds an airy feeling to the room, but it will give little or no protection against the same elements. Think about the different fabrics we describe to emphasize or change the image of your room; do you want the impression to be quiet and matt, shiny and light-reflecting, or plush with rampant luxury? Do you see your windows heavy with dark, rich textures, or made light and airy with gleaming puffs of taffeta or transparent panels of organdie blowing in the breeze?

Our Print Glossary will help you find your way through the enormous number of designs now available. Prints can add colour and liveliness to a room, but some will work better than others in your own particular space. Fashions change, too. Today using pattern with pattern is increasing the chance of creating a strong impact with blending or clashing motifs.

A much-ignored factor in how your curtains will look is the lining and interlining you choose. The glossary provides a list of easily available materials, and should help you make an informed and satisfactory decision.

And the final touch - decorative trims, both *passementerie* (all kinds of braids and tassels) and fabric trims which you make up yourself.

When you consider cost, which most of us have to do, remember that armfuls of inexpensive fabric, made with enough fullness and imaginatively trimmed, can look more luxurious than a skimpy curtain of hand-dyed silk .

Samples

A vital element in your choice, stores often give you tiny samples. You can get returnable, large samples on request which allow you to see how the fabric looks tacked up on the wall. It may take a few days but it is worth the wait.

NATURAL FIBRES

Cotton

The fibres come from the seed pod of the plant. Untreated yarn contains black seeds, which are easy to see in unbleached calico.

Cotton fibres produce a wide range of weights and constructions, and they make strong, durable fabrics.

Linen

Linen is made from fibres extracted from the stem of the flax plant, producing a strong and durable fabric with a crisp handle. Creasing easily, it is often blended with other fibres to correct this. Linen comes in a wide range of plain colours as well as prints.

With a low residual shrinkage, it is the most stable of all natural fabrics. This makes it a sensible choice in kitchens and bathrooms.

Wool

Wool hair from sheep has inherent flame

Madras cotton

Linen print

Professional Tip

Shrinkage can occur in quite ordinary conditions, such as curtains hung in a bay window with a radiator, getting great heat during the day, with frost and cold at night. Buy 5% extra of curtain fabrics which might be affected.

resistant and insulation properties. It will not hold static electricity, keeping it dirt and dust free, and sheds creases easily. It dyes well and has wonderful natural draping qualities.

Woollen yarn is spun from short staple wool. Worsted is spun from long staple wool and so produces a smoother, silkier yarn. Both are manufactured in a wide range of plain colours as well as woven patterns and some prints.

Silk

Silk is woven from the cocoon of the silkworm. The fibre is fine and lustrous, and very, very strong. It responds well to brilliant dyes and drapes extremely well. Silk is also mixed with other fibres such as

Silk taffeta

wool to add shine and finish, which can also increase its resistance to light; if unprotected direct sunlight will fade the colour of pure silk and rot the fabric.

Silk curtains should be protected by lining and interlining; a sensible additional precaution is to fit a blind at the window which is usually kept down when the room is not in use. If you are using a sheer silk then a blind is vital.

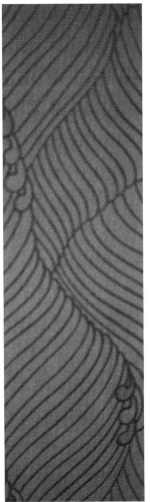

Viscose print

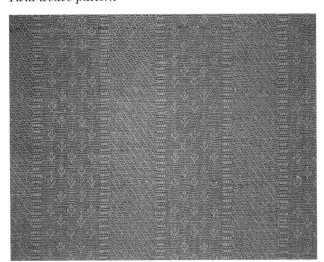

Twill weave pattern

MAN-MADE FIBRES

Man-made fibres fall mainly into two types, regenerated cellulose and synthetics.

VISCOSE

Viscose yarn is made by extruding a cellulose through sieves; the threads harden to form the fibre. As with other man-made fibres, colour can be mixed into the liquid before extrusion.

POLYSTER

Polyester is derived from petroleum. The fibre is inherently flame retardant, and it can be heat set to make a stable, crease-resistant fabric.

It is also used for light weight sheer fabrics. An easy-care polyester and cotton mix is often used for non-iron sheeting and printed bedlinen.

WEAVES

Plain, twill and satin weaves are the three main methods of cloth construction. They vary in the way in which the warp threads, running lengthways down the fabric, are crossed over by the weft threads at right angles.

PLAIN

The simplest weave, the weft alternates under and over the warp. When yarns are the same size and the spacing is even, it becomes a "square cloth", the strongest of all constructions.

HOPSACK

This is sometimes called basket weave; two weft threads go under and over two warp threads to produce a loosely woven but even textured fabric.

RIBBED

The raised, corded effect is created by using a coarser yarn on either the warp or the weft. Reps, grosgrain, taffeta and ottoman are woven in this way. Ribbed fabrics feel good, with a firm body, and are easy to handle.

All ribbed fabrics can be identified by scratching your fingernail lightly over the surface - you'll feel the nail bump over the ribs.

Basket weave

Plain weave
Ottoman rib

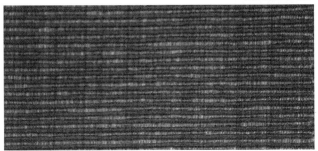

Twill weave stripe

Herringbone check

Damask

TWILL

With twills the weft yarn travels over two warps and then under one. For each row the weft moves on by one which forms diagonal ridges on the face. Twills are useful for plain curtains which rely on braids or fairly heavy ornament.

HERRINGBONE

A variation of twill; changes in the direction of the diagonal produce a herringbone effect.

SATIN AND SATEEN

Surprisingly, these shiny seemingly flat weaves are a twill, but the weft yarn goes over several warp threads producing long 'floats' that lie on the surface of the fabric.

Floats produce a smooth fabric with a shiny surface which looks very tight, although in fact of all weaves it is the weakest. Satin is very popular because of its soft sheen and air of luxury and comfort; it is used traditionally in bed and dressing rooms and for bedhangings.

A satin weave is warp-faced and a sateen is weft-faced. A satin is marginally richer in its finish, and so is used for more expensive plain fabrics, while sateen, a little stronger, is used for linings.

WEAVE VARIATIONS

DAMASK

Reversible patterned fabric usually of one or two colours, the pattern showing up in a variety of plain, twill, and satin figured designs.

Traditionally it was handwoven in white linen as tablecloths and napkins, but now it is made in other fibres.

DOBBY

Dobby looms produce small, often geometric patterns. They have a good body texture.

Dobby wool fabrics are popular for upholstery, but they are also quite suitable for curtains, also working well with larger patterns and as contrast binding on heavy cotton or linen.

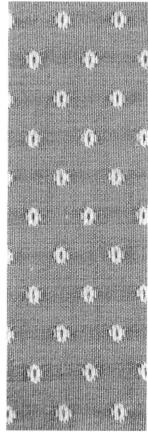

Classic dobby pattern

DOUBLECLOTH

A name for any double weave construction such as matelassé.

The quilted background makes them thick and difficult to drape, so they look best on flat pelmets, as tie-backs, bed-heads and cushions of all kinds.

Matelassé

Jacquard

Gaufrage embossed velvet

JACQUARD

C 1801, Joseph Marie Jacquard invented a loom attachment that now bears his name, which can select warp threads which will make patterns, like damask. This had previously been done only by hand. Jacquard designs can be plain or multicoloured.

LAPPET WEAVE AND CLIP-SPOT EFFECTS

Extra warp threads are bound into the fabric and then the surplus threads are cut away. This technique weaves a dot or small motif onto the surface, a fairly slow and expensive process.

Used often for sheers, clipspots are used to give a hint of texture to an otherwise bland fabric.

PILE WEAVE

The pile is made from loops formed over a wire set into the ground fabric. The loops can be left un-cut as in a terry cloth or chenille, or cut to form a plush finish such as velvet.

PILE VARIATIONS: CORDUROYS

The weft pile is formed in ridges running down the length of the fabric. The ridges can be thin, as in needlecord, or chunky and sumptuous as in a jumbo cord. Often made of cotton and reasonably hard-wearing, corduroy is often used for children's rooms, for floor cushions, for loose covers, and for curtains and upholstery in a study or an office.

GENOA VELVET

Patterns are created within the weaving process. The fabric can be multi-coloured with a cut or an un-cut pile, set onto a satin ground.

GAUFRAGE VELVET

A pattern is embossed onto the surface of the pile using hot metal rollers which bear an etched print.

CHENILLE

A term often applied to a fabric with an irregular pile or patterned pile, often with loops.

VELOUR

A dense pile that is flatter than velvet. It is on a knitted ground and is extremely hard wearing. It is rather shiny and drapes more easily than velvet. Velour also comes in prints mostly in rich deep colours.

VELVET

Two layers of fabric are woven simultaneously interlaced warp threads are cut to separate the layers and make the pile. Trim velvet with embroidery, or braid, appliqué, or contrast bind in satin or silk.

Printed velour

80

Baize

ALPHABETICAL LIST OF FABRIC TYPES

BAIZE

A green, red or brown wool fabric used for covering doors and games tables, small and large. Baize can be battened to cover walls.

BROCADE

Similar to damask, but extra weft threads cover the patterned area of the fabric. Woven in silk or cotton, it lends itself to both formal and elegant styles, which include swags and tails. Chair cushions and cloths can be made up if the cost of curtaining is too great.

BROCATELLE

Resembles damask, made from cotton or blended fibres with supplementary silk wefts on the surface that give a relief effect.

BRODERIE ANGLAISE

Fine cotton embroidered with eyelet designs, traditional in babies' rooms and in feminine bedrooms. Use for light no-sew projects, unlined for summer or over a tinted lining.

CALICO

An inexpensive cotton. Unbleached, it is stiff; part-bleached calico is softer and drapes well.

It can be used for informal curtains and swags, and to achieve the best effect should be used in very generous quantities.

CHAMBRAY

Plain weave with a natural or white warp and a coloured weft. It is suitable for children's rooms and kitchens, as its soft pastel-y colours wash well.

CHINTZ

Colourful floral designs originally from India, most often today printed on a white or pale ground either with or without a glazed finish. The glaze does make it resistant to dirt, but the finish will be damaged by washing.

Plain chintz also makes a good contrast border, as it comes in a positive rainbow of the most luscious colours, both glazed and unglazed.

Brocatelle

Chintz

81

Crewel

Gingham

CREWEL

It takes its name from the wool used to work the embroidered pattern (crewel is a two-ply loosely twisted worsted yarn). The original designs were Indian, then translated into Jacobean motifs, and now once more it is manufactured mainly in India in cotton and wool.

The traditional designs are of scrolling flowers and leaves, worked mostly in chain stitch, in pale, cream or coloured wools onto a loosely woven light-coloured ground.

Crewel wool or cotton has a soft handle, and looks attractive when trimmed with additional wool edgings, rope and tie-backs.

It is also effective as a simple curtain hung from a pole or made into

more elaborate designs for almost any room. It is especially popular as covers and curtains for oak four poster beds.

DRILL

A medium weight twill woven cotton fabric suitable for informal curtains and blinds.

FELT

Traditionally made from wool, the fibres are bonded tightly through a process involving a great deal of moisture, heat and pressure, where they interlock to form a fabric that has no grain and will not fray.

This gives it a weak construction and it will easily pill (with constant friction the fibres form small clusters on the surface of the fabric).

Felt can be used for curtains, borders, and appliqué work. It may

disintegrate if it is dry cleaned although it can be carefully sponged.

GINGHAM

A lightweight, two colour plain woven checked fabric made from either cotton or polyester cotton mix. Unlined, it is washable and very suitable for kitchens and bathrooms. When lined it can be used in any informal room especially with American styles.

GROSGRAIN

A corded silky fabric where the weft yarns are heavier than the warps to give the raised effect.

HESSIAN

Open plain woven fabric produced from hemp and jute fibres and when pre-shrunk can be used for curtains. As hessian frays easily it can be used to advantage to make exciting fringed and tasselled edges. Hessian is quite stiff, and looks best when it is lined and interlined.

LAWN

Crisp plain weave cotton or linen fabric that is used as a sheer.

LINEN

Pure light weight linen can be used as a sheer to give a crisp effect. Heavier weights will crease and this should be accepted as part of its charm. It can be used as a plain fabric and it looks attractive trimmed

Grosgrain

Hessian

with braid or printed. Linen can be suitable for kitchens and bathrooms as well as seaside homes because it is not as absorbent as other fibres.

LINEN UNION

Linen mixed with other fibres to strengthen it. A linen weft mixed with a cotton warp, to give one example, retains the strength of the linen fibre and is softened by the cotton content, improving its draping qualities.

Linen mixed with silk is a luxurious fabric having the weight of linen and the lustre of the silk.

MADRAS

Brightly-coloured checked and striped fabrics, named after the region in India where they originated. It is a light weight fabric and can be used effectively en masse even mixing several designs in one room.

MATELASSÉ

A word derived from the French, meaning 'to quilt' or wad. The fabric is doublecloth construction with extra weft threads woven between the two layers to increase the relief of the pattern.

MOIRÉ

A roller and friction treatment applied to ribbed fabric such as grosgrain and taffeta.

The engraved roller flattens the ribs of the fabric to leave a wavy wood-grained or water-marked pattern.

OTTOMAN

A warp faced fabric with a rib running across the fabric. Originally made with a silk warp and wool weft.

PAISLEY

A fabric woven or printed with a scrolling pear shaped motif, with intense pattern infill.

The Paisley name came from a town in Scotland. There they made and exported block-printed copies of old Kashmiri shawls which were originally woven in India as early as the 15th century.

The French took the lead quickly in creating Europeanised versions, especially after the exciting invention of Jacquard's loom .

Paisley designs are extremely versatile and have been used for furnishing fabrics since the end of the 19th century. They are often printed on thin wool as well as on cotton, and on borders, ribbons, etc.

Shawls make wonderful throws and can be used as swags, dramatically flung over plain curtains or as comforting lap rugs left generously to hand on chairs and sofas.

Moiré Stripe

PIQUÉ

Medium weight cotton fabric with a raised cord effect, at first running across the fabric but now it can also run down. It is used as a textured trim or to contrast with another texture, or in its own right.

SAIL CLOTH

A strong fabric with a weft rib, similar to rep, usually made in cotton and sometimes in linen.

Suitable for casual treatments, but is stiff and does not gather up easily. Good for all the styles of flat blinds and tough-wearing cushions.

Paisley

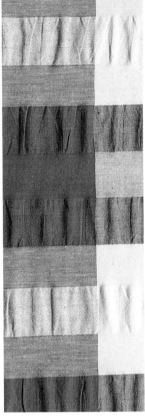

Seersucker

Silk Brocade

SEERSUCKER
A plain woven fabric where the tensions between the warp and the wefts are altered. The fabric then has an applied shrinkage finish which produces crinkly stripes. Suitable for unlined curtains that will be washed often.

SHEERS
These can either be used as a secondary window treatment for privacy or as the main treatment where a translucent effect can be achieved.

LACE
Looks most attractive when used with little or no fullness against a window, making full use of the design. Lace panels were common in Victorian and Edwardian homes made from the heavier Nottingham machine laces, not the hand-knotted or woven lace used for clothes and sometimes for bed linen.

They still look very appealing in the right situation.

MUSLIN
An inexpensive fine cotton fabric which can be used in volume to great effect for informal swag effects and also bed hangings. Very useful for all no-sew treatments and for creating instant curtains for holidays or special events.

ORGANDIE
A fine plain woven transparent cotton fabric with a crisp sized finish. Organza is a silk or rayon equivalent.

VOILE
A general term used for sheer fabrics. Cotton voile has a soft natural handle, polyester voile is not affected by sunlight and polyester/cotton voile has the advantages of both fibres.

Flocked voile is a less expensive version of woven spotted voile.

The pattern is formed by glue printed onto the surface, usually in a dot design. It's the fine fibres which adhere to the glue which create the pattern.

Printed voiles, either in self or in contrasting colours are lovely on their own or as a useful tool; sheer curtains for light and privacy can be co-ordinated with the same print on a heavier fabric used on top, at the side or somewhere else in the room.

SILK
A versatile fibre that is used for most types of cloth. It can be used alone or mixed with cotton or wool to add lustre and strength. Typical silk fabrics include:

BROCADE, described pre-

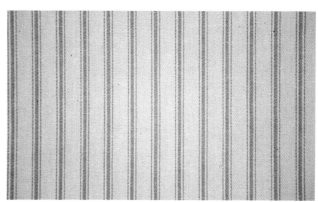

Ticking

viously on page 81, and illustrated on the left.

DUPION
A plain woven fabric using uneven yarn which creates irregular slubs.

DAMASK
see description and illus. p. 79.

FAILLE
Plain woven fabric with a weft ribbed effect that is finer in weight than grosgrain but not as fine as taffeta.

TAFFETA
Plain woven fabric with a fine barely discernible weft rib. It has a high sheen and a light crisp handle. Shot taffeta is woven using one colour for the warp and a second for the weft creating an iridescent light play.

Tapestry

TAPESTRY
Originally hand woven pictorial designs used as wall hangings, the pattern is now made using multi-coloured warp and weft threads brought to the surface of the fabric to make the pattern. It produces a thick, heavy fabric with limited draping ability. It is suitable for simple curtains hung straight from poles, flat pelmets and valances.

TARTAN
Sometimes known as plaid, tartan originated from Scottish clans, each with their designs to identify each other and to determine their status within the family. A clan may have up to four tartans, for the head and family, for relatives, a dress tartan for formal gatherings and a hunting tartan. The older plaids were made with vegetable dyes, more muted than modern versions which use analine dyes. Today tartan is made from wool, silk, cotton or fibre mixes.

All tartans look quite rich when trimmed with wool edgings, rope and tassel tie-backs and can be used for a wide range of window treatments, for a warm, masculine effect. You don't have to be a Scot anymore.

TICKING
A strong twill woven two colour striped cotton fabric traditionally used for mattress covers. For curtains choose a light weight quality with a soft finish that will drape well. Ticking works particularly well in informal settings.

VELVET -
See Pile weaves.

WATERPROOF FABRIC
Mostly for shower curtains, to line other fabrics. Some fabrics can be plasticised and used for tablecloths and mats, but it becomes too stiff for curtaining.

Abstract

Animal

PRINT GLOSSARY

Prints styles evolve over time, progressing with technical innovations and changing taste. These are just a few of the evergreen categories which are found in most fabric shops; in truth, there are as many different print styles and patterns as there are fabrics.

Often the colours change over the years rather than the actual design; for example, many traditional Victorian prints are wildly popular just now, but in lighter and softer colours than they would have used.

Fashion has a part to play in fabric as in everything else, so if you want to make sure your decor will not date, then concentrate on classic designs in classic colours.

Look for inspiration rather than specific designs; this will give you some idea of the possiblities when you start curtain making.

ABSTRACT

Abstracts include all kinds of pattterns which are not obviously based on sources such as flowers or animals.

Geometrics like stripes, checks, tartans and so on are also abstract, of course, but in fabric design terms "abstracts" usually have freer forms and softer lines than a geometric. They may be inspired by an artist's brush strokes or swirls of pigment, or have bold linear forms and shapes. Abstracts were very popular during the 1930-1950s and remain immensely important in modern design.

ANIMAL

Prints based on animal skin patterns or paw-marks. Always very popular in small doses.

ARCHITECTURAL

The flowing repeat designs of architectural motifs are a favourite of textile designers.

Greek, Roman and Islamic scrolls and other similar motifs make effective large-scale patterns, often in neutral colours which reflect the marble originals. The brilliant turquoise blue and yellow of Islamic tiles fascinated the Arts and Crafts and Art Nouveau movements and these were also translated into fabrics.

ARTS AND CRAFTS

William Morris is the best-known designer within the Arts and Crafts Society that flourished in the 1880s. Against the headlong rush towards complete mechanisation, he re-vived the dying art of hand block printing, with vegetable dyes. Softer, darker colours and distinctive patterns

Arts and Crafts; a Morris design

Batik

are typical of his work. Most are highly stylized repeat patterns with elaborate floral shapes and foliage interlacing.

Charles R. MacIntosh's architectural and furniture designs from the same period have also been adapted to fabrics and are increasingly popular with decorators.

BATIK
A resist method of printing where hot wax is painted onto the fabric leaving the areas where the dye is to be taken up. The wax resists the dye, hence its name.

The wax is removed and several more colours can be added using the same process.

The dye seeps into cracks in the wax, and this will create the characteristic grid effect of the pattern. In mass manufacturing the look is simulated.

Batik prints look effective in informal settings, in garden rooms, and made up into accessories such as tablecloths and cushion covers.

BLOCK
An early form of printing where the colour is applied to the surface of the fabric by a wooden block, carved in relief with the design and pre-inked with fabric dye.

These hand prints have an individual charm and irregularity. Individually designed prints are still made today by this method. Simple block printing can easily be done at home, especially if you want coordinated design on the walls and the curtains.

CHINOISERIE
Oriental paintings on silk, embroidery as well as painted porcelain are the sources for these very decorative prints, with gnarled boughs of flowering trees and exotic birds a particular feature. The colours are usually inspired by the oriental originals - strong reds, peach, blue and yellow backgrounds with fairly natural colourings for the motifs. These complex prints look best on full-length curtains and big sofas.

ETHNIC
Hand-woven or printed fabrics made using traditional techniques. The colours are earthy, with Indian, African, Native American, and Polynesian influences. Ethnic styles have become so popular that they have been copied in mass-market production (see Ikat).

GEOMETRICS
Any abstract pattern, printed or woven, based on geometric lines or shapes. Geometrics are now mixed with florals and other patterns to provide contrast and interest.

IKAT
Traditionally a yarn dyed woven fabric where the pattern is created by the occasional absence of dye in the yarn. The yarn is tied-dyed in a pre-determined pattern which is then positioned in the weaving process to form the pattern.

Ikat designs can be identified by the distinctive feathered edges of the pattern. Made in cotton, linen and silk yarns they are most appreciated when the pattern is used flat, for example, on a throw.

INDIAN
Indian traditional filler patterns, in particular small recurring motifs on a figured ground, have influenced English fabric design from the 17th century to the present day.

They were first made to compete against the imported fabrics, but eventually they became

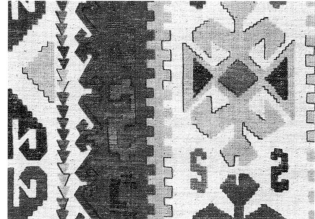

Ethnic

Ikat

much more European encouraged by the use of mineral rather than vegetable dyes in the 19th century.

PROVENÇAL
Brightly coloured cotton prints of small stylized motifs from Southern France, which were originally printed using woodblocks. The colours are bright with strong contrasts; white, red and yellow, green and black, and so on. They have a distinctive look

Provençal

Toile de Jouy

and a country charm, working best in informal settings.

RIBBON, RIBBON AND BOW, Adaptations of 18th century wallpaper and fabric designs, usually featuring curling ribbon weaving in and out of floral motifs. Very often a ribbon design will include a border down the sides with a denser version of the central pattern.

STENCIL
These adaptations of 18th and 19th century American stencils were very popular in the 1980s, characterised by country and floral motifs in simplified colours. Many were originally based on quilts.

TOILE DE JOUY
Traditionally a single colour pictorial print depicting figurative and pastoral scenes. Its name was derived from a small French village, Jouy-en-Josas, where two German brothers set up a factory in 1770 to print imported Indian calico using copper plates. The charm is in the fine detail achieved, best seen when the fabric lies flat, as on bedcovers, cushions and flat pelmets.

When gathered, the pictures are lost in the folds, although the effect is still attractive.

Ribbon Bouquet

LININGS
The lining used on the reverse protects from sunlight and dirt and will extend the life of any curtain. The extra body also adds weight and improves draping quality. Ecru, cream, and white are the standard colours.

COTTON SATEEN lining
This, the most common lining, has floating weft threads and its quality depends on the density of the weave. Most linings have been rolled to produce a sheen, and finished with sizing. An inexpensive lining may be heavily sized to bulk up a loosely woven fabric. It is truly worth investing in quality. Never rip lining as the weft grain is seldom square to the warp threads; cut it to get a square edge.

SOLPRUFE dyed linings
A UK registered process giving colour fastness for light to medium shades.

VAT dyed linings
For medium to dark shades, giving the best level of colour fastness.

COLOURED AND PRINTED LININGS
A coordinated colour or print for lining curtains can be an attractive feature, especially for curtains that are often seen from the outside.

CHINTZ
This comes in a wide range of plain colours as well as printed designs. Glazed fabric resists dust more than other lining fabrics. A plain chintz can be used in reverse with the matt side as the face.

WOVEN, STRIPED OR CHECKED FABRIC
Match or mix for extra impact from the outside.

POLY/COTTON LINING The mix is a stable fabric with little or no shrinkage; the cotton makes it cool to touch.

BLACKOUT LININGS
Specified for hospitals, hotels and dark rooms, as well as blocking out light, these provide extra insulation and are flame retardant.

'2-Pass Blackouts' are for linings; '3 Pass-Blackouts' can also be as unlined curtains on their own. As 3 Pass is coated on both sides, it can make a loose lining.

All are much heavier than conventional lining so you may need metal tracks to support the extra weight.

THERMAL LININGS
These have insulation properties; Pyrovotex has an aluminium finish to reflect the light, protecting the fabric and providing insulation against high temperatures in warm countries.

INTERLINING
Interlinings are firstly attached to the face fabric, and secondly to the lining, at intervals across the entire width of curtain; it improves the drape and hang, provides good insulation and protects the fabric.

All fabrics from light-weight silk to heavy velvet, can be interlined to great effect. The only exceptions are translucent fabrics such as voiles or other sheers. Interlined curtains are not washable and are therefore unsuitable for situations where this must be a consideration. Interlining fabric has a brushed surface that gives it its padding and its insulating quality.

A certain amount of shrinkage may occur (see p. 77); interlining that has been bleached will be less prone to shrinkage.

As the interlining is sandwiched between the fabric and the lining, if they shrink at different rates, this could alter the length and in extreme cases, if the stitches have tightened, it can cause a dimpled effect on the surface.

BUMP
A heavy, loosely woven cotton fabric, made from waste and brushed to give a thick lofty feel. It comes in bleached white or unbleached cream.

When cutting it can be frayed to produce a straight edge and must be laid square onto the fabric, as the looseness of the weave means that it distorts easily.

A certain amount of fluff will inevitably end up on the right side, but this can be brushed off later. A clothes brush will do the job quickly.

SARILL
A stitch-bonded polyester that is naturally flame retardant and being heat set it will not shrink. It weighs less than bump, but it does not hang or drape as well. Iron as little as possible, it creates static between the layers causing them to repel each other. However, this wears off soon.

DOMETTE
A lightweight brushed cotton interlining, woven from cotton yarn, either in plain or twill weave. Thinner and about half the weight of bump, it is used for heavy curtains such as velvet. and to interline swags and tails where there are several layers of fabric.

BONDED INTERLINER
Made by fusing polyester wadding to the back of plain lining, this is used as one fabric. You can make curtains up easily as if they were only lined, yet achieve the insulation properties of interlining.

However, if you want the very best result, bonded interliner will not drape as well as properly lined and interlined curtains. It can be fused to blackout lining when you want to exclude the maximum light.

BUCKRAMS
There are two fabrics, one used in the heading of curtains, the other for pelmets and tie-backs.

HEADING BUCKRAM
A white calico fabric stiffened with size, this sometimes is available with a fusible (iron-on) finish, pre-cut into 10, 13 and 15cms (4,5 and 6in) widths. Heading buckram is used in hand sewn headings.

PELMET TIE-BACK BUCKRAM
GREY buckram is a 2-ply plain woven and starched jute fabric. ORANGE buckram is a twill woven hessian, impregnated with glue, and more pliable .

Use a layer of interlining between either of these buckrams and the face fabric, so that its coarse weave cannot be seen.

SYNTHETIC PELMET BUCKRAMS
There is a vast range of single or double-sided stiffenings, often called interfacing, which can come with pre-printed pelmet designs. Easy to use, they can be doubled up for extra firmness.

POLYESTER WADDING
Polyester fibres are bonded together to form a grain-less lofty and washable fabric. It is sold in a variety of thicknesses; a standard useful weight range for ordinary curtains is 4-6 oz. It is used for bed quilts, wadded edges and hems on curtains and table cloths and for quilted cushions.

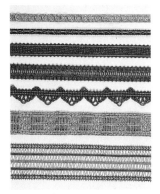

Braids, from extra narrow to extra wide

Fringes, again from very narrow to medium length, one with an openwork top

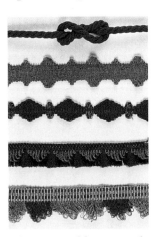

A variety of fringes and edgings; a knotted rope at the top, single and double edged fan, and a fan edge with a braid top and block fan.
Most edgings and braids come in a great variety of mixed colours, but they are also custom made all the time.

PASSEMENTERIE

Passementerie includes braids, fringes, ropes, cords and tassels for soft furnishings.

Although sometimes it may seem a disposable expense, it is worthwhile investing in the best quality that you can afford, to make your curtain look special.

The main growth in its use was in the 18th century, to hide the numerous seams on upholstered furniture, as the early looms could only weave narrow lengths of fabric.

Traditionally of gold, silver and silk threads, passementerie is now constructed from wool, cotton, linen and synthetic fibres.

Custom-made lengths in precious metals are still made for restoration and refurbishment of period homes.

Passementerie can be used to contrast with the curtain or to pick up a colour from another part of the room, or to blend into the curtain fabric, creating a textured contrast.

If stock mixtures are not suitable then there are specialist companies who will make up what you need.

ROPE

Rope is twisted along a "rope walk" several metres long to form any number of interesting corded designs.

Rope can be run along the tops of swags and tails to define the edge, knotted at the base of goblets, made up into rope clovers, and used to trim pelmets and tiebacks. It is made in a variety of standard sizes, from quite narrow to extremely thick.

FLANGED ROPE

The rope is sewn to a flange of woven tape to enable it to be machined into a seam quickly.

Flanged rope is used, like piping, more often in upholstery than in curtainmaking, but it can be seamed into the leading edges and hems of curtains, flat pelmets, and the edges of tiebacks and cushions.

BRAID

Technically referred to as a narrow fabric, it is woven on looms. Some intricate designs are still woven by hand, and can be stiffened with wire to form interesting raised patterns. Braid can look stunning set in from the leading edges of curtain and along flat pelmets. It is also an effective trim for Roman blinds.

FAN EDGING

A braid where the weft is extended to one side in loops, graded in length to form the fan effect. It makes a delicate finish for light curtains, valances, bed curtains and cushions. It can be set onto the seam so that only the fan edge shows, or it can be onset so that the braided edge is also visible.

FRINGE

Woven as a braid, this is extended weft threads to one side to form the loops. The head of the fringe can be very simple or two or three rows of an elaborate braid, The weft loops are cut to make the fringe.

BLOCKED FRINGE

The alternation of colour, usually in two or three tones; a smart finish for the leading edges of plain curtains and the bases of valances and blinds.

BULLION

Woven in the same manner as a fringe, the extended weft loops are twisted to form the skirt. Alternatively the loops of the skirt are tied into a trellis and finished with tassels or 'hangers'. This is generally a thick, bold trimming for big swags and tails, valances and sometimes the hems of curtains, giving a rich sumptuous, finish.

BUTTON TUFTS

A delicate trim for cushions and at the base of goblet or French pleats.

TASSELS

Made in many shapes and sizes, they consist of a wooden core which is decoratively covered by threads. In a big tassel, several sizes of covered wooden cores can be threaded together to form the top.

The skirt is made from a fringe sewn around the base; the join is usually disguised by a ruff. Small tassels are used to trim top treatments and larger tassels are attached to rope to make glamourous tie-backs.

FABRIC TRIMS

Many are derived from 18th century costumes, details revived in the 1960s by John Fowler. As they are often a focal point it is important that they are made with care and well-proportioned.

Trims are used on swags, on some tie-backs, pelmets, as well as valances and blinds.

CHOUX

The crinkly effect is made by stitching. Choux are used like rosettes and also to cover pleated corona boards and the centre of pleated bed testers.

BOWS

Both functional, to tie curtains onto a pole, or decorative trims. Bows can be self or made in contrasting fabric.

TREFOIL

A three pronged bow centred with a fabric covered button .

MALTESE CROSS

Two bows placed at right angles to each other and centred with a fabric covered button. They can have contrast edges, and used with tails make decorative picture bows.

TRUMPET

Cylindrical cone- shaped trim, used for toppings, either set onto pelmets and valances or set between swags and tails. The lower edge can be shaped and they can also be pleated to make double trumpets.

FLUTE

A semi-circular piece of fabric, rolled or folded to form a cone with a tapered base.

The choice of hardware to fit and hang your curtains from is important to make the most of all your time, expense and effort spent on choosing, designing and making up the fabric. The range of tracks, poles, and other possibilities in the shops is quite substantial, and it's improving all the time.

In this section we have given basic advice on various circumstances, but if you have any problems in either finding the hardware or worries about unusual windows or doors, talk to the store where you buy your fabric, to an experienced curtain fitter, or contact the manufacturers direct from the suppliers list.

CURTAIN TRACKS

These are made in plastic and metal, and both come with either plastic or metal runners, and hooks which are often bought separately.

PLASTIC

Suitable for light to medium weight fabrics, which include sheers of all kinds, and most unlined and lined curtains. In general these are inexpensive and can bend around curves and angles, but if you have high ceilings and full length curtains then the track may not be strong enough to take anything but the lightest fabric.

METAL

More costly but stronger, these are suitable for all curtains but especially for heavy fabrics like velvet or chenille, and all interlined or very long curtains. Some are telescopic and can be extended in length.

Metal tracks should be used even for light curtains when the stackback is all on one side, which could happen if the window was next to a wall or a piece of furniture. If all the weight is concentrated in a small area, it might pull the track away from the fixing.

RUNNERS AND HOOKS

Some metal tracks are supplied with either plastic nylon or metal runners, and you can buy hooks in either material. Again the plastic will be perfectly satisfactory on most light or medium weights, but if you have a long drop and a heavy fabric it would be wise to choose the stronger metal runners and curtain hooks.

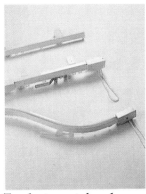

Tracks in metal and plastic, some with easy-fitting circular cords.

BRACKETS

Tracks generally come with their own brackets, which can be adapted to either the ceiling or the underside of a pelmet board, called top fixed, or to the wall called face fixed. Not all tracks are adaptable, though so ask when you buy the track.

Some face fixed brackets can be extended to the front so that the curtains will hang over an obstruction like a deep sill moulding or a radiator.

CORDING

Tracks can be bought with or without cording in place. In public or hotel rooms the curtains may be yanked about, so the corded style might jam. Uncorded tracks should be used for fixed curtains and also small sections like dressing table skirts.

Corded tracks do prevent the leading edges of the curtains from being soiled by constant handling, and they help greatly in smooth running when the curtains are long or heavy.

COMBINED TRACKS

Tracks can be found with valance rails attached on extended brackets. They suit light to medium weights only, but they are very useful for small windows, sheers, and unlined curtains.

BAY WINDOWS

For lightweight curtains plastic tracks can be curved to most bay windows, but the angles musn't be so great that it stops the runners. A bay can have a simple, concave curve, making it a one-way bend, or it may bend back at the ends to return onto the wall; for this you need a more flexible two-way bend track.

Metal tracks can be bent in your home by a professional fitter, but if you can supply the manufacturer with the dimensions they will pre-set the bend of the tracks at the factory.

Corded tracks are available for bays, usually with drawcords at either end because the window is too wide for one. For a really large bay with three substantial windows, consult your fabric store or a manufacturer for the best combination of tracks and cording.

ARCHED WINDOWS

These also need special tracks. With a template of the arch, the supplier will be able to set the track at the factory; and they will also supply locked runners so that the curtains won't fall down the curve! Inside the recess, a plastic track can easily be fitted into the reveal, although in some cases it might be better to make up a wood frame first and screw the track to that. (see Fitting and Installation).

SHOWER CURTAIN TRACK

Most shower curtains hang from a tension rod over the bath recess. However, special cubicle tracks only require one supporting wall. They are made from rust-free aluminium with plastic runners and hooks.

BOW-FRONT PELMETS

Tracks hung from a bow-fronted pelmet board should follow the curve . Most tracks will bend in a concave shape, so you might need to set the track back to front.

CORONA TRACKS

Half-circle tracks for bed hangings are crescent shaped and fitted directly to the wall. If you are planning a heavy interlined valance as well as side hangings, then a shaped pelmet board will do a better job. Fix the track to its underside.

FIXING TRACK TO PELMET BOARDS

Tracks should measure less than the length of the pelmet board so there is room for the curtain to be wrapped around the end of the track. Tracks are usually fixed onto the underside of the board.

PELMET BOARD BRACKETS

Shelf brackets are the obvious choice to provide adequate support. You will need one at each end, and with any window over 170cms (5'7") wide, you will need a centre support as well. See Fitting and Installation .

POLES

Pole brackets are made in various finished to match the poles (see opposite page). The bottom bracket on the left is an overclip, used where there is no space to lift the pole above the bracket.

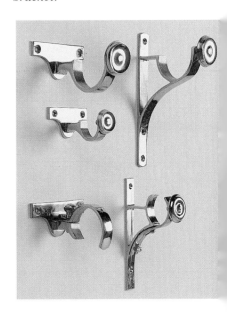

POLES

Decorative poles come in all shapes and sizes. They are made from wood and metal, finished in brass, bronze, pewter, iron, and come in a variety of diameters and with a large selection of finials at the end.

The material should blend with the rest of the room and look appropriate with the finials. You will need to buy either telescopic poles which can be extended to fit a given range of sizes, or have the poles custom made to the right length. The main rod should extend the full width of the window treatment between the outside of the brackets; finials usually screw into the ends.

WOOD

These are extremely versatile as they can be stained, painted, inlaid or stencilled, or gilded. Ready-made poles vary in diameter and custom-made poles can be ordered thicker or narrower.

Some wooden poles are corded with a groove in the underside of the pole fitted with a narrow track. There are no rings.

Wood poles can be used for bay windows, but these are custom-made so that the dowel is mitred at each angle. The curtains hang one at each side and two in the middle in, for example, a two-angled bay, the most common design. You cannot pull a pair of curtains right around the bay because of the brackets which support the corners.

BRASS AND BRASS EFFECT

These are widely available in a complete range of sizes for both ready-made and custom-made designs. Many are corded and telescopic which makes them easy to fit in almost any situation. New improvements include ready-made brass poles for bay windows which have adjustable angles. But remember that each angle will still require a bracket for support.

Narrow brass tubing is a neat way of hanging lightweight curtains at small windows, or around a four-poster bed. It is also available with special fixing brackets.

Iron poles come narrow medium or thick, either in black, bronze or pewter finish. They can be painted or gilded, and decorated with tassels, ribbons, etc.

POLE BRACKETS

There are several types of pole brackets for awkward places - for recesses, over-clip (see illus opposite) and circular brackets which are fixed into the ceiling. Make

Slim wrought iron poles with decorative finials

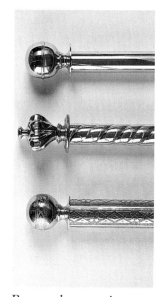

Brass poles come in a wide variety of designs

sure your store or supplier knows exactly how the curtain design works and they will advise you.

FINIALS

These come separately or with a pole, and are usually made from the same material. Check that they will fit the diameter of your pole.

*Three ombras, showing narrow stem
Assortment of fancy wooden poles*

OTHER FITTINGS

PORTIÉRE RODS

For door curtains, and available in painted metal or in brass tubing. They have rings or runners for the curtain, and are fixed to the top of the door. The hinged bracket rises when the door is opened and lifts the curtain off the floor.

DORMER RODS

These swing flat back against the wall during the day, letting in all possible light.

MERRICK & DAY
CURTAIN MAKING WORKSHOP

American Glossary

UK	US
Bedcovers	Bedspreads, Quilts
Bed valances	Dust skirts/ruffles
Binding	Banding
Blinds	Shades
Curtains	Drapes
Curtain track	Traverse rod
Cushions	Pillows
Frill	Ruffle
Pelmet	Upholstered Cornice Board
Pelmet Board	Cornice Board
Piping	Cording/welting
Selvedge	Rough Edge
Tails	Cascades/jabots
Trumpet	Trumpet/bell

PARTS THREE – FIVE:
THE COMPLETE CURTAIN MAKER

PART THREE: CURTAINS TOPS & BLINDS

GUIDELINES

Here are some points to think about when you are choosing your designs, curtains, fabric, and fittings.

BUDGET

If you have a tight budget, try quick and easy unlined curtains. If there are existing fittings in place, plan to use them to cut the overall cost.

LIGHT

How much daylight are you prepared to lose? Curtains hung from poles or covered laths lose the least from the top, but all curtains will block out light where they extend over the glass. Try to make them pull back; the wall area they cover is the 'stack back'.

Any sort of pelmet, swag or valance will block out some top light, but as with Roman and gathered blinds, they can be fitted in the dead space above the window frame. Roller blinds block out very little light, even when they are fitted inside the window.

FITTING

Blinds are usually the best solution where there is very little room at either side of the window. If there is stack back room on one side of the window only, go for a single curtain treatment. If there is very little dead space above the window it is sensible to use a pole or a fabric covered lath (see bottom of next column).

You must also check for obstructions underneath the window (furniture? radiators? window seats?) that will need to be taken into account.

WINDOW SHAPE

If the window is tall and narrow you can choose almost any classic treatment. If it is very wide, a serpentined top treatment will soften the horizontal line. If it is small and needs to blend into the wall, keep the design simple. If the window is shaped at the top, the pelmet or top of the curtain can be shaped to match.

THE ROOM

Additions, extensions and alterations usually result in a muddle of windows in different shapes or sizes. If you want different treatments in the same room, link them by using the same fabric and decorative details.

STYLE AND DESIGN

For classic, formal rooms, you will probably think about swags or elegantly trimmed valances. Softer treatments seem suited to quiet bedrooms, creating pools of tranquillity in a busy life. Simple treatments suit everyday rooms and kitchens. None of this need

mean boredom - a subtle touch of country charm can be just as inspiring as a grand flourish.

PROPORTIONS ON TOP

Correct proportions are vital. Mock up the finished valance, swag or pelmet in calico, and pin it up at the window. If it blocks out too much light don't compromise by making it shorter, or it will end up looking skimpy. Choose another design; a decorative heading on a pole is just one possibility.

FULL LENGTH VERSUS SILL LENGTH

If there isn't enough room for full length curtains we would normally advise using a blind instead. Sill length curtains rarely make enough impact in a decorative scheme. However, there are some exceptions, such as stairways, kitchens, hallways or bathrooms, where practical considerations mean that shorter curtains should be used. With attention to detail, they can look very attractive indeed.

OUTSIDE THE WINDOW

Blinds easily control the amount of light that comes into a room. If the window has an ugly outlook, keep an unlined blind permanently down, shutting off the view but letting the light filter through.

LIVING WITH YOUR CURTAINS

If you need to wash your curtains, they should be unlined and made up in a washable fabric. Lined and interlined curtains which are full and overlong will keep frosty night air at bay. If old doors fit badly, interlined door curtains made up in thick fabric will again keep out draughts.

TO SEW OR NOT TO SEW

If you want a temporary solution, or simply like changing your schemes regularly, do not choose time consuming, hand sewn, fully trimmed curtains. Concentrate on unlined designs which are easy to make and quick to install. Bear in mind though, that many are only for effect and won't open or close easily.

FABRIC COVERED LATHS

This is a trade term for narrow pelmets which are covered in the same fabric as the curtains and usually blend into the wall. They are a discreet method of concealing the curtain track, and do not restrict light.

Laths are a good choice when ceilings are low and there is little or no dead wall space above the window. The best heading to use with a lath is French - it is narrow and stacks back into a compact area.

POLES

A versatile and decorative fitting. You can use them to hang simple curtains, or they can look sumptuous if they are decorated, finished with exotic finials. Formal swags and tails can be attached to a pole, or thrown over to exciting and dramatic effect.

Poles do not restrict light from the top. The pole should be extended beyond the window frame and the rings you choose should move easily along it.

Poles are also suitable when there is little or no dead wall space above the window; they can be used in most rooms, and with most windows. Valances can be attached to curtains hung from poles. If you choose a slotted heading, you will find the curtains cannot be drawn back, because the pole is threaded directly through the fabric; use tie-backs to hold them open.

PELMET BOARDS

These are useful for many curtain treatments. Tracks can be set underneath, and valances and pelmets can be hung from the front edge. Fixed curtains and swags and tails are also attached to the front edge.

PELMETS

Flat pelmets show off patterned or printed fabric, and can be padded or quilted to give a softer appearance. They are also economical in fabric. The lower edge can be cut to any appropriate shape. Pelmets use up dead space above the window and, at the same time, increase the apparent size of the window. A pelmet should be roughly $1/6$ of the curtain length. If the ceiling is low, then $1/8$ is possible, but anything too shallow may look mean.

LAMBREQUINS

A type of flat pelmet in which the sides come down to at least $1/3$ of the window to make a stiff frame; they are useful on dormers or in deep recesses.

VALANCES

A valance is a gathered or pleated pelmet which is hung from the front edge of a pelmet board. It gives a soft finish and also hides the track and the curtain heading. If you intend to have a valance, choose a decorative heading which complements the curtain fabric and the style of the room.

If the pelmet board is set above the window frame, the valance should hang down just enough to cover the top of the frame, letting in all possible light and making the window look taller at the same time. Its proportions are usually $1/5$ of the curtain length, $1/6$ if the ceiling is very low. Valances can be shaped, arched or given a serpentined edge, or fringed, or frilled...the possiblities are endless. In common with other aspects of curtain design, gathered and frilled valances give a light appearance, while French and goblet headings are more tailored.

SWAGS AND TAILS

This is the design style that most people associate with grand ballrooms, elegant dining rooms and restaurants, as well as stately homes. But in fact swags and tails are surprisingly versatile, they are easily adapted to casual and informal rooms, and in the right fabric can be delightful in kitchens and bathrooms too. Swags and tails suit the no-sew technique because they can look brilliantly creative, as if they were just thrown into place.

Swags and tails can be draped over poles, or hung from a pelmet board. They follow the same rule of proportion as valances, that is, the top to bottom of the swag should be $1/5$ of the curtain length. Tails, which should be at least twice the length of the swags, can be softly gathered or sharply cut into folds, and lined in contrasting fabrics to bring out accent colours.

All swags and tails, including no-sew styles, depend on good pattern cutting for their effect. Although it looks like a continuous length of fabric, each swag and tail is made up separately and then assembled.

BLINDS

These are now more popular than ever, with a host of different styles and designs, from the absolutely plain roller to a frilly festoon gathered blind. They can suit any room, even the most formal living room, and work well in company with all curtain treatments to control the outside light, and protect more delicate fabrics from fading.

Professional Tip

SPECIAL FITTINGS

Many awkward situations can be overcome with the appropriate hardware - dormer windows, door curtains, skylights and arched and bay windows can all have well-designed fittings, which solve the practical problems but may limit your choice of curtain design. Choose your fitting before choosing your style or your fabric.

QUICK & EASY: NO-SEW

Quick and easy curtains are unlined, and can even be unseamed. They should be cut out and constructed on site (usually with a staple gun) for the best labour saving results. With a little ingenuity and imagination most styles can be adapted to this technique for instant effect. The trick lies in using generous quantities of fabric.

You can begin with easy yet elegant designs for fabric hung from clips, hooks or a pole. Remember that most no-sew styles are non-functional, for decoration only. For privacy, fit a roller blind as well. If you can't decide what to do, or you have to save up for your dream curtains, don't make an expensive mistake with sale 'bargains'. Try something fun and cheap, live with it for a while; you may find your original ideas have changed completely and with these inexpensive designs, you won't have paid out large sums. Or if you have just moved in, make your bare house more like home, by stapling fabric onto existing pelmet boards while you work out a programme of permanent decoration.

Because these are fairly broad concepts rather than advanced skills, we have provided three basic projects for you to adapt or improve.

FABRICS
The only real cost of these projects is the fabric, so use inexpensive muslins, calicos and cottons in quantity to produce the best results. Sheer fabrics look especially good when used lavishly. Hessians can be frayed at the edge, and wide felt can be pinked to avoid hemming.

HARDWARE
These designs do not need complicated or expensive curtain hardware. Often the fabric can be stapled to a wooden batten or hung from cup hooks using rubber bands. Improvise with all kinds of fixtures and fittings; the attachments can be crude as long as you cover them with drapes, bows, etc.

Curtain clips, also called 'café' clips, are like rings on a pole; they are available in various diameters to suit pole sizes. Clips are suitable only for light to medium weight fabrics. The heavier the fabric, the more clips you will need.

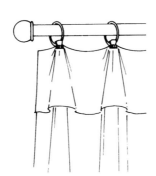

Swag holders, swag formers and rings are some of the new devices now on the market, making it easy to swathe fabric around a window. Made of metal or plastic, they can be bought in various sizes. Some are transparent and become almost invisible when they are up in place.

EQUIPMENT
Staple gun	Tape measure
Scissors	Pinking shears
Rubber bands	EXTRAS (Useful for some
Needle and cotton	of the designs)
Pins	Iron-on hemming tape
	Iron-on heading tape

EDGES, HEMS AND SEAMS
A quick technique is to use iron-on hemming tape on edges, then fold up and press to neaten. Another option is to cut with pinking shears. This works extremely well on closely woven cotton fabrics such as chintz and, of course, felt. Iron-on hemming and heading tape are both widely available; follow manufacturer's instructions for correct use.

On plain fabrics, turn the top edge over to the front to make a frill. If the fabric is firm it will not need a hem. If it is a loose weave, you can unravel it by pulling away the threads, making a small fringe.

On printed fabrics, where the wrong side would be obvious, turn the top edge over to the back of the curtain, with enough fabric to allow it to stay there. Selvedges are more obvious on prints; turn in and hem with tape, or trim away entirely with pinking shears.

To use several widths of fabric together, simply overlap the panels and fix at the heading. Alternatively, panels can be joined with iron-on hemming tape. You can make a decorative seam by punching eyelet holes down each length, then lacing them together.

FAN TOPPED PLEATED CURTAINS, HELD IN RIBBON TIE-BACKS

Fan topped pleats are made by gathering fabric into elastic bands. These clip onto cup hooks fixed into a wooden batten, and are then decorated with ribbon bows. This technique works especially well with a sheer fabric. The curtains can be opened and closed using ribbon tie-backs; see picture on p70.

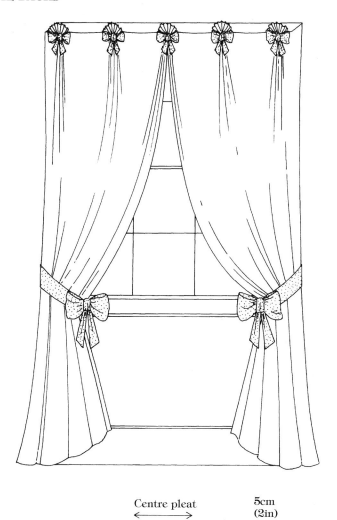

FABRIC QUANTITIES

You will need two times fullness across the curtain; this means a fabric quantity twice the width of the area you are covering. Allow extra to 'return' around the ends of the batten. Add 30cm (12in) to the length of each panel for the heading at the top, and for extra to trail on the floor.

Fabric
Narrow ribbon, 75cm (30in) per top bow/pleat
Wide ribbon, 4m (4yd) per pair of tie-backs
Wooden batten 5cm (2in x 1in) as long as the window frame, plus 7.5 cm (3in) each side
2 or 3 small angle brackets
Cup hooks, one for each 20-30cm (8-12in) of batten
(You must have an odd number to have a central hook)
A pair of cup hooks for the tie-backs

1 Paint the wooden batten, or cover with fabric. Fix cup hooks into the front, then put up on wall over window with the small angle brackets. A large window may need three brackets, one in the middle, two set in from either end.

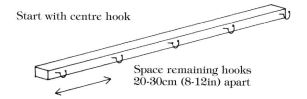

Start with centre hook

Space remaining hooks
20-30cm (8-12in) apart

2 Cut out the required number of fabric widths.

3 Neaten the top and bottom edges of the fabric, and if required, join panels with iron-on hemming tape.

4 Lay out the fabric panels, butting them together in the centre. With pins, mark the spaces between the hooks and the pleats to be gathered into the elastic bands. Leave a 7.5cm (3in) flat space at each end.

Centre pleat   5cm (2in)

Space

5 Gather up the pleat sections and wrap each one into an elastic band. Pull out 5cm (2in) of fabric above the band into a small fan. The central pleat is made from the two leading edges.

6 Hook each pleat onto a cup hook. You may need to readjust the elastic bands so that the distance between each of the pleats is the same.

7 Cut 75cm (30in) of the narrower ribbon and tie around each elastic band into an attractive bow. Staple the outside edges of the curtains round the ends of the batten to cover the wood.

8 Cut the wider ribbon into two 2m (2yd) lengths and tie a large, loose bow around each curtain. Slip onto a cup hook, fixed to the wall at a suitable height. Finally dress the curtain into attractive folds.

PUFFED HEADED CURTAINS

An attractive heading; amazingly it is achieved with only a single row of running stitches and a staple gun. The puffed heading, stuffed with petticoat net to make it even fuller, works especially well in crisp cottons and silks. As the heading is fixed, the curtains need to be held back during the day. Depending on which style you prefer, choose one or two tie-backs, ombras (see p93 for some examples) or curtain bands. These are usually metal, and are u-shaped. The fittings hold the draped curtains neatly to the sides.

FABRIC QUANTITIES

You will need two times fullness across the curtain, which means twice the width of the batten, plus 7.5cm (3in) extra to 'return' around the ends of the batten. Long strips of petticoat net, 20cm (8in) deep, two per curtain width.

Wooden batten, 5cm x 2.5cm (2in x 1 in) as long as the window frame plus 7.5cm (3in) each side
2 or more small angle brackets
Staple gun
Iron-on hemming tape (optional)
One or two tie-backs, ombras or curtain bands

1 Paint the wooden batten or cover with fabric and fix to the wall with small angle brackets.

2 Cut the number of fabric lengths you will need. Cut the strips of net, two for each width of fabric.

3 Neaten the bottom edge of the fabric and, if you prefer, join panels with iron-on hemming tape.

4 At the top of each curtain, fold over 20cm (8in) of fabric to the back. Insert the two layers of net, and pin in place. Take a long piece of strong thread and sew a running stitch at the bottom of the doubled fabric, 2.5cm (1in) in from the raw edge. This is your gathering thread. Alternatively, you can use an iron-on gathering tape, but first you will have to stitch the doubled fabric together.

5 Pull up the gathering thread to the length of the batten plus the sides, and tie off the thread. Staple the curtain onto the front of the batten just above the gathering thread. Start at one side, close to the wall and go straight across to the other side.

6 Dress the heading by opening out the fabric to make the puffed effect. Fix the one or two tie-back hooks, ombras or curtain bands onto the wall and dress the curtain in place.

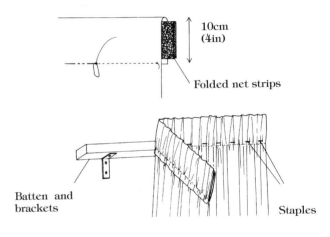

10cm (4in)

Folded net strips

Batten and brackets

Staples

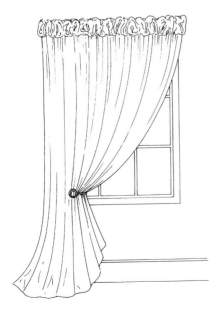

Left, curtain held by a single curtain band.

Right, curtains held by two curtain bands

BLINDS

These are one of the most versatile no-sew projects. At very little expense, since they use such small amounts of fabric and trimmings, you can have decorative windows, privacy, and a splash of colour, all in a couple of hours. Their only disadvantage, compared to commercial roller blinds, is that you need to take a little more care in pulling them up and down. But the results can be so spectacular that this is a tiny price to pay.

FABRIC QUANTITIES

You will need a piece of fabric which is slightly wider and slightly longer than the window. If it is an extra-wide window it might be better to make two blinds, or choose curtains.

FITTINGS AND MATERIALS

Wooden batten 5cm x 2.5cm (2in x 1in), cut as long as the window frame plus 7.5 (3in) each side.
2 small angle brackets to secure batten to wall as shown, and 2 screw eyes
Iron-on hemming tape
Decorative tape or strong ribbon, for ties

1 Cut the fabric to the width of the batten, plus 5cm (2in) for side turnings, by the finished length, plus 5cm (2in) for a hem.

2 Neaten the sides and the hem with iron-on tape.

3 Lay the fabric over the batten and pull tight; staple it to the top.

4 The blind is rolled up and tied at each side with tape or ribbon. Fix two screw eyes to the underside of the batten. Thread a length of ribbon - double the drop of the finished blind - through each eye. Cut small slits in the top of the fabric, in line with the screw eyes. Bring one end of each ribbon through to the front. Tie the ribbons in a pretty bow, pulling up the blind at the bottom to give a little shaped hem. When you want to open the blind, untie and pull each side further up and tie in a bow again; see p51.

Another idea is to fix cup hooks onto the batten and press out eyelets on the top of the blind. Sew tape or ribbon loops in vertical lines onto the front of the blind. Hook them up onto the cup hooks when you need to raise the blind.

Now that you have seen how easy it can be, why not be more adventurous and try your hand at some of the other styles?

All of the projects are graded for difficulty from one to four needles, so if you are a beginner start with the one needle projects, such as a gathered machine tape heading.

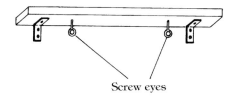
Screw eyes

Blind tied with contrasting ribbon

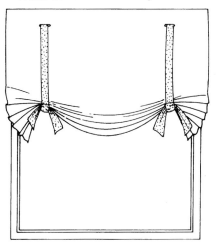

Blind with eyelets

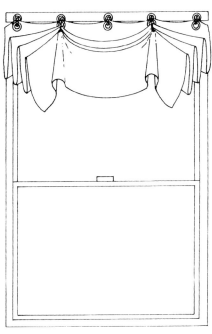

GET READY TO SEW

To ensure the very best results, you should first get ready to sew. Plan your curtain making project throughout beforehand; make sure you have the right equipment to hand and set aside an organised work space. You should devote some time to measuring your window, to decide what kind of fittings and where to place them, and the proportions of your swags, valances, pelmets etc. Estimating fabric quantities and cutting out will also take a little time. Get Ready to Sew includes all the things you need to know to get you started.

Of course it is perfectly possible to make beautiful curtains on your dining table, using whatever equipment is to hand. But if you want to make it easy for yourself and still achieve a really professional finish, then a little bit of planning and organisation before you begin will bring great rewards in time, temper and the end result.

Even if making one set of curtains, you'll benefit from a dedicated working area where you won't have to put things away every evening. It is almost essential for your own comfort especially if you are planning to work on several sets of windows.

Any space big enough to hold a sturdy table is the answer. Lay a sheet of firm board on top. Make sure it is at a comfortable working height; add blocks under the legs if it needs to be raised. This will be your measuring, cutting and ironing table; it is also useful for laying out fabric to avoid creasing and folding.

Make sure there is room for the sewing machine against the edge of the table at one end; a portable that sits on top of the table must have enough support. Cover the table with brown paper, taping it neatly underneath to give you a dust-free surface; replace as often as necessary. Boxes stored underneath can hold lining, interlining, and supplies for the job. Lay fabric rolls horizontally.

Permanently fix measuring tapes along both sides in order to work quickly and accurately. The same board can be temporarily covered with a blanket; use lining fabric or an old clean sheet for ironing.

If your plans include making swag drapery, fix a large pinboard to the wall. This will be like having a second pair of hands when draping fabric.

The right tools produce the best results. Keep groups of tools together, so that you can find them easily.

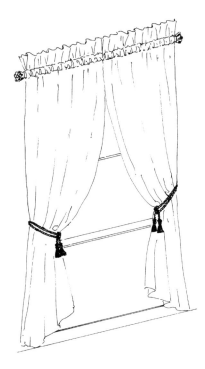

CUTTING ESSENTIALS

METAL RULER at least 1m (1yd)
SET SQUARE for cutting fabric squarely
SCISSORS 20-23cm (8-9in)
FABRIC MARKER PENCILS white, yellow

USEFUL EXTRAS

WOODEN BATTEN 150cm long x 4cm x 2.5cm (60in x 1¹/₂ in x 1in) for cutting piping on the true cross
SCISSOR SHARPENER
SET SQUARE for mitred corners

SEWING ESSENTIALS

PLASTIC TAPE MEASURE
EMBROIDERY SCISSORS
FINE STEEL PINS for silk and light fabrics
GLASS-HEADED PINS 5cm (2in) long
HAND SEWING NEEDLES

> Sharps: general purpose needles with round eyes
> Milliners or straw needles: longer and finer
> Darners: a long eye, easier to thread if using a thicker cotton

SMALL PLIERS for pulling a needle through several thicknesses and for sewing buckram pleats
THIMBLE invaluable to push a needle through more than one thickness of heavy fabric
MASKING TAPE used on machine plate to make seam and hem guides
STEAM/DRY IRON only use steam for badly creased fabric; dry iron whenever possible to reduce the risk of water damage

USEFUL EXTRAS

Table clamps keep the fabric secure; or use bricks, covered in interlining and fabric
PINKING SHEARS for frill edges

PATTERN MAKING ESSENTIALS

PATTERN PAPER
PATTERN CARD for frequently used patterns, such as tie-backs
POLYTHENE or PVC HEAVY-GAUGE SHEETS are transparent, and will make placing the patterns much easier
HB PENCILS
COMPASSES
INEXPENSIVE LINING FABRIC for draping swags patterns
PERSPEX SET SQUARE with measurement rules for seam allowances
LIGHTWEIGHT CHAIN 3m (3yd), for swag drapery; alternatively you can use a length of lead-weight tape

---

Professional Tip

A lot of time is invested in making patterns; they should be kept for future projects. Store them in large, labelled envelopes in a safe, dry place.

Pattern paper is perfectly suitable for infrequently used patterns. For swag or tie-back patterns that will be used often, it is better to cut the patterns from pattern card or heavy-gauge polythene.

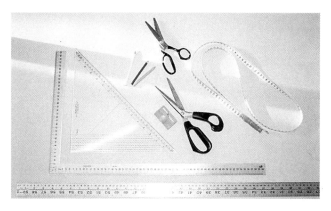

Above, a simple group of items you will find essential when cutting and measuring. We have shown cutting scissors and pinking shears, a set square in clear plastic so that you can see any pattern or weave through it, and two rulers, a steel metre ruler for measuring.

Left, sewing equipment, ranging from an assortment of needles, threads, pins, pliers.

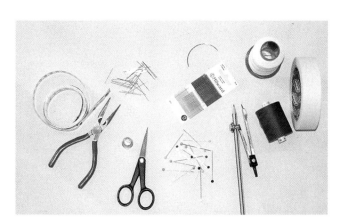

ABOUT YOUR MACHINE

Domestic machines are suitable for most curtain work and can be put away when not in use. Interlined curtains with buckram pleated headings are usually too thick for a domestic machine and will strain the motor, but these can easily be sewn by hand.

Machines with a swing needle stitch are useful for neatening edges, and some have additional features such as a blind hemming foot.

EXTRAS

A domestic overlocker with three or four threads is not essential, but useful if you plan to make lots of cushions, unlined tablecloths, bed valances and covers, unlined blinds and curtains.

THREADS

There is a vast choice of threads; you should not only match the thread with the colour but also the weight to the fabric. Many sewing problems are caused by thread which is incompatible with the fabric.

Mercerised 100% cotton thread is suitable for sewing most furnishing fabrics. Polyester thread, sometimes with a cotton core, is a strong, general purpose thread useful for any fabric. Polyester sheer fabrics should, ideally, be sewn with a fine polyester thread. Invisible monofilament thread saves having to stock numerous colours, but when ironing take care not to melt the stitches. It can also be tricky to handle, slipping out of needles easily.

Standard dressmaking thread (120 denier) is recommended for domestic machines and will accommodate fabrics from sheers to velvet. See Machine Needle and Thread Guide opposite, for alternative thread sizes and their uses.

MACHINING HINTS

The first rule of good sewing is to have your machine serviced regularly, every two years.

Never take the work out from the machine unless the take-up lever is at the top of its position. The threads are halfway through a stitch cycle and still under tension; there will be unnecessary stress on the needle and it may bend. For the same reason, always pull the work out towards the back of the machine.

Allow the feed mechanism of the machine to take the work through at its own rate. It should be *guided* but not *pulled* through the machine.

When sewing large pieces of fabric, the weight must be supported so that it does not pull against the needle. Pins placed at right angles to the seam can be machined over when seaming. See diagram, p120.

To sew a precise seam allowance, place masking tape onto the machine at the required distance from the needle. Use this as a guide.

When two pieces of fabric are sewn together, the fabric in contact with the teeth of the feed mechanism is sometimes taken through at a faster rate than the top fabric, creating a gathered effect. Gently hold onto the lower piece, applying a little pressure so that both fabrics are taken through at the same rate.

If the top and spool tensions are not balanced, it may cause puckered stitching and tight seams. The spool case has a small screw on the side; if this becomes loose, adjust with a small screwdriver. It's useful to keep the screwdriver handy in your sewing box near the machine.

Professional Tip
The size of needle and thread should both be compatible with the work. The finer the needle the less damage it makes, reducing thread breakages and puckering. But if too fine a needle is used to sew a thick fabric, it will become blunt, and break. Change the needles frequently. Use sharp needles for all woven fabrics, and ballpoints for knitted fabrics. If, when matching thread colour to fabric, you are unable to find an exact match, a thread one shade darker is less noticeable than a lighter one.

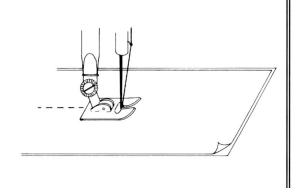

When sewing different weights of fabrics together, such as a chintz border to a heavier cotton fabric, place the lighter fabric underneath, next to the feed teeth. If this still puckers, gently hold the lighter fabric, applying a little pressure, so that both go through the machine at the same rate.

THREAD BREAKAGES

> Upper machine tension too tight.
>
> Sewing thread too fine for the weight of fabric.
>
> Blunt or bent machine needle.
>
> With high speed sewing the needle becomes hot, melting the thread.
>
> Worn spools with nicks in the outer edges prevent smooth turning.

Spray the machine bed with a silicone spray and wipe over the area when you are sewing leather, suede and coated fabrics.

MIS-STITCHING

> Machine incorrectly threaded.
>
> Blunt or bent needle.
>
> Needle inserted incorrectly.
>
> Incompatible needle and spool threads.
>
> On knitted fabrics change to a ballpoint needle.
>
> Placing tissue paper under lightweight fabric will help the thread to form the loop which creates the stitch.

HAND SEWING

There are some jobs which will have to be done by hand. 120 threads are suitable for the finer fabrics such as sheers and chintzes, but they are seldom strong enough for medium to heavyweight fabrics. They are likely to get tangled when doubled up; you'll spend more time unknotting than sewing. So we advise using a stronger, ticket or denier thread, size 36, often used for buttonholes. It is sensible to store your machine and hand sewing threads separately and in an accessible place.

Tangles can usually be avoided by running the thread over a white candle, or a piece of soap before sewing with it.

MACHINE NEEDLE AND THREAD GUIDE		
FABRIC	NEEDLE SIZE	THREAD DENIER
LIGHTWEIGHT SHEER FABRICS	Singer 10-12 Metric 70-80	180s-120s
MEDIUMWEIGHT FABRICS	Singer 12-14 Metric 80-90	120s
HEAVYWEIGHT FABRICS	Singer 14-16 Metric 90-100	75s

Professional Tip

Industrial machines will withstand constant use and are capable of sewing at great speed. Free standing and set into their own table, they deserve a permanent home in a workroom.

There are many types available, but a standard lock stitch, drop feed machine is capable of sewing medium to heavyweight fabrics and should cope with most situations. An alternative feed mechanism for lock stitch machines is 'needle feed', recommended for several thicknesses of fabric such as buckram headings and piping details. A 'walking foot' feed mechanism holds both the top and bottom layers of fabric, and will cope well with difficult fabrics.

To make curtains in great quantities there are specific machines such as blind hemmers, which will replace hand sewing the hems and the sides. Three and four thread overlockers, and frilling and pleating attachments will gather and sew the frill into a seam in one operation.

These machines require a substantial investment, so need to be fully utilised to be cost effective.

Sewing thread tensions can be set up (by a qualified mechanic) to sew nets perfectly using a fine needle and a fine thread (180 denier), and re-set to sew several thickness with a stronger thread (75 denier). Contact the large sewing machine manufacturers for more information.

MEASURING

THE BEST ADVICE ANYONE CAN GIVE YOU IS TO MEASURE TWICE AND CUT ONCE

Measuring is sometimes claimed to be the single most important part of fine curtain making. It is true that, with the correct measurements, the simplest window dressing will look just right. One of our most valuable tools is the Measuring Chart, which we devised for our own use. Now we have adapted it for you to use, so that you can measure with confidence and have a convenient place to put all the necessary information. It will help to make your work easier, quicker and more accurate.

Measuring a window is important for two reasons. First, for its size and location in the wall and its relation to the rest of the room. Second, to find the quantities of fabric, the sizes of the hardware you will need to buy, and the finished measurements of your curtains and tops. Always take a full set of measurements. You may change your ideas, and remeasuring can be a great waste of time.

When you are measuring have a few fabric samples available to help you imagine the design and colour scheme you are considering.

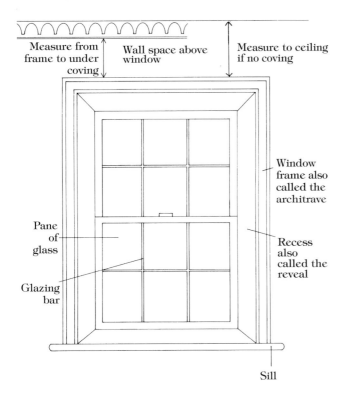

GOLDEN RULE 1
MEASURE CAREFULLY

Measurements are used not only for making up curtains but also for estimating the quantities of fabric, lining and trimmings you will need. This will give you an accurate indication of the final cost, so that if you change any of the individual items, you can quickly see how it affects your budget.

Allow plenty of time – roughly 10 minutes per window. A house of approximately 12 windows will take you at least 2 hours. This will be enough to take a full set of measurements for curtains, blinds and sheers. Then no matter what style or design you eventually choose, you will have all the measurements to hand.

Think of it as an investment - measuring properly with the right equipment will take you a few minutes per window. With a little basic care and cleaning, your curtains may hang there for a minimum of 10 years and, if you choose a fine fabric and it wears well, perhaps even a lifetime!

Well worth it!

GOLDEN RULE 2
MEASURE EVERYTHING

Never make the assumption that two apparently identical windows have precisely the same dimensions. Measure each window individually, and as carefully as if they were in separate rooms. For rooms with more than one window, sketch a floor plan, mark in the windows and number them.

When you make each curtain, sew a little tag on the back with its window number.

Keep the Measuring Charts for future reference: they may be needed at a later date for new or replacement curtains, and they are also useful to hand on to any new owners.

MEASURING CHART

Floor plan and diagram

Style and design	
Track corded LH/RH	
Architrave depth	
Radiator depth	

Existing track and pelmet board or pole

Window	Length of track or pole	Hook to sill/floor	Hook to top	Return of track or pole to wall	Length of pelmet board	Return of pelmet board
1						
2						
3						
4						

No fittings in place

Window	Coving/ceiling to floor/carpet	Coving/ceiling to top of window frame	Top of window frame to sill	Sill to floor	Width of window inc frame	Wall space either side LH/RH	For blinds and sheers Inside reveal	Outside reveal inc frame
1							wide / drop	wide / drop
2							wide / drop	wide / drop
3							wide / drop	wide / drop
4							wide / drop	wide / drop

MEASURING ESSENTIALS

RETRACTABLE STEEL TAPE MEASURE with a 2.5cm (1in) wide tape. Especially useful when measuring high ceilings by yourself – it will stay upright without flopping over.

SPIRIT LEVEL to check for uneven fixing points for blinds; these need to be level or they won't pull evenly and might snag on the sides.

STEP LADDER even in a low-ceilinged cottage it can be difficult to make sure the top of your tape measure is really at the corner.

EXTRAS

HOOK DROP STEEL TAPE MEASURE useful if you are making curtains regularly. It hooks into the glider of the track to take precise measurements when the track is already installed.

PATTERN PAPER for templates of arched windows, window seat cushions, etc.

ANGLE PROTRACTOR for measuring the angles of bay windows.

CAMERA for awkward windows that need some thought, especially if you haven't yet moved in.

MEASURING EXISTING FITTINGS

Measuring is quite straightforward when existing tracks and other fittings are already in place, but it is still a good idea to use the Measuring Chart. You can use it for estimating fabric quantities and for keeping all the necessary information together.

If you are refurbishing, moving into a new house, or just changing your style, you can add new ideas to old fittings; a pelmet board can be set over a wall-fixed track or you can extend an existing board or pole, or change their height for longer, more elegant curtains.

WALL-FIXED OR CEILING-FIXED TRACK OR POLE
1 Length of track or pole
2 Return of track or pole to the wall
3 Hook to floor or sill

ADDITIONAL MEASUREMENTS NEEDED FOR A TRACK FITTED TO A PELMET BOARD
4 Front edge of pelmet board
5 Return of pelmet board to the wall

Wall-fixed pole

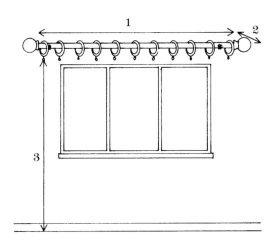

Pelmet board and track

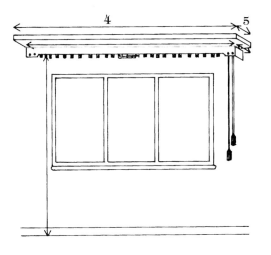

> **Professional Tip**
> Where there are multiple windows on one wall, measure the distances between them. If you plan separate curtains, check whether you want to allow space for paintings or a mirror hanging between the windows.

MEASURING BARE WINDOWS

1 UNDER COVING/CEILING TO FLOOR/CARPET
To check for uneven floors measure at each end and in the middle. If there is no carpet yet, make a note to deduct carpet thickness.

2 WALL SPACE ABOVE WINDOW
This is from the under coving or ceiling down to the top of the window or architrave. Many kinds of hardware will be fixed here. This space can be covered with decorative top treatments.

3 TOP OF WINDOW OR ARCHITRAVE TO SILL
For sill length curtains or outside blinds. If you want to keep out the light and draughts, add an extra 7.5-15cm (3-6in) to the curtain length.

4 SILL TO FLOOR
When added to 2 and 3, this should equal 1. It's worth double checking.

5 WIDTH OF WINDOW (including frame)

6 AVAILABLE WALL SPACE EITHER SIDE OF WINDOW FOR CURTAIN STACK BACK
Note any doors, built-in furniture, etc. and planned changes. Measure on the right and left; a track or pole will usually be the width of the window plus 30%. The extra is equally divided into a left-hand stack back (LHSB) and a right-hand (RHSB) stack back, one on either side for a pair of curtains, or at one side only for a single curtain treatment. The curtain pulls back against the wall when open to let in the light.

7 DEPTH OF ARCHITRAVE
A pelmet board or a pole on the wall needs to be in front of the window frame (architrave) to allow curtains to hang freely. Pelmet and pole brackets may need to be extended so that curtains don't catch, and can glide easily when they are opened and closed. The depth of the architrave is added to the usual depth of the pelmet board or brackets.

8 WIDTH OF WINDOW RECESS (inside reveal)
Blinds and sheers can be fitted inside the recess and curtains where space is limited.

9 DEPTH OF THE WINDOW RECESS (inside reveal)
For both 8 and 9, measure at the top, centre and bottom of window to check for an uneven frame. Work to the smallest measurement for roller or Roman blinds, fixed nets, or sheers which hang directly over the glass. Otherwise they will not hang straight.

10 WIDTH OF WINDOW (outside reveal)
Allow an extra 2.5-10cm (1-4in) at each side to the width of blinds.

11 DEPTH OF WINDOW (outside reveal)
Allow an extra 2.5-10cm (1-4in) to the top and bottom of the finished length of the blind. Record the fixing point above the window on the Measuring Chart.

12 TYPE OF WALL AROUND WINDOW (concrete lintel, wooden beam, brick, etc.) Ensure you have suitable wall plugs and screws, see p224.

Window and surrounding wall

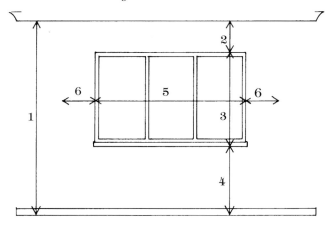

Detail of window and frame

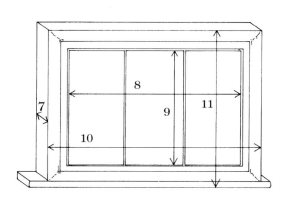

MEASURING BAY WINDOWS

Tracks can usually be bent one way to the angles of the bay. If you also want the curtains to turn back onto the walls you will need a two-way bend track.

MAKING PAPER TEMPLATES FOR BAYS

1 If there are no fittings in place, follow Steps 1-12 on p111 for each individual window; if there are existing fittings, follow Steps 1-5 on p110. Then make a diagram (Step 1, right) of the whole bay, and letter each corner, starting at the left-hand side of the window. Measure each section, e.g. for the two-angle bay, A to B, B to C, C to D.

You will need to take the measurements where the track or pole will be fixed, in case the walls are uneven. Cut some strips of card the width of a pelmet board. The standard width is 15cm (6in). Then cut the strips to convenient lengths.

2 Take two strips and hold them into the angle of the wall, overlapping the card. Tape the cards together to make a template and mark it with the letters, A-B-C, B-C-D. Do this with each angle. Show where the curtain will return to the wall to close any small gaps (the dotted line).

3 Use both the measurements and the card angles to make a full-sized paper template of the shape of the pelmet board. Draw a line on the template to indicate the position of the track.

Using your template as a guide, cut out the board. Measure and mark on the length of the curtain track and work out the returns. Measure the front edge and returns of the board.

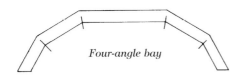

Four-angle bay

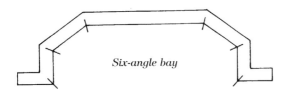

Six-angle bay

Step 1 *Measurement No 5 includes the spaces between the windows when working with bays.*

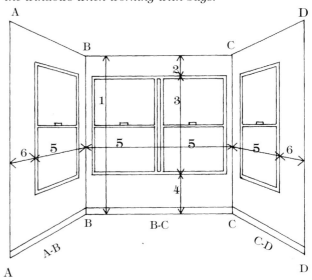

Step 2 *Full sized paper template*

The board will be shaped to the wall at the dotted line

Step 3 *Pelmet board seen from underneath*

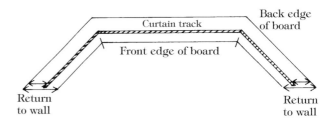

The four-angle bay, like the two-angle bay which is shown above, can be fitted with a track that bends one way only. Extend the curtain round the corner to close the gap.

The six-angle bay will need a two-way bend track since it looks best when it turns back to the wall. For bays fitted with poles, you will need a curtain at every angle. For problems with an unusual bay, ask the fabric store or the hardware manufacturers to advise you. See p234 for major suppliers.

ARCHED WINDOWS

Where curtains are fitted to the shape of an arched window, a paper template is required, not only for shaping the heading but also for the hardware.

Some fitting options are listed on p226 in the Arched Fittings section.

First you need to take the basic measurements of the bare window:

1 In the centre (of the arch), its top to the floor
2 In the centre, top to the ceiling/undercoving
3 Width of the window at the widest point
4 Depth of the architrave, if present
5 Width available either side of the window

MAKING PAPER TEMPLATES FOR ARCHES

1 Pin or tape a large piece of paper over the arch, either on the frame or on the wall. A roll of brown paper will do if you can buy one wide enough. If you cannot find the full width you need, make a template of half the window by lining up an edge to the centre of the arch, then fix the paper over one side.

2 With a spirit level, mark a horizontal line at the widest part of the window. Trace the shape of the arch above the line onto the paper. Measure the distance from the horizontal line to the floor on both sides. Put it on the Measuring Chart but also onto the brown paper for quick reference.

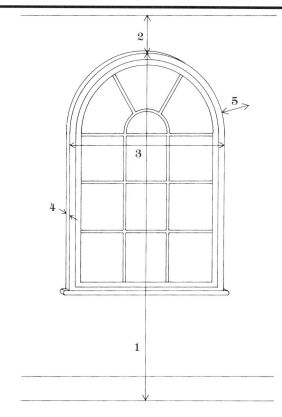

If the curtains are to hang inside the arch, use the curve on the paper to shape the heading. If they are fixed onto the wall, increase the size of the arch to where you want to fit the track. Remove the paper and keep it safe. Check all the measurements on each window - there may be subtle differences.

Professional Tip

Most often the curtain hangs from a track on the wall, fitted around the arch.

A quick way of establishing the shape of the track you need is to take the radius from the centre of the arch to the line on the paper above the window. This gives you a radius to use for bending the track, and to help make up a paper pattern for the heading.

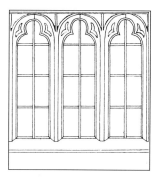

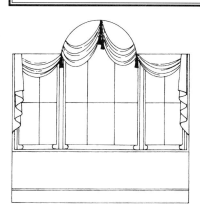

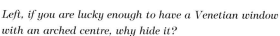

Left, if you are lucky enough to have a Venetian window with an arched centre, why hide it?

You can use dramatic swags and tails on their own, leaving the architecture to shine without curtains.

Shape the swag to the arch of the window, and make up separate swags and tails for the side windows.

Above, windows like this Gothick set were originally medieval but they became popular in the 19th century.

You can leave them uncovered to show off their delicate shape. If you do curtain them, don't try to curve around the arches, but let the curtain hang straight, over the whole frame.

Design decisions include how far on either side of the window to extend the pelmet board or pole, how long to make the valance, and so on. All play an important part in the success of any window treatment.

Once you understand how the curtain proportions can be altered to suit the window, where to position the brackets or poles, then the finished curtains will make a beautifully balanced statement. Here are some questions for you to consider while still at the measuring stage and before you make up your mind about fabric, hardware, style, and design. Make a note on the Measuring Chart of any appropriate suggestions. Before purchasing your tracks, boards or poles, see Fitting, pp225-227.

PELMET BOARDS
What height above window?

Any dead wall space above the window can be fully utilised and covered with a valance or pelmet to achieve a more elegant effect. In an ideal situation, the pelmet board should be positioned directly underneath the coving or cornice; the pelmet itself or the valance or swag should be between $\frac{1}{5}$ to $\frac{1}{6}$ of the finished curtain length – it should just cover the frame to lose as little light as possible during the day. See p99 for the ideal proportions of other top treatments.

If the valance you have planned doesn't quite cover the top of the window, lower the position of the pelmet board until it does. You can use a piece of lining fabric tacked in the right position to see how it looks.

TRACKS OR POLES
How long, including stack back, should they be?

STACK BACK is the area where the curtains hang against the wall when they are pulled open. By covering the wall and not the glass, during the day, it allows the most light into the room.

Corded tracks and poles require more wall allowance than un-corded. The curtains can only stack back on the track or pole between the cord housing and the overlap arms.

EASY FORMULA
To determine the length of the track or pole, increase the width of the window glass area by 30%. Very full curtains need more stack back space than flatter ones, and heavier fabrics will also take up more stack back area. You can adjust the 30% to take this into account.

POLES AND LATHS
What height above window?

Laths and poles have the advantage that they can be fixed at window level if there is no available space above. They can even be ceiling fixed if necessary. Ideally, the top of the lath or pole should be fitted 10-20cm (4-8in) above the window.

Poles can be fitted into the ceiling joists, with brackets that have a top fitting. The pole is slotted through the brackets. Make sure the fitting is secure, because a set of lined and interlined curtains can be a considerable weight, and simple plasterboard or unsupported boards will not hold them. Poles can also be fitted up to the ceiling with overclip brackets. They are held by the clips, rather than resting on brackets.

CURTAINS
How long should they be?

Curtains look their most imposing when they are full length, either touching the floor or falling generously onto it. If they are going to be held in tie-backs, ombras or curtain bands, make them 2.5-5cm (1-2in) longer, so they can be bloused above the holder.

Curtains that puddle onto the floor will need arranging each time they are opened and closed, or they can look messy. Corded tracks should not be weighed down with too much extra length as it may strain the fixing. Covered laths look tailored and smart when the curtains just touch the floor.

Sill length curtains can be recessed into the frame and touch the sill, or fixed outside the frame, and hang 10-15cm (4-6in) below the sill. This is sometimes called 'apron length' and ensures light and draught exclusion.

NOTE:
Measurements for finished curtains: To convert your window measurements to the finished width and length of your curtains, and to estimate fabric quantities, see the relevant sections:
For finished width see p134, and for finished length see p126. Fabric quantities are on pp116-17.

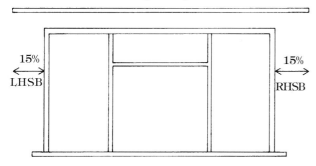

Length of track or pole = window width + 30%

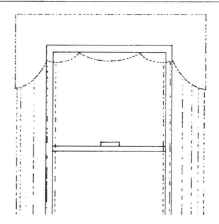

Shaped pelmet – the shortest drop just covers the window frame to let in maximum light

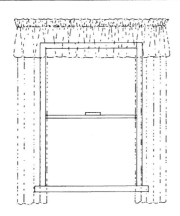

Valances are ¹/₅ length of curtains, and just cover the top of the frame

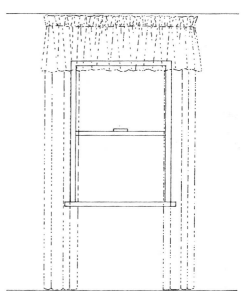

The longer valance and curtains look more elegant than the sill length pair

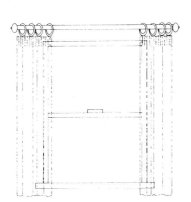

The pole is hung above the window to allow the top of the curtains to cover the window completely when they are closed

A blind hung inside the recess. It must fit tightly, yet allow free movement when it is pulled up and down.

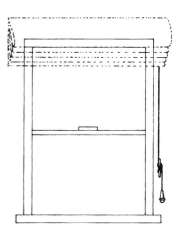

A blind set outside the recess. The track is fixed as flat to the wall as possible to cover any gaps at the side. The window looks larger.

115

Check the measurements you will need before you begin your calculations. A calculator is useful.

> NOTE: we have simplified the fabric quantity formulas to make it easy to work on your calculator by using the following symbols: + (plus) and x (times).

CURTAINS

1 Length of the track or the pole

2 Curtain fullness ratio

3 Usable width of the fabric:

On *plain* fabric this is the width minus seam allowances (allow approximately 1.5cm ($^1/_2$in) seam allowance on each side)

On *patterned* fabric, match the pattern first at the sides. For the repeat, measure from point to point where the motif or pattern starts again. See p119 for the technique.

4 Fabric cut drop:

On *plain* fabric work out the finished length of the curtain from your window measurements + heading and hem allowances. See chart below. On *patterned* fabric take the fabric cut drop and divide by the pattern repeat. Round up, never round down, and multiply the result by the amount of the pattern repeat. For a drop pattern see p119.

Professional Tip

ALMOST INSTANT FABRIC FORMULA

Use centimetres or inches, but make sure you don't use both. This is the formula for any plain fabric. The length of the track or pole is multiplied by the appropriate fullness ratio. See below.

Divide the result by usable width of fabric, which will give the number of widths you need to cut. Round up to the nearest width.

Multiply the number of widths required by the measurement of the cut drop (see left). Remember to take the pattern into account if necessary. The result is the total fabric quantity for that window.

The hardest part of estimating is in marginal cases where, for example, three widths will not quite give sufficient fullness, and yet four might be too much. But most extra fullness is absorbed by the side turning, overlap and return allowances which add up to nearly half a width of normal furnishing fabric.

Unless the cost is critical, it's always better to round up rather than down.

This FABRIC QUANTITIES table will show you how to find the exact quantities you need for the Almost Instant Formula, above. The fullness ratio gives you the *number of widths*, add the allowances to the *length* of each panel.

MACHINE HEADINGS	FULLNESS

On machine gathered tapes the fullness ratio can be flexible as the draw cords are pulled up to the required measurement. Even if a finished heading has slightly less than 2 x fullness, it will look attractive.

TAPE HEADINGS	
Gathered	2.00-2.50
Pleated, pinch/goblet	2.00
Pleated, box	3.00
Frilled/puffed	2.00-2.50
OTHER MACHINED HEADINGS	
Slotted	2.00-2.50
Ties and café clips	1.50-2.00
Tabbed	1.00-1.50

HEM ALLOWANCES	
Full length curtains	allow 24cm (10in)
Sill length curtains	allow 14cm (6in)
Italian strung curtains	allow 25cm (10in)
Lining and interlining	allow 20cm (8in)
Valances	allow 10cm (4in)

HAND SEWN HEADINGS	FULLNESS

Here the fullness is more critical as it dictates the size of the pleats and spaces. With less than 2 x fullness, spaces will be wider than pleats, and the curtain will look skimpy. Especially on patterned fabrics, allow plenty of fullness so the pleats can be positioned over a particular area, see p140.

Hand sewn French pleats	2.25-2.50
Hand sewn goblet pleats	2.25-2.50
Hand sewn box pleats	2.50-3.00
Hand sewn gathers	2.25-2.50
Hand sewn smocked	2.25-2.50

HEADING ALLOWANCES

A standard allowance for machine tape and hand sewn pleats is 6cm (2in).

For frilled, puffed, slotted and other decorative headings, see individual suggestions pp 134-48.

VALANCES

1 Finished width of valance – that is, the measurement around pelmet board or valance rail including sides.
2 Heading fullness ratio. See table, opposite page.
3 Usable width of the fabric. See opposite page.
4 Fabric cut drop = finished depth of valance + heading and hem allowance. See opposite page.

Do your calculations as given in the Almost Instant Fabric Formula, opposite page.

GATHERED VALANCES These need to be full to be successful and the valance may require one more width of fabric than the curtains beneath.

SERPENTINED VALANCES A graceful proportion is for the shortest and longest measurements to be ⅙ and ⅕ respectively of the finished curtain length. Calculate the fabric quantities as for a straight valance based on the longest measurement.

ARCHED VALANCES The finished depth of the valance at the shortest point should be ⅙ or ⅕ of the curtain length. The longest point at the sides is determined by the design. If the longest point hangs over the curtain stack back area, there will be no loss of light.
Cut drop = deepest measurement of valance + a heading and hem allowance. Adjust the cut drop for pattern repeats if necessary.

PELMETS

The finished width of a flat pelmet is the measurement around the pelmet board or rails including the sides. Divide this figure by the usable width of the fabric to establish the number of widths you will need.
Cut drop = deepest measurement of pelmet + 15cm (6in) turning allowance.

INFORMAL SCARF DRAPERY, SWAGS AND TAILS

For estimating quantities, see p166 and p182 respectively.

FABRIC TRIMS

For contrast edging, frills and fabric trims, see individual instructions in Finishing Touches pp150-65. These apparently minor quantities will add up to more yardage than you imagine; never assume you will be able to find enough from leftover fabric. For piping and binding cut on the cross, see p121.

BED CURTAINS

These are estimated in the same way as window curtains. For specific details, see p213.

TABLECLOTHS

For round tablecloths, see p218. Obviously there will be some wastage with round cloths, but you can use the corners for the smaller fabric trims, appliqué on cushions and so on.

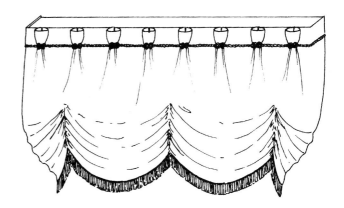

An Austrian blind with a goblet pleated heading and drop down sides

BLINDS

ROLLER and ROMAN BLINDS will need only the flat measurement across the window, see pp199-200.

GATHERED AUSTRIAN BLINDS vary in fullness from 1.5- 2.5, according to the heading required. They are usually made a little overlong so that you can have pretty scalloped hems even when they are dropped down.

FESTOON BLINDS as above, but they also have extra vertical fullness; for more details see pp203-4.

Professional Tip
If fabric is sold as imperfect, then buy as much extra length as you can afford, up to 15% or 20%.

A good store will not charge you for obvious flaws when they see them, but at home you may find smaller, additional imperfections: these should be cut out and discarded.

CUTTING PLAIN AND PATTERNED FABRIC

Now that most of the preparation has been done, it is finally time to start making up! But before you wield the scissors for the first time, read through these important notes:

As soon as you unpack the fabric, check the reference number and the colourway with your original sample and order. This is especially vital if you ordered by telephone or by post. Many companies make similar designs in the same or slightly varied colours, but once you have cut into the fabric they are very reluctant to change it.

Roll out the fabric right to the end and check for flaws, and that the correct quantity has been sent. Again, manufacturers will not replace fabric once it has been cut.

Remember to work in either centimetres *or* inches!

CUTTING PLAIN FABRIC

1 Calculate the cut drop by adding a heading and hem allowance to the finished length. See table on p116 for the fabric quantities you will need. The diagram, right, shows how you lay out the roll to begin cutting.

2 Always cut out the fabric using a metal ruler and an L or a set square, otherwise the curtains will never hang straight. Keep the ruler firm and, with a fabric marker pencil, draw right across the width below it.

3 Check that you recognise the right and wrong side of the fabric, and as soon as you have finished cutting each drop, mark the top of the length and the right side of the fabric with a fabric marker pencil.

4 Before cutting linings and interlinings, check that they are the same width as the fabric; if not, you will have to cut more or less to match up the total width.

5 Ideally, you should cut each fabric or lining for a pair of curtains from the same batch, as colours do vary.

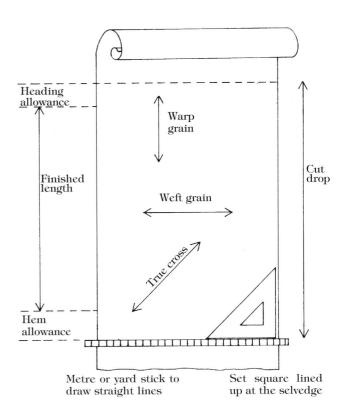

Metre or yard stick to draw straight lines

Set square lined up at the selvedge

6 If the selvedges are tight before you cut out the lengths, release any puckering by snipping to just within the seam allowance. If this is not done, the fabric will not lie straight and you will find it difficult to cut straight lines.

Snipped selvedges

7 The cut panels of fabric are joined together with a plain seam.

NOTE: If you are working on a patterned fabric it will make it more accurate if you match the pattern on the cut lengths, and then quickly slip-tack the seams before you machine them.

FABRIC WITH BORDERS

If you have a border printed down each selvedge, you should cut away one border per seam. This will show off the design, but will also reduce the usable width; so bear this in mind when you calculate fabric quantities.

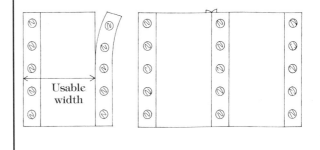

Usable width

CUTTING PATTERNED FABRIC

When you lay out the fabric, start your measurements at the hem and count up. It's unlikely that a finished length will incorporate a full pattern at the top and bottom. An incomplete pattern is less obvious in a heading – it's better to put a full pattern at the hem. The diagram shows the adjusted cut drop measurement to use when you cut out all of the lengths. All the cut lengths have to start at the same part of the pattern so that they match at the seams when they are joined.

1 Check the pattern repeat. This is the distance before the pattern repeats itself. A simple pattern repeat will usually match horizontally across the fabric.

2 Adjust the remaining lengths to allow for the pattern to be matched. You can do it by physically laying out each length, or just by measuring if you have calculated the adjusted cut drop accurately.

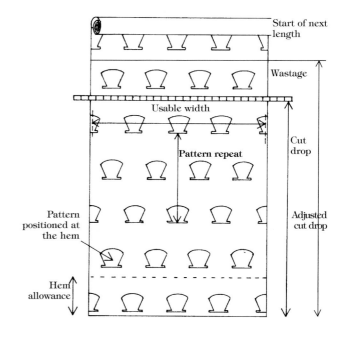

DROP PATTERNS

This repeats itself diagonally across the width. To match the panels, the cutting measurement is the adjusted cut drop + ½ a pattern repeat.

The pattern will alternate on the cut panels, so as you cut each one, number it at the top. Seam them up in this order.

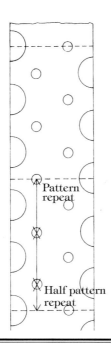

Professional Tip

CUTTING OFF GRAIN PATTERNS

When fabric is printed 'off grain', the pattern does not match side to side. You must still cut square, or the curtains will not hang straight. Cut your first length, match up the pattern as best you can at the selvedge, and cut the next length. Continue, numbering each panel as you cut it, and seam the panels together in that order to make the best of a difficult job.

SEAMING UP DROP PATTERN FABRIC

If you have an even number of widths, the central opening, called the 'leading edge', will fall between whole widths.

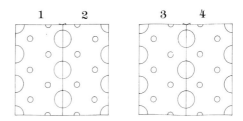

If you need an odd number of widths (there are three in the diagram below), allow an extra full repeat on the final width. Cut down the centre and match the right-hand half to the outside of the first panel. Trim the excess from both halves. This keeps whole widths at the centre.

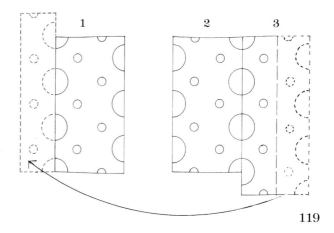

Seams are the main building blocks of sewing, and are usually sewn by machine rather than by hand. For those who have little or no experience, these are the three major seams that you will need to make curtains.

PLAIN SEAMS

Place the cut fabric panels . right sides together and machine a line of stitching, taking the necessary seam allowance.

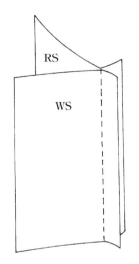

Flat fabrics without a prominent weave need only a narrow 1.5cm (½in) seam allowance.

Thick, loosely woven fabrics may need a wider seam allowance.

FRENCH SEAMS

For sheer curtains and lightweight or unlined curtains where a plain seam would look untidy. (It is not practical for patterned fabrics that have to be matched.)

1 Place the two pieces of fabric wrong sides together and machine, taking a 1cm (⅜in) seam. Trim the allowance down to 0.5cm (¼in) and press.

2 Fold, placing right sides together, and then machine 0.6cm (a generous ¼in) in from the fold of the seam, making sure that the raw edges are enclosed.

Step 1

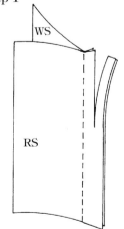

Step 2

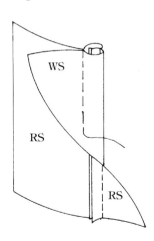

SINGLE LAPPED SEAMS

Interlining can be joined using a plain seam but an overlapped seam will give a flatter finish. This is important when using the bulkier interlinings.

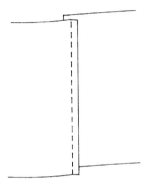

Overlap the selvedges and machine together.

SEAMING PANELS

Never have a seam in the centre of a panel; it looks very unprofessional. Always split a width and put half on each side.

A pair of curtains, 1½ widths in each curtain

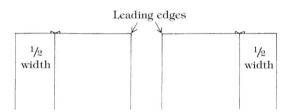

4 width valance

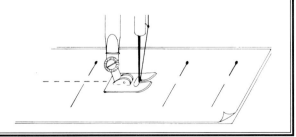

Professional Tip

Machining over pins placed at right angles is easy to do and it helps to keep all the fabric neatly in place, particularly when the fabric is slippery.

Watch out for a blunt needle. When it goes over the pin it may be slightly nicked, and it should be replaced frequently.

CUTTING ON THE TRUE CROSS OF THE GRAIN

For piping and curved contrast bound edges, the fabric is cut at 45° to the selvedge. This is the 'true cross of the grain' and it uses the 'give', or the stretch, of the fabric to let the trim lie flat. It may then be sewn around curves without puckering.

Loosely woven fabrics have the best stretching properties and, although chintz is popular because of its colour range and sheen, it is too tightly woven to give. Try to choose a more open weave. Some fabrics, such as silk, have a lot of give; as it is stretched, the strips get narrower, so you will need to cut wider strips than usual.

PIPING is usually cut 4cm (1½in) wide. Check this is sufficient for the piping cord you want to use, and cut wider strips if necessary. Thicker fabrics need heavier piping cord and wider strips. Make a piping ruler from smooth timber to quickly mark out the strips.

BINDING is cut four x the finished width measurement. There is a limit to the width that can be used and still lie flat. It is usually cut between 5-8cm (2-3¼in) wide. When binding a deep curve, make up a test piece to find the maximum width which will work.

FABRIC QUANTITIES

Add together the length of all the proposed bound or piped edges.

HOW MUCH WILL IT MAKE?

0.5m (½yd) of fabric will make 12.50m (13yd) of *piping.*
0.5m (½yd) of fabric will make 7.5m (8yd) of *binding.*

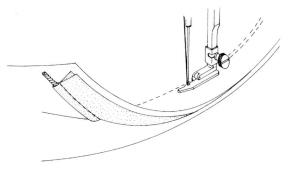

CUTTING AND SEAMING STRIPS

1 Fold a corner up to the opposite selvedge in a triangle. The fold should lie at 45° to the selvedge. Crease the fold and cut. Pin the two pieces together; with a fabric marker pencil, mark and cut out the strips.

2 To join the strips together, cut the ends to a right angle and place two ends, right sides together, at right angles to each other. Machine across the diagonal, trim off the corner and press. Turn the bottom strip over to the right side. Repeat with the other strips. Follow the instructions below to make piping.

Step 1 *Cutting strips*   Step 2 *Seaming strips together*

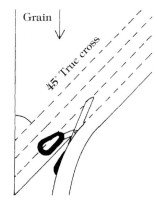 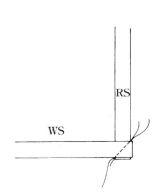

PIPING SEAMS

1 Lay the cord in the centre of the wrong side of the strip and fold in half. Using a zip foot, machine as close to the cord as possible.

2 With the raw edges together, machine the piping onto the right side of the fabric with a second row of stitching, taking the correct seam allowance. Snip the seam allowance to let the piping lie flat.

3 Lay the other fabric underneath, right sides together, and machine, following the stitch line made when attaching the piping.

This has involved three rows of machine stitching. With experience, you can place the cord into the centre of the strip and insert it into the seam in one operation, with a single row of stitching.

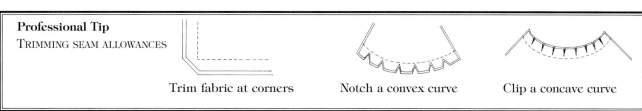

Professional Tip
TRIMMING SEAM ALLOWANCES

Trim fabric at corners   Notch a convex curve   Clip a concave curve

SLIP TACK STITCHES

On patterned fabric, slip tack along the seam for a perfect match.

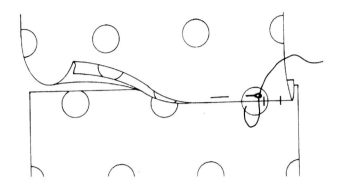

On the right side, fold under the edge of one piece and place over the other so that the pattern matches perfectly before tacking.

SLIP STITCHES

These have many uses, but they are always used for sewing a mitred corner, and for sewing the lining to the fabric up the sides of curtains.

1 For a mitred corner, secure the thread and take a short stitch through the fold of the fabric, and the next stitch through the other fold, starting opposite the previous stitch. Pull the thread taut to keep the two pieces of fabric together and to conceal the stitches without puckering.

2 When attaching the lining to the side of a curtain, the slip stitches can be 2cm (^{3}/4in) long. Make sure that the thread is not pulled, otherwise the edge of the curtain will become tight and won't hang straight.

When taking the stitch through the fabric, take care not to go through to the right side.

1

2

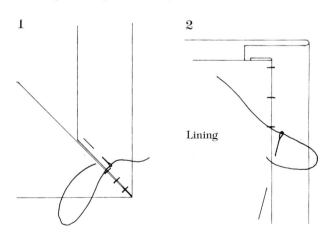

Lining

HEMMING STITCHES

For stitches which can be seen on the right side, secure the thread and take a 2cm (^{3}/4in) stitch through the fold of the hem. Take a small stitch directly above and then a long stitch back into the fold. The small stitches will be barely noticeable.

HERRINGBONE STITCHES

Worked from left to right, the needle points to the left, keeping the thread on the right-hand side of the stitching.

INTERLOCKING STITCHES

Long and loose, they tie the fabric to the interlining, and the interlining to the lining, holding the layers together while allowing some slight movement between them. Use a continuous length of thread, no matter how long the curtain or panel. Work from the hem to the top; the stitches should be barely visible on the right side, loose enough to avoid dimples but not so loose as to be ineffective.

TACKING STICHES

To hold the fabrics firmly together and still work quickly, use as long a thread as you can manage. Take a long stitch on top followed by a shorter stitch underneath rather than even stitches.

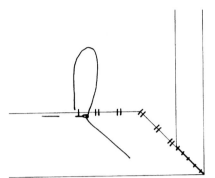

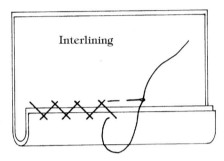

Interlining

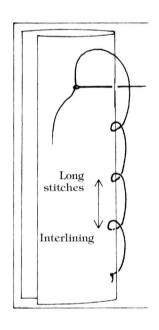

Long stitches

Interlining

BACK STITCHES

To take each stitch, place the needle into the work behind the thread. The stitches look like running stitches on the right side but are overlapped on the reverse side, making a strong seam.

SMOCKING STITCHES

These decorative stitches can be worked in cotton, silk or wool embroidery threads. Silks can be used on most types of fabrics but wool is easier to use on loosely woven fabrics. Select a hand sewing needle that can be easily threaded but which is sharp enough to sew through all the layers of fabric. An embroidery needle is almost a necessity for the wools and heavy cottons.

Smocking stitches use a reasonable quantity of thread, so buy plenty of skeins, most shops will give a refund on unused skeins. Thread the needle with a normal length of thread with a secure knot. Take the thread from the back of the work to the front, to a point where the stitch is to begin. (If you are left-handed turn the book upside down and the diagrams are converted for you. The stitches are then worked from right to left.)

To embroider over machine tape the stitches must cover the depth of the tape, usually 7.5cm (3in). However for a hand sewn heading, the depth of gather stitches and smocking stitches is optional, which makes them very versatile for creating different effects.

For example, on a sheer fabric a single row of chevron smocking 2.5cm (1in) deep will give a light look. Two rows of smocking 5cm (2in) in depth, and featuring a stand up frill above it, is an attractive heading for a valance or for curtains on a pole. Deeper smocking, 15cm (6in), looks stunning on a full length curtain or on a fixed heading; see pictures on p139. Only one disadvantage, smocked headed curtains will not stack back well - they are too thick at the top.

PREPARATION

Smocking stitches are worked from left to right. Place the fabric on a table, with the heading parallel to the edge. The heading is effectively sewn upside down. When sewing, use either the machine lines or the hand sewn gather rows as a guide to keep the stitches straight and at an even depth. The two most frequently used stitches for smocked headings are Honeycomb and Chevron.

The difference between the stitches is that Chevron smocking travels up and down on the surface of the pleat, rather than inside it as it does in Honeycomb.

HONEYCOMB STITCHES

Start the thread at the left-hand edge of the first pleat and take a stitch through the right-hand side of the second pleat (2). Travel down the pleat coming out on the left-hand side (3). Move along to the next pleat (4). Take the needle up inside the pleat (5) and so on. Make sure you pull the thread with an even tension after each stitch to bring the two adjoining pleats together. Subsequent rows are worked mirrored top to bottom, so that a second stitch is worked over points 3 and 4 and so on.

Honeycomb stitching

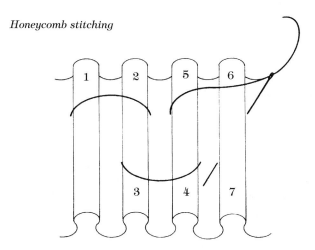

CHEVRON STITCHES

Start the thread at the left-hand edge of the first pleat and take a stitch through the right-hand side of the second pleat (2). Move down that pleat and take the next stitch (3) directly below 2. Move along to the right-hand side of the next pleat (4) and make a stitch through the pleat. Move up that pleat for the next stitch (5) and so on. Make sure you pull the thread with an even tension after each stitch to bring the two adjoining pleats together. Subsequent rows are worked mirrored top to bottom so that a second stitch is worked over points 3 and 4 and so on.

Chevron stitching

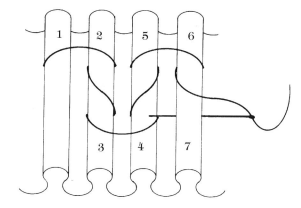

FINISHING CORNERS

There are two methods of folding the hem allowance inside the corners of the curtain. One is a 'true' mitre, the other is known as a 'mock' mitre.

A true mitre distributes the fabric evenly, and should be used on the hems of all curtains, and particularly for interlined ones. A mock mitre can be used at the top of the panel, and on valances, pelmets, etc.

MITRING CORNERS

1 Mark the corner of the mitre with a pin; this is where both the hemline and the side fold line of the curtain converge.

2 Turn up the corner of the fabric at an angle of 45° so that the fold runs through the mitre point. Check that the raw edge of the fabric at the top of the fold lies at 90° to the side of the curtain.

3 Turn up the first and second hem folds, and pin.

4 Cover a lead weight with lining fabric and sew into the corner.

5 Fold in the side turning allowance to complete the mitre. There will be excess fabric in the corner, so tuck it inside with a pin to make a clean point. Check the corner with a set square. Slip stitch in place, see p122.

Step 1

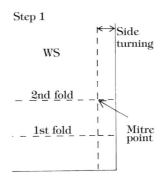

Step 2

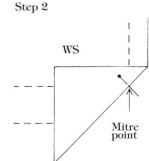

Step 3

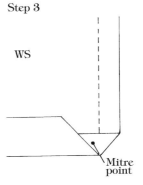

Steps 4 - 5

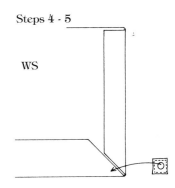

MOCK MITRING CORNERS

1 Turn in the side of the curtain. Turn up the first hem fold and turn up the corner at an angle of 45°.

2 Turn up the second hem fold turning to complete the mitre. Place lead weight in corner and slip stitch.

Step 1

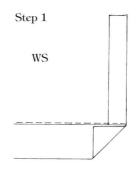

Step 2

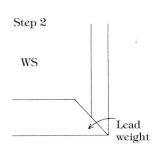

Professional Tip

To cover several lead penny weights in lining once, machine double vertical rows, a little apart. Slot the weights down the rows and machine two rows across to enclose them securely.

Cut between the stitched lines and use individually. When you have some spare time, make up a big batch in standard ecru lining, and keep them until needed.

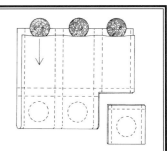

ATTACHING MACHINE TAPES

Turn over the raw edge at the top of the curtain to the wrong side and pin. Trim the raw edge so that it will be neatly enclosed by the tape.

1 Pull 10cm (4in) of draw cords out at one end of the tape and tie in a secure knot.

2 Pin part of the tape onto the curtain; check back to your Measurement Chart to make sure the hook loops are correctly placed to match your hook to top and hook to hem measurements.

3 Machine up the side of the tape and along the top. Stop machining 15cm (6in) from the edge of the curtain; keep the work in the machine. Cut the tape, leaving a 10cm (4in) turning allowance. Pull the drawcords out at the outside edge and tie in a secure knot. Trim and tuck underneath the raw edge of the tape, enclosing the cords so that they will not pull loose.

Machine down the side and along the bottom so that the tape is secure.

4 From the centre of the curtain pull up the draw cords evenly to the finished width. Tie them into a bow or wrap around a cord tidy, which you can buy at a sewing shop.

Insert hooks into the tape pockets every 15cm (6in), or according to manufacturer's instructions.

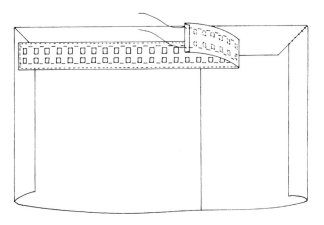

Attaching pencil heading tape

CHAIN STITCHING LININGS TO HEMS

Start with a long piece of thread brought through from the back of the lining. Make a big loop around the first three fingers of your left-hand, holding the thread taut in your right hand. You can take the needle off, or let it lie at the other end of the thread.

Reach through the loop with your left fingers to catch the taut thread and pull it back through the loop, tightening gently until the chain stitch is formed.

Repeat 12 times – you will now have a length of very strong chain stitch. To tie it off, thread the needle through the loop and pull. Secure the end to the hem of the fabric. A chain every half width will make sure your lining and fabric hang together professionally.

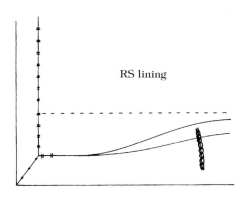

RS lining

Finished chain linking fabric hem and underside of lining

PREPARING LININGS AND INTERLININGS

Machine the lining panels, right sides together, using plain seams. Press the seams open and keep flat without creasing.

If working with an odd number of widths, remember to seam half widths onto the side of each curtain lining. See p120 for diagrams.

Fold up the hem 7.5cm (3in) and press. Fold up the same amount again, and pin in place, ready to machine.

A quick way to press up the hem without measuring is to cut a strip of card 7.5cm (3in) deep over which the fabric is folded. Slip the card out, pin and machine.

Interlining can be joined using a plain seam but an overlapped seam is flat and less bulky. Overlap selvedges 1.5cm (½in) and machine together.

CURTAINS OF ALL KINDS

There are no rigid rules to curtain making and our methods can be adapted to suit your specific needs. Methods and techniques are graded from very easy to quite difficult, using one to four needles. But even if you are an absolute beginner, do remember that lack of experience can almost always be made up by patience, and by allowing yourself plenty of time.

VERY EASY: ONE NEEDLE   EASY: TWO NEEDLES   MODERATE: THREE NEEDLES   NEEDS EXPERIENCE: FOUR NEEDLES

NOTE: If you do not understand a term or phrase used anywhere in the book, look in the glossary on p236 and then in the index for specific descriptions of individual projects which will put the term in context.

On diagrams, RH refers to the right as you are facing the curtain, LH refers to the left. RS is the right side of the fabric, WS is the wrong side. Most work is done on the wrong side, and both diagrams and instructions will show any exceptions clearly.

So that you can see the whole curtain at a glance, the diagrams are usually of a single width sill length curtain.

CHECK LIST: SIX THINGS TO DO BEFORE YOU MAKE YOUR CURTAINS.

1 Measure your windows and fittings. From these work out the finished curtain width, p134 and length, see right.

2 Estimate the quantity of curtain fabric, see p116.

3 Choose the curtain heading. At this stage it may be worthwhile to read through the relevant make-up notes, see pp134-147.

4 Choose your curtain make-up method. Make sure you understand the instructions before you start.

5 Cut out and seam up your fabric, lining and interlining panels, see pp118-120.

6 If you are planning to edge your curtain with a contrast border, frill or braid, it may need to be added to the curtain panels before you begin, see pp150-158.

Now you are ready to make your curtains.

NOTE: MACHINED CURTAINS
Fold the panels neatly. Place a table (or a friend) by the machine to take the weight and minimise creasing.
HAND SEWN CURTAINS Place the fabric, lining and interlining on a table. Let any widths that will not fit on the table fall neatly on the floor. Work on one section at a time. Widths that have been sewn and ironed should be concertinaed and placed at the edge of the table.

Professional Tip

FINDING THE FINISHED CURTAIN LENGTH

Finished curtain length = hook to top + hook to hem measurements

HOOK TO TOP MEASUREMENT

1 Track fitted to a pelmet board = 1cm (^{3}/8in)

2 Track fitted on a wall without top treatment = 4-6cm (1^1/2 - 2^1/4in)

3 Pole = 2cm (^{3}/4in)

4 Fabric covered lath = 7.5cm (3in)

NOTE: For puffed headings, the hook to top measurement is 15-20cm (6-8in)

HOOK TO HEM MEASUREMENT

Take the hook to floor/sill measurement and increase or reduce according to the required curtain length. For options, see p114.

FITTINGS IN PLACE

Take the hook to floor/sill measurement and reduce or increase as appropriate for hook to hem measurement; for the finished length, add the hook to the hem to the relevant hook to top measurement.

FITTINGS NOT IN PLACE

This is more difficult. You have to work out where the top of your track, pelmet board, or pole will be positioned. Work backwards from this measurement to get the hook to floor/sill measurement. Reduce or increase as appropriate for hook to hem measurement; for the finished length, add this to the relevant hook to top measurement.

MACHINING UNLINED CURTAINS

A quick, easy make-up method, useful when frequent washing outweighs the need to keep out draughts.

MATERIALS
Fabric, seamed up into panels
Heading tape

1 Fold in the side edges 2cm (³/₄in) and fold over a further 4cm (1¹/₂in). Pin in place and machine along the folded edge.

2 Fold up the hem 12cm (5in) and fold up again 12cm (5in). Pin in place and machine the hem.

3 Measure the finished length up from the hem and mark with a line of pins. Transfer the pins to the right side. Fold over the top of the curtain, level with the pins. The raw edges will be covered by the heading tape, see p125 for details.

Steps 1 - 3

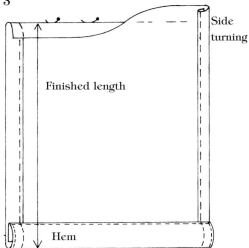

MACHINING LINED CURTAINS

Lining adds body and weight. Options include thermal lining for extra warmth or if the curtain lining can be seen from outside, through a patio window for instance, try lining with a light, complementary pattern or colour.

MATERIALS
Fabric, seamed up into panels
Lining, seamed up into panels and hemmed
Heading tape

1 Fold up the hem 12cm (5in) and fold over 12cm (5in) again. Pin in place and machine.

2 On patterned fabrics trim the selvedges at the sides of the curtain, leaving a 1.5cm (¹/₂in) seam allowance.

3 Trim the outside edge of the lining, so that the panel measures 7.5cm (3in) less than the curtain fabric.

4 Place the lining onto the fabric, 4cm (1¹/₂in) up from the hem, right sides together. Machine up each side, taking a 1.5cm (¹/₂in) seam allowance.

5 Turn the curtain through to the right side. Press 4cm (1¹/₂in) of fabric over onto the wrong side of the curtain at each side, so that the lining lies flat.

6 To mock mitre the raw edges at the hem, fold up and into the sides to neaten. Slip stitch in place.

7 Measure the finished length up from the hem, and mark it with a line of pins. Transfer the pins to the right side of the fabric. Fold over the top at the pin line; the raw edges will be covered by heading tape. See pp125 and 134 for the different types of heading tape.

Steps 1 - 6

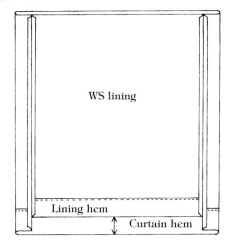

Step 7 *Curtain right side out*

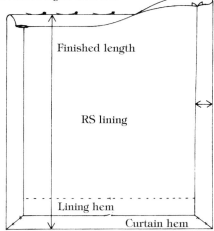

HAND SEWING LINED CURTAINS

Use this method when you want rounded edges but it is not practical to fully interline. Strips of interlining are placed in the sides and hem of the curtain to soften the edge.

MATERIALS

Fabric, seamed up into panels

Lining, seamed up into panels and hemmed

Strips of interlining 7.5cm (3in) wide for sides of curtain

Strips of interlining 14cm (5^1/$_2$in) wide for hem

Fabric covered weights (one for each corner and seam)

1 Lay the fabric panels right side uppermost and mark the hemlines with pins 12.5cm (5in) and 25cm (10in) up from the raw edge. Mark the mitre points of the corners with pins, 25cm (10in) up from the bottom and 6cm (2^1/$_4$in) in from the side.

2 Place the leading edge, wrong side uppermost, parallel to the side of the table and weight the fabric down to prevent it from slipping off the table. (Fabric covered bricks make very good weights.) Let any widths that will not lie flat on the table sit neatly on the floor.

3 Cut and join strips of interlining 7.5cm (3in) wide, long enough for each side of the curtain and also strips 14cm (5^1/$_2$in) wide for the hem.

4 Fold up and mitre the corners of the hem. Place the strips of interlining inside the second hem fold and into the side turnings. Place the fabric covered weights into the corners and slip stitch the mitres, see p124. Slip stitch along the hem catching alternate stitches through the interlining to the fabric.

5 Fold over the 6cm (2^1/$_4$in) side turning and herringbone stitch to the interlining. Stitch up to the top, just below the depth of the curtain heading tape or buckram.

6 Measure the finished length up from the hem and mark with a line of pins. Transfer pins to the right side of the fabric.

7 Starting at the leading edge, lay the lining onto the curtain right side up. Where possible, match the seams with the main curtain and place the lower edge of the lining 4cm (1^1/$_2$in) up from the hem of the curtain.

8 Fold back the lining and interlock to the fabric every quarter width, half width, on the seams and 15cm (6in) in from the side edges.

Steps 1 - 4

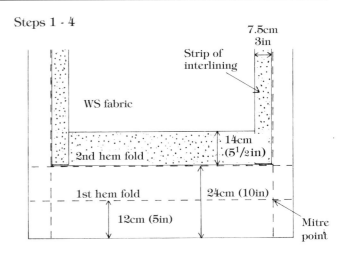

Steps 8 - 12

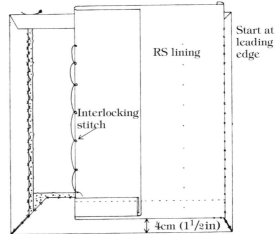

9 Trim the lining level with the side edges of the curtain and turn under the raw edge to within 2.5cm (1in) of the edge and slip stitch. At the hem, continue to slip stitch around the corner for 2.5cm (1in).

10 At the hem, sew chains between the lining and the fabric every half width across the curtain, see p125.

11 Fold over the top of the curtain at the pin line. The raw edges will be covered by the heading tape. Mock mitre and slip stitch the corners. If making a pair of curtains, check that the lengths are exactly the same.

12 Either machine attach the heading tape, or hand sew a decorative heading. See pp134-48 for variations.

HAND SEWING INTERLINED CURTAINS

A layer of interlining is sewn between the main curtain fabric and the lining.

The extra body and weight of the interlining ensures that the curtain drapes well, and provides additional insulation.

Instructions for the hem vary slightly according to the weight of interlining. Bump is heavier and thicker, domette is lighter and thinner.

MATERIALS

Fabric, seamed up into panels

Interlining, seamed up into panels

Lining, seamed up into panels and hemmed

Fabric covered weights (one for each corner and seam)

1 Follow Steps 1 and 2 for Lined Curtains, opposite.

2 Lay the interlining onto the wrong side of the fabric, placing the side edges together. Either place bump 24cm (10in) up from the lower edge or domette 12cm (5in) up from the lower edge. Smooth out the interlining so that it is completely flat.

3 Carefully fold back the interlining lengthways and interlock to the fabric every quarter width, half width, at the seams and 15cm (6in) in from the side edges. Always work the interlocking stitch from the hem upwards and stop 10cm (4in) below the top.

4 Mitre the corners of the hem and insert fabric covered weights, see p124.

5 Fold over the 6cm (2¹⁄₄in) side turning allowance and herringbone stitch to the interlining. Stitch up to the top, stopping just below the depth of the heading tape or buckram.

6 Measure the finished length up from the hem. Mark the top line with a row of pins. Transfer these to the right side of the fabric. Trim the interlining to this line.

7 Starting at the leading edge, lay the seamed and hemmed lining, right side uppermost, onto the curtain.

8 Fold back the lining and interlock to the interlining as before, every quarter width, half width, and on the seams and 15cm (6in) in from the side edges.

9 To finish the curtains, follow Steps 9-12 for Hand Sewn Lined Curtains opposite.

Steps 1 - 4

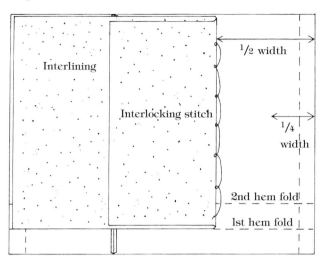

Steps 5 - 7

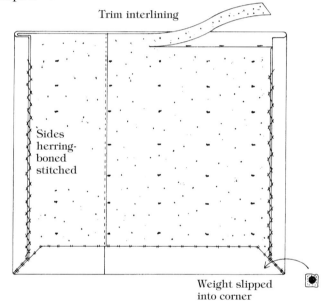

Steps 8 - 9

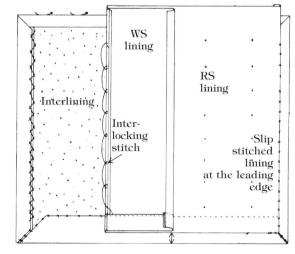

Door curtains help to prevent cold draughts. Double sided curtains hung in passageways will also help to keep the house warm. To be effective, they should be made of a heavy fabric and interlined. Decorative curtains hung at an inner door can be lined, but do not necessarily have to be interlined. Follow instructions for Lined and Interlined curtains on pp127-9, using the door frame as your measurement base instead of a window.

Interlined curtains can be weighty. They are best hung from portiere rods, which are thin brass or painted metal poles with rings and special fixing brackets; see p93 for details. These are fitted to the top of the door, so that the curtain lifts when the door opens. Check the recommended weight; hollow metal tubing will carry decorative lined curtains, but a solid brass rod is much better for a heavy interlined curtain.

Door curtains should be made approximately 5cm (2in) overlong to prevent floor draughts. You can tie them back at the hinge side in summer. Curtains in passageways will be visible from both sides, so you need to make a double sided curtain in the same or contrasting fabric. The leading edge at the opening side can be decorated by inserting piping, a frill or fan edging into the seam, or by sewing on bullion fringe or rope.

INTERLINING DOUBLE SIDED CURTAINS

MATERIALS

Fabric, seamed into two panels, one face and one back
Interlining, one panel seamed up
Fabric covered weights (one for each corner and seam)

1 Place the two fabric panels right sides together. Machine down the leading edge. If it is in the design, insert a frill or piping to make a decorative edge.

2 Interlock the interlining to wrong side of the face fabric, see p129. Fold the interlining over 5cm (2in) at the leading edge. To hold it in place, interlock along the fold of the interlining to the seam of the leading edge.

3 Make a 12cm (5in) single hem fold on the face fabric and sew in place. Continue to fold up the hem of the backing fabric and sew in the same place.

4 Fold the backing fabric over onto the curtain and interlock it to the interlining. The hems of the face and backing fabrics should be level. Sew chains along the hem, see p125.

5 At the outside edge of the curtain, fold in the raw edges of the face and backing fabrics to bring them level and slip stitch together.

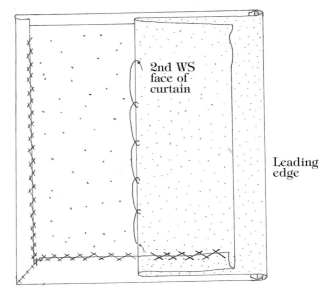

2nd WS face of curtain

Leading edge

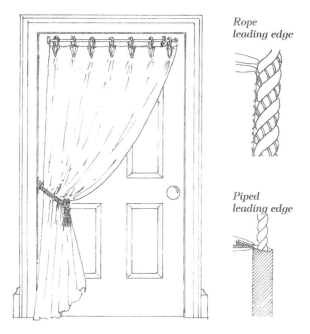

Rope leading edge

Piped leading edge

DOUBLE SIDED HEADINGS

Hand sewn goblet and French pleats look neat with only the pin hooks showing on the reverse. The back fabric can be brought round to the front to make a contrast leading edge.

DORMER WINDOWS

Dormer windows built out from a sloping roof line are often quite small, so it is important that the curtains block out as little light as possible. You can use long curtains for added impact. Hang the curtains from a pole and use a second, slightly longer pole, to hold them back to the wall.

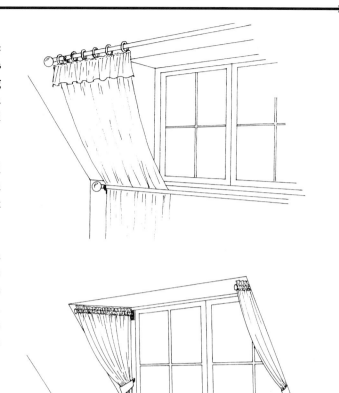

For large dormers, if the space allows, hang sill or full length curtains from inside the recess. Make sure you have enough stack back so that they can be pulled back completely.

The ideal solution, where space is restricted, is a dormer rod or swing arm fitted inside the recess. The rod pivots from a bracket fitted to the side and lies against the wall or swings out in front of the window. The curtain will have to be double sided, as both faces show. Or use a decorative lining as your second face and bring it around the front edge to make a contrast.

A slotted heading works well; the rod is simply pushed through. Pleated and gathered headings can also hang from the rod and look attractive on both sides.

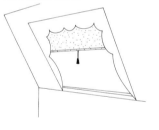

Skylight with lambrequin and roller blind

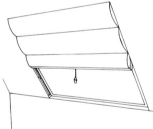

Skylight with Roman blind

SKYLIGHTS

Set into the roof line or ceiling, they can be fitted with special roller or Roman blinds. These have runners adapted to hold them on the slope. See the Suppliers Directory on p234. One attractive idea would be to frame the window and blind within a stiff lambrequin in a toning colour or pattern. See left.

BATH AND SHOWER CURTAINS

Decorative curtains can be made for the bath or a shower recess. The simplest solution is to buy a plain shower curtain and to use it as a lining for the main fabric. Leave the sides and hem open so that the plastic can hang inside the bath to catch any drips, while the face fabric hangs outside.

Alternatively, line cotton fabric with plastic to make valances and side curtains for a feminine, framed bath.

Fabrics rarely endure hot, steamy conditions for long. Bathroom and kitchen curtains will need replacing more often than those in the rest of the house.

SHEER FABRICS

The primary use for sheer fabrics is to provide privacy while letting in more or less light, depending on their weave and design. They were traditionally used behind heavy curtains, but interior designers are increasingly using sheers as the main fabric. When not required to provide extra insulation, sheers create a delightful light, airy effect.

A sheer curtain hanging next to the glass will absorb atmospheric dirt, protecting the main curtains. If you live in the heart of a busy town, it is worth making two sheers per window – one to hang and another to wash.

A light, open fabric such as muslin is inexpensive and can be used in generous quantities. Traditionally sheers were used around beds and dressing tables. Today sheers cover a wide range from lace to spotted muslins and printed voiles. See Fabric Glossary and Quick & Easy: No-Sew for more ideas.

FABRIC QUANTITIES

Sheer curtains only look sumptuous when the fabric is used plentifully. 2 x fullness should be the minimum, and 3 x fullness is even better.

Some voiles are manufactured up to 3m (3yd) wide, so that the fabric can be cut in either direction to eliminate the need for seams. As any doubling will show through, avoid unnecessary seams or side turnings; a neat selvedge is less conspicuous.

HEADING CHOICES

Use a slotted heading with a small stand up frill for a net wire or net tension rod.

For pencil gathered heading use special transparent 5cm (2in) deep heading tape.

Puffed headings will give a light, fluffy look and can be made up above a gather tape, a slotted pole channel, or a net suspension rod. Use either white or cream fine net inside the heading to match the colour of the sheer fabric.

Smocked headings using self or contrast coloured thread are charming in nurseries and children's bedrooms.

DESIGN VARIATIONS

Two or more tucks sewn across the hem of the curtain will give a more tailored finish. Use a cool iron to press the fold of each tuck and then sew in place. The raw edge of the hem is folded up inside the lowest tuck.

Italian stringing is very effective with sheers; they form beautiful swathes as a single curtain or as a pair. The stringing is done in the same way as for heavier fabrics, (see p197) but use small, clear plastic rings instead of brass rings.

To make large bows for tie-backs, use two or more layers of net inside the fabric to hold the shape.

Puffed headed and Italian strung sheers

HARDWARE

Net wire is a coil with a plastic coating. The wire is cut with pliers, and small screw eyes are fitted into either end. It stretches between two hooks at either side of the window. Net wire is sold in packs which 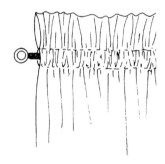 indicate how far it will stretch; for narrower widths, cut the wire short, or the curtains will droop. The tension must be enough to hold the wire straight when the nets are up.

By placing enough hooks around a bay window, a single sheer curtain can be hung from net wire. After threading it through the fabric, lift the wire into a cup hook. It will raise the hem of the curtain a little, but with sufficient fullness in the fabric the uneven hemline is barely discernible.

SPRING LOADED RODS

Simply wedged into the recess of the window, they are easy to put up and take down and you can adjust the length of the curtains by moving the rod instead of re-hemming. They can only be used in recessed straight windows.

Make the slot in the curtain heading twice the diameter of the rod. The frill above the rod is optional.

CORDED OR UN-CORDED WHITE PLASTIC TRACKS

These tracks offer many installation options. They can be wall-fixed, ceiling-fixed or fitted to the underside of a pelmet board. They fit inside or outside the window recess or to the underside of a pelmet board.

Where a pelmet board carries tracks for both inner sheers and outer curtains, the width of the board must be increased by 5cm (2in) to make sure that the curtains do not catch the sheers.

Check with your supplier for suitable tracks; use a lighter one for sheers and a heavier one for curtains. They will need good fixing points to hold the weight.

MAKING SHEER CURTAINS

Follow directions for the particular style or design you have chosen, keeping these points in mind.

Cutting sheer fabrics is sometimes awkward as they are often slippery and difficult to cut accurately. To cut a straight edge on a plain sheer, pull a thread from one side of the fabric to the other and cut along this line. Measure the cut drop and pull another thread to find the next cutting line. If there is a woven or printed pattern, follow that when cutting. For hem and heading allowances, see p116.

Seam widths together with French seams, see p120. Then neaten the raw edges at each side by turning over 1cm (³/₈in) twice, and machining along the fold of the fabric. If the side selvedges of the fabric are neat, i.e. tightly woven with no small pin prick holes, they can be left without turning.

The size of slotted heading channels is based on the width of the screw eyes, rather than the thickness of the net wire. To make it easy to thread, make a channel twice the width of the screw eye.

To make a sheer hem, fold and press a double 7.5cm (3in) allowance in the same way as for curtain lining,

see p125. Weighted hems are useful to stop billowing when the window is opened. Place lead-weight tape into a double hem fold, 1cm (³/₈in) wide. Machine along the hem using a zip foot. Use a light to mediumweight tape, according to the length of the curtains. The airy effect of the sheers is a vital part of their charm.

Professional Tip

DECORATIVE HEM TUCKS

Make at least two or three tucks in a band – just one would not be as effective. Machining tucks can be made easier by drawing threads 10cm (4in) apart. Use the spaces as a machining guide.

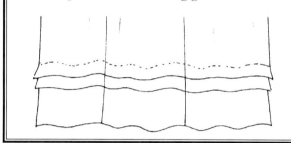

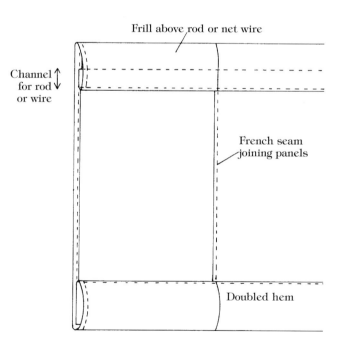

Frill above rod or net wire

Channel for rod or wire

French seam joining panels

Doubled hem

NOTE: PUCKERING

You cannot alternate thick and thin fabrics on a machine without adjustments. For sheers, use a fine needle, and thread the machine with a lighter weight thread; see p107 for troubleshooting.

DECORATIVE HEADINGS

All gathered or pleated curtains, valances or blinds require a heading. The heading affects everything - fullness, how the curtain pulls open or closed, and how the fabric is displayed. If you plan to hang the curtains without a valance, pelmet or swag, then make the most of the heading because it will always be in full view. Almost all the designs have many possible variations, so there are plenty for you to choose from.

Decorative headings can be machine taped or hand sewn. The table on p116 shows how much fabric each group of headings will need across the width, and gives a standard machine tape heading allowance. Frilled, puffed and slotted headings have allowances given in their individual instructions.

FINDING THE FINISHED WIDTH
You have planned your curtains, chosen your design and heading, and made up your curtains. Now you need to find the finished width of the heading.

HEADINGS FOR CURTAINS THAT OPEN AND CLOSE
For each one of the pair, measure half the track or pole, add half the overlap at the centre, plus any return at the side, and a little extra for tolerance. Unless you have an unusual window, these are the standard width measurements.

A central overlap to keep out light and draughts is usually 7.5cm (3in)

Return to the wall either side = 7.5cm (3in), but increase if pelmet board or brackets are extra wide

Tolerance = 2cm (^{3}/$_4$in) per width of fabric

FIXED HEADINGS
These can be used on valances, gathered blinds or Italian strung curtains.

Measure around the front edge of the pelmet board or valance rail from wall to wall, so that it includes the return on either side. Add 4cm (1^1/$_2$in) tolerance to the width to allow for easing around corners.

MACHINE TAPE HEADINGS
There is a wide range available from traditional gather and pencil tapes, to triple or pinch pleats. Goblet, box pleats and smocked tapes are also now on the market. They are attached with rows of machine stitching which will be visible on the right side of the heading, see p125 for advice about how to attach them.

Most tapes have pockets for hooks to be inserted. Some tapes also have a looped surface that can be fixed directly onto the hook side of Velcro fastening tape.

With gathered tapes, the draw cords can be pulled up to the finished width. Triple pleats, goblet, cartridge or box pleated tapes are usually made to 2 x fullness.

Smocking tape is attached with three rows of machine stitching and pulls up into a honeycomb effect. It usually requires 2 x fullness.

Narrow tape, top frill

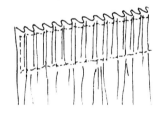

Pencil tape

Triple pleat tape

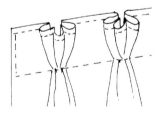

Goblet tape

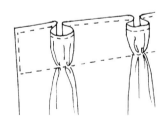

Smocking tape

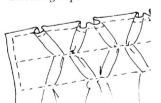

Box pleated tape

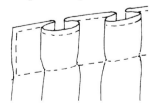

FRILLED HEADINGS WITH MACHINE TAPE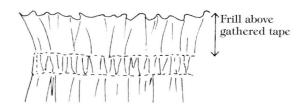

A versatile heading which can be contrast bound. The frill is formed by setting the tape down from the top edge. Any fabric above the tape forms a frill. A standard frill size above the tape is 5-7.5cm (2-3in).

HEADING ALLOWANCE 2 x frill depth + seam allowance

To make the gathers and frills of lined curtains more rounded, cut a strip of interlining or wadding to the depth of the frill and insert in the heading. For a crisper look, insert two or more layers of net instead.

Measure up from the hem to the hook drop + depth of frill. Fold frill fabric over to the back of the heading. Trim as necessary.

Pin the 2.5cm (1in) tape over the raw edge of the fabric and machine attach, see p125.

NOTE: For a contrast bound top, sew the contrast strips onto the frill, see p151. Fold over to the back of the heading, and attach the tape as usual.

PUFFED HEADINGS WITH MACHINE TAPE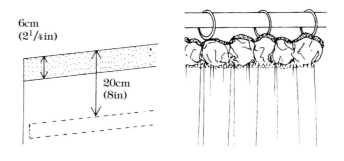

A puffed heading is created in the same way as a frilled heading. The frill is 15-20cm (6-8in) deep and is stiffened with net to make the puffed effect.

HEADING ALLOWANCE 30-40cm (12-16in) + seam allowance

NET QUANTITIES 2 layers, each 2 x depth of frill x flat width of finished panel

1 Measure up from the hem to the hook drop + depth of frill. Fold the frill fabric over to the back of the heading. Insert the net into the fold.

2 Trim the fabric. Place 2.5cm (1in) tape over the raw edge and machine attach, making sure to catch through to the edges of the net to hold it in place.

3 Pull up the tape draw cords to the finished width measurement. Open out the frill and organise the folds into rounded puffs. Some fabrics, such as chintz and silk, will naturally retain this puffed shape, but others, such as linen, will need stab stitching in place.

NOTE: To stab stitch, take a stitch every 10cm (4in) along the heading, from the top of the fold down inside the frill, to just above the top of the tape. Secure the thread to finish.

Frilled heading

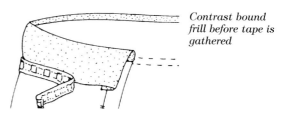

Frill above gathered tape

Contrast bound frill before tape is gathered

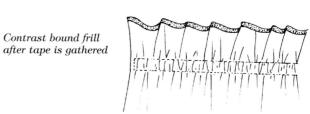

Contrast bound frill after tape is gathered

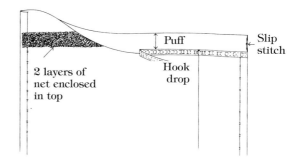

Puffed heading

2 layers of net enclosed in top — Puff — Slip stitch — Hook drop

Puffed heading with contrast top

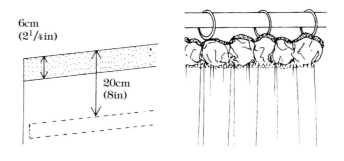

6cm (2¼in) — 20cm (8in)

Stab stitch

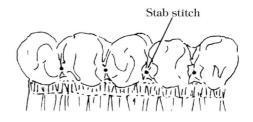

GATHERED DROP DOWN FRILLS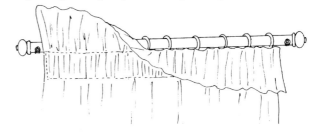

This heading is similar to a plain frill, but the frill is much deeper and folds down onto the right side.

The weight of the frill may tip the heading tape forwards, making it visible from the front. To prevent this, use a good quality gather tape that is reasonably stiff, preferably a 7.5cm (3in) pencil tape, which will be more stable than a narrow gather tape.

For curtains, the minimum frill depth is 13cm (5in) (so that it covers the tape) and the maximum depth can be up to $^1/_6$ of the finished length. For valances, the frill can be as much as $^1/_3$ of the finished length.

HEADING ALLOWANCE 2 x frill depth + seam allowance

Measure up from the hem to the hook drop + depth of frill. Fold fabric over to the back of the heading. Trim the fabric as necessary and place the tape over the raw edge and machine. At the top of the tape, machine as close as possible to the edge so that the white tape does not show on the front of the heading.

For fabrics with a *one way* design, the frill must be reversed so that when it is folded down the pattern falls in the same direction as the curtains (see right).

Cut the frill allowance off the top of the curtain, leaving a 2cm ($^3/_4$in) seam allowance. Fold the frill in half and sew it back onto the curtain upside down. Position the tape over the seam and sew in place (see right).

Simple drop down frill, just covering the tape

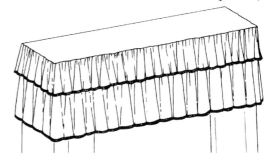

Contrast bound valance with contrast bound drop down frill

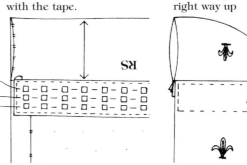

Cut frill off the length and reverse. Cover the seam with the tape.

When frill folds over in front, the pattern will be right way up

Drop down frill on full length curtains

BOX PLEATED DROP DOWN FRILLS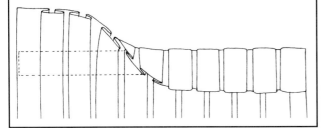

This is made in the same way as the gathered drop down frill, but using a box pleated tape. Follow the make-up instructions as above.

For strong *vertical* patterns, such as stripes, pleat them up by hand to show off the pattern. Machine pencil tape over your stitching to hold the pleats in place and to provide pockets for the curtain hooks.

SLOTTED HEADINGS

These are for a fixed heading slotted onto a pole, either with or without a frill above the stitched channel. The curtains are held open using tie-backs, ombras, brass curtain bands or Italian stringing.

To find the finished length of the curtain, measure from the top of the pole to the hem, and add the depth of the frill.

The depth of the machined channel must be considerably wider than the pole or rod to accommodate the fullness of the fabric.
Width of channel = 2 x diameter of pole or rod

SLOTTED FRILLED HEADINGS

To look balanced, make the depth of the frill either the same size as, or greater than, the diameter of the pole.

HEADING ALLOWANCE 2 x frill depth + channel depth + seam allowance

Measure the finished length up from the hem, and mark the bottom row of stitching with pins.

Measure the depth of the channel and frill and fold the fabric over to the back of the heading. Turn under the raw edge and machine the row.

Measure up and mark the top row of stitching with pins. Machine as before. It is important to machine all the rows in the same direction to avoid twisting.

SLOTTED PUFFED HEADINGS

Stiffened with net, the puffed effect is made in the same manner as a frilled slotted heading. The puff is 15-20cm (6-8in) deep.

HEADING ALLOWANCE 2 x frill depth + channel depth + seam allowance

NET QUANTITIES 2 layers, 2 x depth of frill x width of heading

Fold the net in half and insert into the fold of the heading. When machining the channel, make sure to catch through to the net with the top row of stitching.

Slot the pole through the channel and arrange the frill into rounded puffs. Spread the gathers evenly along the pole and, if necessary, stab stitch along the heading. See Puffed Headings p135 for instructions.

Measure pole

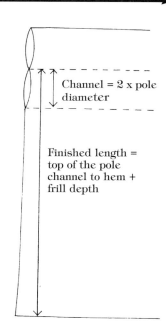

Channel = 2 x pole diameter

Finished length = top of the pole channel to hem + frill depth

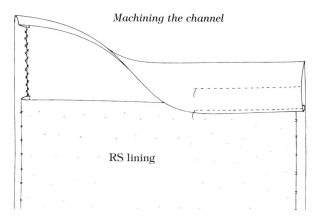

Machining the channel

RS lining

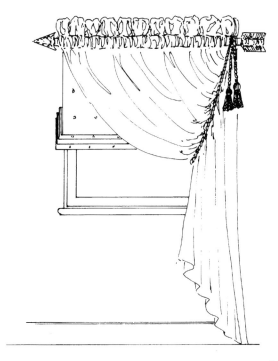

STITCH TEMPLATES FOR GATHERING

The advantage of hand gathering is that there is no machine stitching visible on the right side of the heading. Rows of running stitches are sewn across the top of the heading and these draw threads are pulled up to the finished width of the heading.

Whether the hand gathered heading is narrow, deep or a trellis design, they are all made in the same way, using different stitch templates. Make a set of card templates by tracing over each one, then glue the tracing paper onto a thin piece of card. Cut around the shape, pierce a hole at each dot and label each template. Put them away carefully to use again another time.

For gathered frill headings, set the 2.5cm (1in) gathering template 5-7.5cm (2-3in) down from the top of the curtain. For puffed headings, place the stitch template 15-20cm (6-8in) down from the top of the curtain. For the trellis heading, the rows of stitching are staggered to create alternating pleats.

Pencil gathers are normally 7.5cm (3in) deep, but they can look very attractive up to 15cm (6in) deep on a fixed curtain. For the deeper heading, increase the depth of the template.

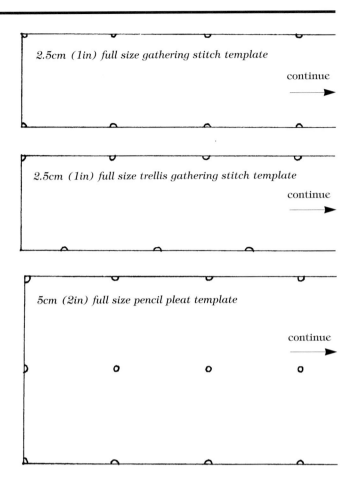

2.5cm (1in) full size gathering stitch template

continue

2.5cm (1in) full size trellis gathering stitch template

continue

5cm (2in) full size pencil pleat template

continue

HAND GATHERED HEADINGS

1 Fold fabric over to the back of the heading. Bring the lining up over the fabric, fold under the raw edge level with the hook drop measurement, and slip stitch.

2 Place the appropriate stitch template level with the top of the lining. Mark dots onto the lining with a fabric marker pencil.

3 Using strong thread (no. 36 buttonhole quality) long enough to finish a width, sew a line of running stitches, taking a small stitch through to the right side of the heading, either side of each dot.

4 Use a new length of thread for each width. Start each one by overlapping the last stitch, preventing a 'flat spot' when the gathers are pulled up. Complete all the rows across the heading.

5 Pull up the threads, a width at a time, and temporarily anchor around a pin. It is important to do this evenly. Divide the finished heading by the number of fabric widths in the heading and check that each width is pulled up to the exact measurement.

Step 1

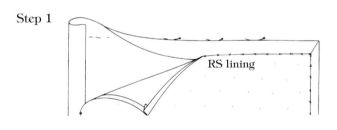

RS lining

Steps 2 - 3

Step 4

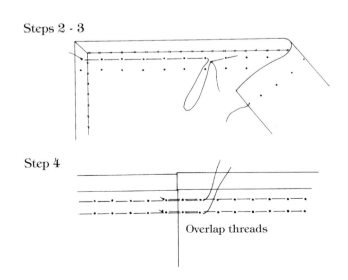

Overlap threads

138

6 At the back of the curtain, encourage the pleats to form neat, evenly spaced 'tubes'; for the trellis heading, there will be alternating smaller tubes top and bottom.

7 As these stitches are not taken out, tie off the ends of the threads by sewing them securely.

8 To make a backing for the heading, cut a piece of iron-on heading buckram or stiffening the same size as your template, and cover it with lining. Slip stitch the buckram in place.

To hang from a track, insert pin hooks.

To attach to a pelmet board, pre-sew Velcro onto the lining which covers the stiffened band.

> **Professional Tip**
>
> The pleats are prone to slip along the threads while you work, producing some areas that are sparsely gathered and others that are bunched. Pin the buckram every 15cm (6in) in place over the gather stitches.
>
> For serpentined valances, keeping the gathers even will keep the hemline even.

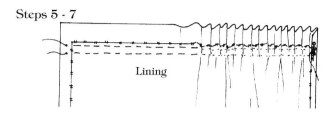

Steps 5 - 7

Lining

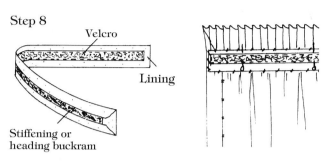

Step 8

Velcro

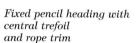

Lining

Stiffening or
heading buckram

*Fixed pencil heading with
central trefoil
and rope trim*

SMOCKED HEADINGS

1 Make up as for a gathered heading up to Step 7. The heading is smocked before the buckram or stiffening band is sewn onto the back.

2 Embroider rows of smocking stitches on the right side of the curtain. The stitches create a honeycomb effect, and look effective when worked in either embroidery silks or tapestry wools according to the type of fabric. See smocking stitches on p123.

3 Make and attach the backing as in Step 8 above.

4 Finally, from the right side of the heading, take out the draw threads. The smocking stitches and the backing will hold the pleats in place.

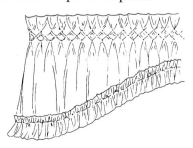

CALCULATING THE SIZE OF PLEATS, AND SPACES

Start with the width of the finished heading; see p134 for instructions. Lay out the seamed panels and measure across the top. As a standard rule, allow four pleats per width.

Individual pleats should be between 15-20cm (6-8in), with the spaces between them 10-15cm (4-6in) wide. In simple terms, all the space measurements must add up to the finished width of the heading; whatever is left is the fullness, which is then divided evenly into the pleats.

On curtains, the first and last flat space measurement is the overlap and the return respectively. On a valance the first and last flat space measurements are the returns. The valance returns should be greater than the return of the board or rail, so that the pleats begin on the front edge of the board rather than at the corner.

PLEATING PLAIN FABRIC

1 Subtract the finished width of the heading from the flat width. This gives the fullness to be pleated.

2 Divide the fullness by the number of pleats to find their size. If the pleat size is too small, i.e., less than 15cm (6in), re-calculate, dividing by one *less* pleat. If it is too big, i.e., over 20cm (8in), re-calculate dividing by one *more* pleat.

3 To find the size of the spaces, take the finished width of the heading and subtract the first and last flat space measurements. Divide this figure by the remaining number of spaces between the pleats to find the size of the spaces.

PLEATING PATTERNED FABRIC

Establish the finished width of the heading, the flat width of the heading, and the first and last space measurements as above. The calculation will be different as the number of pleats is dictated by the pattern. Decide on which part of the pattern to position the pleat. This is what you will see when the curtains are pulled back and the pleats compressed.

1 To establish the number of pleats, place a pin at the centre of each motif or stripe across the width.

2 Measure the horizontal pattern repeat - the distance between the pins.

3 To find the size of each space, take the finished width of the heading, subtract the first and last space measurements and divide this figure by the number of spaces *between* the pleats (one less than the number of pleats).

4 To determine the pleat size, subtract the space measurement from the horizontal pattern repeat.

Flat panel

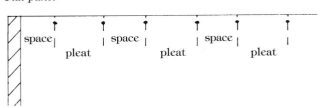

After pleating

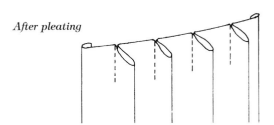

Pins mark the line of small motifs which will be the front of the pleat, while the stripe will be less prominent inside the folds when the curtain is pleated up

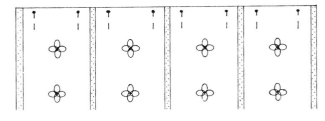

5 Mark the pleat and space measurements with pins along the top of each panel; see above.

If there is insufficient fabric at the sides to achieve either the first or last flat space measurement plus a side turning allowance, rework the calculation with one less pleat. Any excess fabric over and above the side turning allowance should be trimmed away.

With some fabrics it is difficult to both pleat and display the pattern properly. Some large horizontal repeats can be double pleated, see p176. If in doubt, or with limited time, make it simpler by switching to a gathered heading.

BUCKRAM PLEATED HEADINGS

French, goblet and box pleated headings are all made in the same way, using buckram stiffening to allow the fabric to hang in crisp folds. The depth of the buckram depends on the choice of the heading and the finished length of the curtains or valance.

The standard pre-cut size range available is 10-15cm (4-6in). The heading should be proportionate, deeper on long curtains and smaller on sill length. However, for goblets whatever the length of the curtains or valance, the buckram should be approximately 7.5cm (3in) deep to echo the shape of a goblet wine glass. French, goblet, and box pleats all begin with steps 1-5 below.

1 Measure the finished length of the curtain up from the hem and mark with a row of pins on the right side.

2 At the top of the heading, fold over the turning allowance. On the right side, mark with pins the pleats and space measurements, as diagram p140.

3 With a row of interlocking stitches sew the buckram onto the interlining across the lower edge. If you are only using lining, sew the buckram as invisibly as possible to the fabric to hold it in place.

4 Fold in the raw edge of the lining and slip stitch to the fabric.

5 Pin the pleats together, ensuring that the top edges are level, and sew down to the bottom of the buckram. As there are several thicknesses, hand sew the pleats with a small back stitch rather than strain the sewing machine.

There are three ways of finishing the pleats: French (below), for goblet and box see p142.

FRENCH PLEATS

Divide the pleat into three folds. Hold the centre fold, and push it down gently to form three equal sections. Bring them together at the base and hand sew through the bottom of the pleat, just beneath the buckram. Sew the side pleat, either side of the seam, to the top edge of the curtain, and sew the top edges of the middle pleat together.

Professional Tip

If the size of the pleat is rather small due to lack of fullness, make it into a double rather than a triple pleat to look more substantial.

DEPTH OF HEADINGS ACCORDING TO CURTAIN LENGTH			
Heading	Full Length	Sill length	Valances
French	12.5-15cm (5-6in)	10cm (4in)	5-10cm (2-4in)
Goblets	7.5-10cm (3-4in)	7.5cm (3in)	7.5cm (3in)
Box Pleats	15cm (6in)	10cm (4in)	7.5cm (3in)

Steps 1 - 4

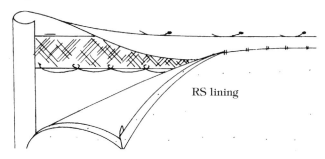

RS lining

Step 5   *Pinned and sewn pleats*

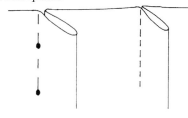

Making a French pleat

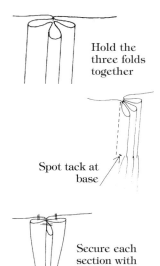

Hold the three folds together

Spot tack at base

Secure each section with small stitches

French pleats on curtain

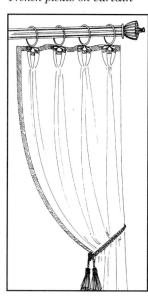

For goblet and box pleats, begin with Steps 1-5 on the previous page:

GOBLET PLEATS

Fold the bottom of the pleat as for a French pleat and sew through the base to secure. Shape into a tube, and hand sew the top of the goblet, either side of the seam, to the top edge. In order to retain the shape, cut 5cm (2in) strips of buckram, coil inside the goblet and stuff it with waste bump or wadding.

If the top of the goblet can be seen, for example on a landing, cut a circle of fabric, larger than the diameter of the goblet, place it over the stuffing and tuck down the sides.

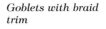

Goblet pleat

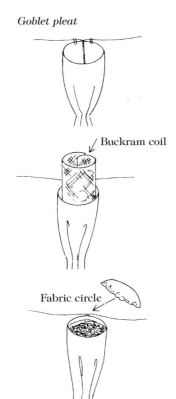

Buckram coil

Fabric circle

Professional Tip

Goblets are one of the most attractive details and can make curtains and valances look elegant and special. You can incorporate them into almost any design. Look out for scraps of antique rope, braid, tassels, and other kinds of passementerie to decorate your finished heading. See p149 for rope knotted over goblets.

Goblets with braid trim

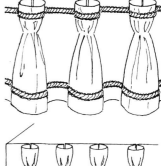

Goblets with a pleated frill

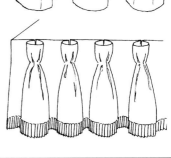

BOX PLEATS

Flatten out the pleat and hand sew the outside edges near to the top of the curtain. Secure the base of the pleat at the outside edges with very small stab stitches taken from the back of the heading.

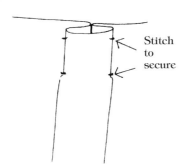

Stitch to secure

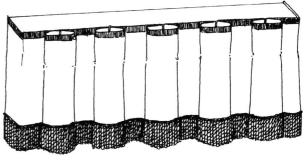

ADDING HOOKS TO PLEATED HEADINGS

Pleated headings are fixed to the hardware with pin hooks, sewn brass hooks or Velcro fastening tape. Pin hooks are stabbed into the buckram at the side of each pleat, at a level which will give you the required hook to hem measurement. Take care not to stab through the stitches as they may break. Brass hooks can be sewn to each pleat; ensure you secure them to the buckram.

If the track or pole has overlap arms, position the hooks at the leading edge of the curtain to correspond with them. Hooks are not put on the overlaps of uncorded poles with rings, as this will prevent them from closing. Place hooks onto the curtain returns as required.

The quickest and easiest solution for valances and fixed headed curtains is to sew a wide Velcro to the back of the heading.

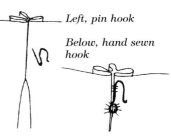

Left, pin hook

Below, hand sewn hook

Velcro sewn to back

SHAPED PLEATED HEADINGS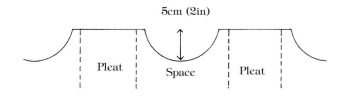

Design variations for buckram headings include scalloped French pleats and scooped out goblets. The buckram is shaped before the pleats are sewn. This is time consuming and has to be accurate. You have to decide whether it is worth the effort.

SCALLOPED FRENCH PLEATS

This is a pretty heading, often used for café curtains.

1 Calculate the pleat and space measurements p140 and make the curtains up to the heading stage pp141–2.

2 Cut the buckram to the required length and mark out each pleat, space, overlap and return measurement.

3 Make a paper template of the scooped shaping for the spaces. It is a good idea to start the shaping 1.5cm (¹/₂in) in from each side of the space to provide an anchorage point for the wings of the pleat. The depth of the scallop is usually 5cm (2in).

4 Cut out the scallops along the buckram, then lay it at the top of the curtain, leaving a seam allowance above.

5 Cut and seam together some strips of fabric, the width of the curtain by the depth of the buckram, to make a facing. Place this at the top of the curtain, right sides together.

6 With the buckram uppermost, put the facing and the curtain right sides together at the top. Pin in place and sew around the buckram shape. Do not sew through the buckram itself as this will make it difficult to turn inside out. Clip and notch the seam allowance and turn the facing fabric over to the back of the curtain. Pull out the corners and press the seam.

7 Turn in the sides of the curtain and then turn under the raw edge of the facing and slip stitch to the lining.

8 To finish the French pleats, see p141. Sew or insert pin hooks in place as required.

SCOOPED OUT GOBLETS

Goblets which are scooped out to reveal the inside, look most effective when a contrast fabric is used for the facing. They are made in the same way as described above for Scalloped French Pleats, except that the *pleat* section is shaped, rather than the *space* between the pleats. When deciding the depth of the scooped shaping, mock up a sample goblet in some waste lining fabric and pin it to the curtain top to see the full effect.

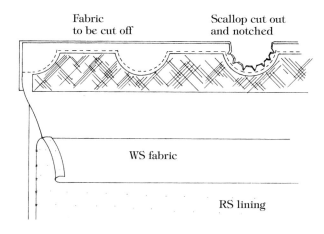

5cm (2in)

Pleat · Space · Pleat

Fabric to be cut off

Scallop cut out and notched

WS fabric

RS lining

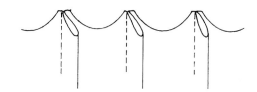

Pleats sewn in place

Scalloped pleats hung from a pole

Scooped out goblets: seen from the front and the side, the contrast lining will show off the heading

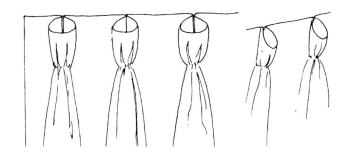

ARCHED WINDOW HEADINGS

Decorative headings for arched or Gothic shaped windows have to be cut carefully. The method suggested below applies to any arched or tiara shaped heading at the top of a curtain, valance, or shaped blind.

Arched headings are static. The curtains are joined at the centre and the sides held back with tie-backs, ombras, or Italian stringing.

MAKING ARCHED PAPER PATTERNS

1 Calculate the fabric quantities (p116) as for a standard window, but use the top of the curtain arch to the floor as the finished curtain length.

2 Make a paper template of the arch as described in Measuring Arches on p113.

3 Make a paper pattern of half the arch and draw vertical lines parallel to the leading edge every 10cm (4in) apart. Number each section and cut out each one.

4 On a large sheet of paper, mark a horizontal line and place the lower edge of each section onto the line. Leave a space for the fullness between each section.
10cm (4in) space = 2 x fullness.
12.5cm (5in) space = 2¼ x fullness
15cm (6in) space = 2½ x fullness

Draw a smooth curved line to join the sections together. Add a return to the side edge of the curtain and then add 6cm (2¼in) turning allowances to the side, leading edge and top. Cut out the paper pattern.

GATHERING ARCHED HEADINGS

Cut out the curtain fabric and seam up. Position the pattern at the top and cut round. Make the curtain up to the heading stage, see pp126-29.

For a tape gathered heading, turn over the allowance at the top of the curtain and attach a 2.5cm (1in) gather

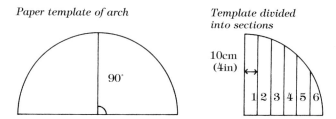

Paper template of arch

Template divided into sections

10cm (4in)

1 2 3 4 5 6

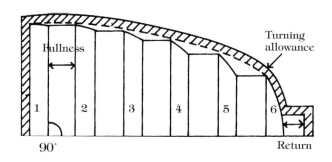

Paper pattern

Fullness

Turning allowance

1 2 3 4 5 6

90°

Return

tape in the usual way. Make small tucks as necessary. If you have allowed fabric for this, the tape can be set down to leave a small frill above it.

When pulling up the tape draw cords, make sure the fullness is evenly distributed along the arch. It may be easier, although more time consuming, to gather by hand so that the gathers are fixed in place.

PUFFED ARCHED HEADINGS

These can be made using either 2.5cm (1in) tape or by hand gathering.

Due to the curve of the heading, it is not possible to extend the puff fabric allowance above the position of the tape.

Instead, cut out the puff allowance from straight pieces of fabric, and seam onto the top of the curtain. The seam line should correspond with the top line of the tape or gather stitching, where it will be hidden.

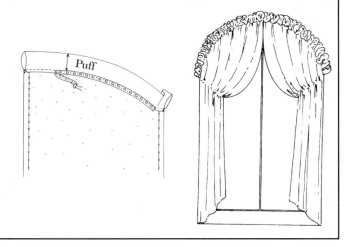

Puff

HAND GATHERING

The lines of the gather stitches should follow the curve. Ease the stitch template gently around the curve. Sew and pull up the gather stitches, see p138.

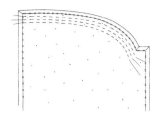

Lay the original template over the heading to check the shaping is correct. For the backing, cut buckram to the finished shape of the heading (joining pieces of buckram together if necessary) and cover it in lining.

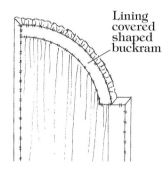

Lining covered shaped buckram

Professional Tip

In most cases the heading will project from the wall, by the depth of the architrave, wood frame or track brackets. A return is added to the side of the curtain to close the gap. To conceal the top of the arch, cover a strip of buckram or interlining, the required width by the length of the heading, and tack in place.

HAND SEWN FRENCH OR GOBLET PLEATS

Calculate the pleats and spaces, see p140. Make the paper pattern as described opposite. Cut the sections to the required width of the spaces. Do not join the sections with a curved line. The space between each section will be the pleat.

Cut the buckram to the shape of the heading. To sew the pleats, lay the paper pattern over the heading and mark the position of the pleats with a fabric marker pencil. Sew the pleats and finish as you would for a straight heading.

If the curtains are joined in the centre cover the join with a false pleat made out of waste fabric. Alternatively, cover the join with a small trim, such as a Maltese cross or a rosette.

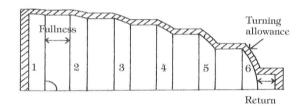

Fullness

Turning allowance

1   2   3   4   5   6

Return

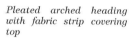

Pleated arched heading with fabric strip covering top

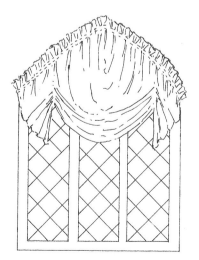

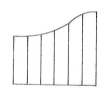

Make templates of your arched window (left) or tiara top (right) and divide into sections to make the heading

This is a popular style with no rules or restrictions. With the exception of hand sewn rings, they should really be considered as static headings as, for example, curtains tied on a pole cannot esily be opened and closed.

The curtains can be held open with tie-backs, curtain bands, ombras or Italian stringing. Alternatvely, use this kind of heading on dress curtains, with a functional blind set behind. Most informal headings need only double fullness and sometimes even less than that.

Informal headings are often used when remaking curtains limits the amount of fabric available. Genuine antique curtains were often made with less fullness than modern styles. Possible styles include sewn rings, scalloped looped rope, fabric ties, eyelets and rope headings.

SEWN RINGS

Decide how many rings you want to put on the pole. Allow about one ring per 10-15cm (4-6in). Space the rings evenly across the top of the curtain, leaving an overlap allowance of approximately 7.5cm (3in) at the leading edge and a return allowance at the side edge. If the calculated distance between the rings on the pole is 10cm (4in) and they are spaced 20cm (8in) apart on the curtain, this will give 2 x fullness.

ATTACHING RINGS

If the rings have eyes, set them down from the top edge, so that the bottom of the ring is flush with the top of the curtain. Remove rings before cleaning.

Sew through the eye, picking up all the layers - the thread will take the entire curtain weight. For rings with no eyes, make some fabric loops, thread these directly through the rings, and sew to the fabric on both sides of the curtain, again making sure you catch all the layers.

Thread the rings onto the pole and place it on the brackets. At either end, leave one ring between the fnial and the bracket to hold the curtain in place.

The loose fabric between the rings is the curtain fullness

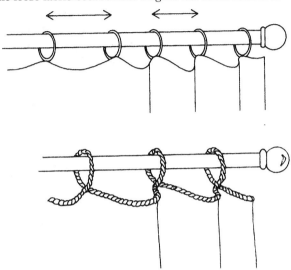

SCALLOPED LOOPED ROPE

Spaces between rings can be shaped into scallops. The depth of the scallop should be 5-7cm (2-3in) deep. Make a paper template for the scoop. Mark the curves onto the fabric, leaving a seam allowance above them.

Cut and seam together strips of fabric 15cm (6in) deep by the width of the curtain. This will make a facing. Pin the facing, right sides together, to the top of the curtain, and sew to the top, following the curves. Clip and notch the seam allowance, and turn the facing over to the back of the curtain. Pull out corners and press. Sew rope to the top of the curtain, making loops which will be threaded onto the pole. The loops should be generous in size so that they slip onto the pole easily.

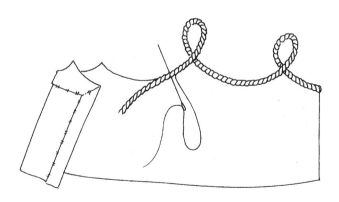

FABRIC TIED HEADINGS

Fabric loops tied around a pole are an attractive heading but the curtains will not run easily.

For curtains that you want to open and close often, it is better to choose another style.

The ties can be positioned in the same way as sewn rings, so that the number of ties is calculated by the length of the pole and the distance between them is dictated by the fullness required.

Make the required number of fabric ties. To find the length of a tie, pin a length of tape to the top of the curtain and tie it around the pole into a bow. Measure the tape, and also note the length of each tie, as the one which wraps around the pole behind the bow is longer than the other.

Cut strips of fabric 4 x finished width x required length. Fold the raw edges into the centre, fold over the ends, and then fold the strip in half lengthways. Machine the side edges together and across each end. Position the ties across the top of the curtain, the shorter in front and the longer at the back. Stitch in place securely, and then tie them carefully into bows, knotting them at the front.

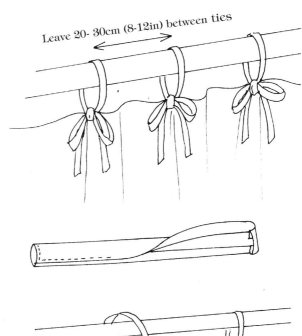

Leave 20-30cm (8-12in) between ties

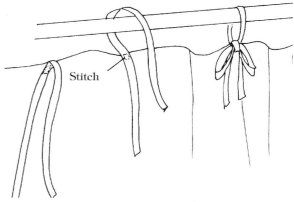

Stitch

MOCK TIES

For gathered curtains hung from rings on a a pole, sew fabric ties to the top of the curtain. Thread them through the rings, and tie into decorative bows. If this looks too cluttered, put ties on alternate rings.

Ties threaded through rings

EYELET HEADINGS

When buying an eyelet kit, choose a size large enough for the rope you want to use. Calculate the number and spacing of the eyelets in the same way as for sewn rings.

To work out the rope measurement which looks best between each eyelet, wrap rope around the pole and through an eyelet pressed into a sample piece of waste fabric.

When threading the rope, measure the distance between each eyelet. Sew the rope firmly in place at the back of the curtain, directly above each eyelet, so that the curtain hangs evenly. Finish the ends of the rope with tassels or knots.

TABBED HEADINGS

Tabbed curtains often have no fullness; the flat tabs are extended above the heading and wrap over the pole. This heading is normally used for short café curtains which stay in place on the lower half of the window. Although tabs can be used for full length designs, they will not move easily along the pole.

Each tabbed heading may be slightly different; to make the pattern, experiment first with some spare paper. The length of the tabs should be long enough to go round the pole with ease, plus a 2.5cm (1in) seam allowance. Make a paper pattern of the tab shape for one width.

Finished length = top of pole to floor/sill measurement

Starting with fabric and lining panels, turn up the hems and sew. Put them right sides together, and lay the paper pattern on top so that you will end up with the correct finished length measurement.

Use a fabric marker pencil to draw around the pattern. Machine up each side of the curtain and the top, following the line. Clip and notch the seam allowance, turn the curtain through to the right side, and press. Fold the tabs over to the back of the curtain and stitch in place. Thread the curtain onto the pole.

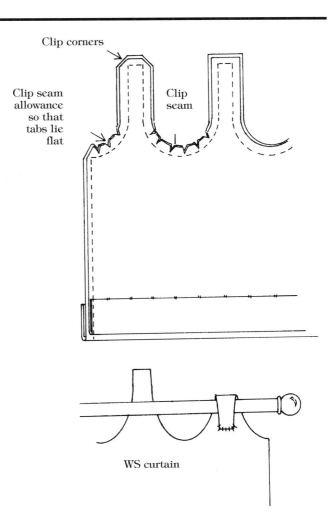

Clip corners

Clip seam allowance so that tabs lie flat

Clip seam

WS curtain

Making tabs

Tabs set between fabric and lining

Tabs centred on pleat

WS curtain

Tabs seen from the front of curtain

TABBED HEADING WITH BOX PLEATS

Turn up the hem allowance on both fabric and lining and sew in place. Place the fabric and lining right sides together and pin the position of the box or inverted pleats across the top of the curtain.

Make some fabric tabs the width of the pleat. The length of the tabs should be long enough to go around the pole with ease, plus a 2.5cm (1in) seam allowance.

Insert the tabs between the fabric and lining, in the centre of each pleat position. Machine up the sides of the curtain and along the heading.

Trim the seam allowance, clip the corners and turn through to the right side. Press the seams.

Fold the pleats in place, making either a box pleat or an inverted pleat on the right side of the curtain. Stitch across the top of the pleat to secure, and press the top if necessary.

HAND SEWN ROPE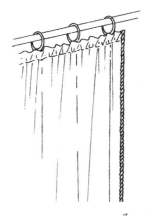

Rope simply sewn to the leading edges and hems of curtains makes a smart and luxurious finish. Traditionally, it was sewn around curtains to protect the edges of the fabric from wear and damage from sunlight. It must be attached with small stitches.

KNOTTED ROPE

Knotted rope can be sewn at the base of French or goblet pleats, sewn along gathered headings, or used to conceal the joins of coronets and trumpets. A convenient rope size is 12mm (1/2in) diameter.

Make an overhand loop and then a second loop. Pull the ends of the rope to form the decorative knot. The right side is with the figure of eight uppermost.

Tie the number of knots you need, leaving the correct spacing between them. Sew the rope to the heading, either side of the knot and also between them. Sew rope through from the front to the back of the heading, or you can let the rope fall in scoops between the knots.

BUTTON TUFTS

Small button tufts made from matching or contrasting silk or wool, are a subtle trim for goblet or French pleats, see p 223 for instructions.

ROPE CLOVERS

These are often used in the centre of fixed headed curtains to disguise the seam that joins the curtains together at the top. They can be used on valances, at the top of Roman blinds, or over any static heading.

Make the left hand loop measuring 19cm (7 1/2in) and then make the centre loop behind it measuring 27cm (11in). Make the right hand loop to mirror the left. Pin and sew through the base to secure.

Allow about 65cm (25 1/2in) of rope per clover, although of course it can be made smaller or larger.

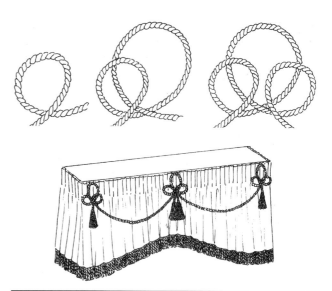

> **Professional Tip**
> If the rope is quite soft and will not hold its shape, wrap some floristry wire around it before looping.

FRINGE

Fringe can be either machined in place or sewn by hand. It is prone to stretching during the process can easily pucker. To avoid this, ease the fringe onto the fabric when tacking or sewing it down.

For gathered treatments such as valances, it is easier to attach the fringe onto the flat valance before the heading is gathered or pleated.

Fringes come in such a wide variety of sizes, colours, weights and patterns that you should spend some time looking through the catalogues of fine passementerie suppliers, see p233. They can also be made to order in relatively small quantities, or bought as remnants, or found in antique shops. For more information, see pictures and explanations on p90.

FINISHING TOUCHES

There are many design elements that can be added to a basic curtain, pelmet, valance, swag, or blind. Finishing Touches covers wadded and contrast bound edges, frills, ribbon and braid. Highlighting the edges in this way is a simple but effective detail that can turn ordinary curtains into something exceptional. This section also includes various fabric trims which can be used to further embellish your window treatment.

WADDED EDGES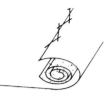

The leading and outside edges of curtains can be emphasised by inserting wadding or interlining into the side turning allowance, to make rounded edges. A wadded edge will give lined curtains the appearance of being interlined. It will also create an even more luxurious finish on interlined curtains. Avoid wadding curtains which are intentionally overlong as it stiffens the edge and the hem will not break gently on the floor, but will kink and crease the curtains.

To begin, increase the side turning allowance from 6cm (2¹/₄in) to 10cm (4in). Cut a piece of wadding 7.5cm (3in) wide x the finished length of the curtain (butt pieces together if necessary). Insert into the side turning allowance of the curtain prior to mitring the corner, see p128. Herringbone stitch down the side of the curtain. For a fuller effect, cut the wadding 15cm (6in) wide, fold in half and insert into the side turning allowance.

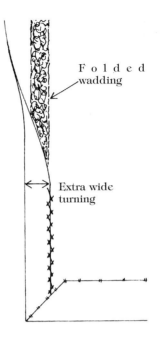

Folded wadding

Extra wide turning

For interlining used as wadding, cut a piece the finished length of the curtain and make a roll the required size. Stitch along the roll to hold it together, then tuck it into the side turning. Herringbone stitch along the edge.

Roll of interlining inserted in leading edge

Professional Tip

For the ambitious, wadded edges can be attached to quilted bed covers, to create an even more luxurious, feminine effect. Cut contrast strips and wadding as above. Seam on the contrast edge. Insert the wadding and slip stitch. For a ruched border, cut twice the amount of contrast. Gather it onto the edge of the quilt. Insert the wadding and slip stitch in place.

CONTRAST EDGES

These include straight contrast borders and decorative binding. They emphasise a colour or a pattern in contrast to the main fabric. Contrast borders are a useful device to define the edges of curtains and valances. Decorative binding is used to neaten the hems of bed covers and swags.

The size or width of the contrast can be varied, for instance a narrow edge adds a light touch, a wide embroidered or clashing border creates visual excitement. All four sides of the curtain can be edged, or just the leading edge.

If you are sewing a border onto more than one edge, the top should be narrower than the leading edges, whilst the hem contrast border should be deeper. Occasionally, with a small area such as a Roman blind, an even contrast on all sides will look smart and tailored.

For lined or lined and interlined curtains and valances, follow the notes for a contrast border. Once you have sewn the contrasting fabric onto the edge of the panel, it simply becomes a larger panel. For unlined curtains, a contrast binding neatens the raw edge of the fabric; use the make-up method for bound edges.

STRAIGHT CONTRAST BORDERS

For a single, two, three or four edged border, follow the relevant notes below. Note the seaming sequence for a multi-edged design; it's important. Add the contrast borders after you have cut out and seamed up your curtains or valance panels.

FABRIC QUANTITIES

For a vertical border, allow the cut drop measurement of the fabric by 2 times the finished width of the border + seam allowances. Never have a seam in a vertical border – it will look unsightly.

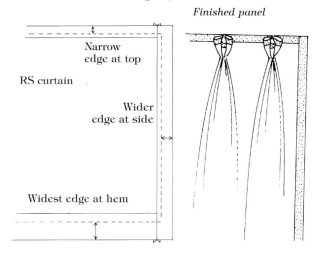

Finished panel

Narrow edge at top

RS curtain

Wider edge at side

Widest edge at hem

For a top border, allow the same number of contrast widths as fabric widths. If you are using fabric narrower than the curtain fabric, measure the contrast out to make up the difference. You'll need 2 x the finished depth of your border + a heading allowance.

For a hem or lower edge border, allow the number of widths as above 2 x the finished depth, + a seam and hem turning allowance.

If your contrast fabric is a tight, plain weave like chintz, you can minimise seams in the top and hem edgings by cutting longer strips *down* the fabric.

SEAMING CONTRAST STRIPS ONTO A CURTAIN OR VALANCE

1 For tops and hems, seam the contrast strips together. Trim seam allowance to 1cm (3/8in) and press open.

2 Seam the strips onto the curtain or valance in the correct order; top and bottom edges first, leading edges and sides second.

3 Continue to make up the curtain or valance.

Professional Tip

MITRED CORNERS

If you are using edges that meet at the corners, you can mitre the corners to avoid crossing seams. To be at 45° the adjoining edges must be the same finished width – so ignore the rules about larger top and bottom bindings. The mitre must be accurate, otherwise the fabric will not lie flat.

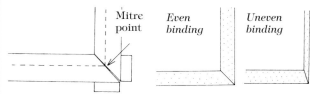

Mitre point   *Even binding*   *Uneven binding*

1 Sew the two strips onto the fabric to the corner point at which they meet.

2 Measure the finished width of the strips to find the outer mitre point or finished corner.

3 Fold the raw edge of each strip under, at either 45° or an acute angle, making a line that runs through the mitre point and lightly finger press the fold lines.

4 Slip tack along the mitre and machine together. Press the seam open and trim away excess fabric.

Design ideas

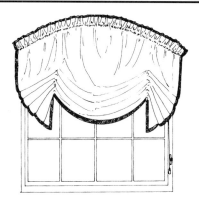

ALL KINDS OF BOUND EDGES

A binding encloses the edge of a fabric to which it is sewn. If the edge to be bound is straight, then the binding fabric is cut on the straight grain, either down or across.

If the edge is curved, like the hem of a swag, a round tablecloth, or a serpentined valance, the binding is cut on the true cross, see p121. You can either bind an edge in the same fabric for a subtle finish, or in a contrast for emphasis.

STRAIGHT BOUND EDGES

A contrast binding is not only decorative but it also neatens the raw edges of the fabric. It will also define the outline of an unlined curtain, valance or blind.

Keep it narrow; a finished width of 2cm (³⁄₄in) will suit most designs very well. Binding on bed covers can be up to 6cm (2¹⁄₂in) deep.

FABRIC QUANTITIES

For side edges, cut strips which are as long as the cut drop measurement of the curtain or blind, and 4 x the finished width of the binding.

For top and lower edges, cut as many strips as the number of widths in the treatment (+ an extra width if the contrast fabric is narrower than the face) and make them 4 x the finished depth of the binding.

NOTE: A 2cm (³⁄₄in) or wider fabric binding is used to neaten the tops of swags, tails, trumpets and swagged valances. The binding is either attached with Velcro, or tacked to the top of the pelmet board.

1 Seam the strips together. Trim seam allowance to 1cm (³⁄₈in) and press open. The edge to be bound does not require a seam allowance, so trim away any excess fabric if necessary.

2 Sew the strips onto the fabric panels in the correct order as for contrast borders; top and bottom first, sides second. Lay the contrast strip right side down onto the right side edge of the fabric and seam, leaving an allowance the finished depth of the contrast. On the sides of patterned panels, trim away the blank part of the selvedge before you measure the seam allowance.

3 Press. On the wrong side of the fabric, fold the binding fabric over to mirror the seam allowance, and fold over a second time so that it just covers the line of machine stitching; pin and slip stitch by hand.

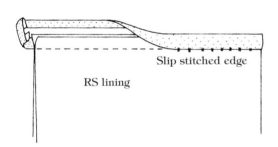

Slip stitched edge

RS lining

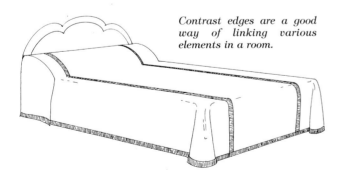

Contrast edges are a good way of linking various elements in a room.

Professional Tip

SINK STITCHING

Another way of finishing the binding is to sink stitch it in place by machine, rather than slip stitching by hand.

Make sure the binding at the back covers the machine line on the right side, pin the binding in place with the pins placed at right angles to the seam.

On the right side, machine a row of stitching in the groove created by the seam of the main fabric and the contrast. The stitches will sink into the seam and hardly show.

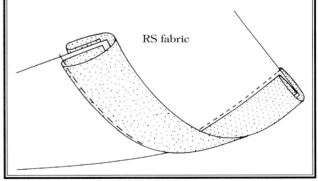

RS fabric

CURVED BOUND EDGES

These are treated in the same manner as straight bound edges, except that on curved edges the binding must be cut on the true cross of the grain and joined together to make a continuous strip, see p121.

Apply in the same manner as for a straight edge.

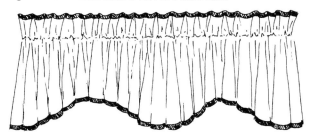

Swag with bound edge

Serpentined valance with a curved bound hem

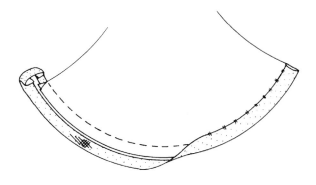

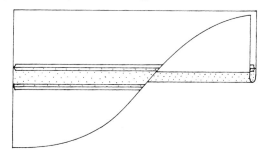

Professional Tip

Binding that is too wide will not lie flat around a curved edge. A finished width of 2-4cm (³⁄4in-1¹⁄2in) is standard.

Straight bound edge, machine bagged out

Notched curved edges

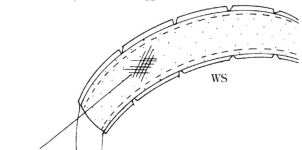

Curved bound edge, machine bagged out

WS

Binding cut on the true cross of the grain

MACHINING 'BAGGED OUT' EDGES

This method is used for lined treatments, especially for valances of all kinds. It can also be used for curved hem lines and round tablecloths, where the binding again needs to be cut on the cross.

1 Cut (and seam together if necessary) the binding strips. Cut the strips on the straight grain for straight edges and on the true cross of the grain if the edge to be bound is curved, see p121.

2 Lay the seamed (and shaped) fabric and lining together. Clip notches along the line/curve and use as reference points when inserting the contrast lining.

3 Lay the contrast strip right sides together with the fabric and seam together; take a seam allowance the finished depth of the contrast binding.

4 Seam the lining onto the other edge of the contrast strip, taking care to align the notches on the fabric and lining either side of the contrast.

5 Press the seams and turn the fabrics through to their right sides. If the cloth or valance is to be interlined, simply lay the interlining into the fold of the binding and pin in place.

FRILLED EDGES

Frills can be gathered for a pretty look or pleated for a tailored finish. They can either be set into a seam or set onto the finished edge of the treatment. They should always look crisp and light, even when they are double sided. Double sided frills are a good idea if the back of the frill might be seen as on a leading edge.

All frills should be generous in fullness, between 2.5 to 3 x to be really sumptuous. With the exception of pleated frills, they should not be too narrow, or they will look unattractive.

A frill that is too shallow, irrespective of fullness, will look mean and stubby, but a deep frill with ample fullness will make the treatment look bold and confident. A good frill depth for most window dressings is 7.5-10cm (3-4in).

INSET FRILLS

An *inset* frill looks smart when the seam is piped, although this does create extra thickness to sew through. The outer edge can be also bound with the binding folded over to the back.

ONSET FRILLS

Frills *onset* to an edge are particularly attractive. They give the effect of two frills, one above the stitch gather line and one below. A variation is to bind both edges, continuing the contrast fabric at the back of the frill.

PLEATED FRILLS

These are not as flouncy as gathered frills, and they can be narrow or deep, inset into a seam or set onto the edge. To make knife and box pleats, see p157.

PINKED FRILLS

Pinked onset frills are light and fluffy. As only a single layer of fabric is needed, it should be made to 3 x fullness – any less and it will look limp. A variation is a double frill where a second contrast backing frill is cut 1.5cm (1/2in) wider than the face fabric. Only fabrics with a tight weave are suitable for pinking, as a loosely woven fabric will fray and the decorative effect will be lost. Glazed plain or patterned chintz fabrics are ideal for pinked edges or for a fun look, felt frills with pinked edges either gathered or box pleated.

> **Professional Tip**
> Frills take a huge amount of fabric, time and patience to make properly. Think about one frill, perhaps on the valance, rather than attempt a complete round-the-curtain frill on all edges.

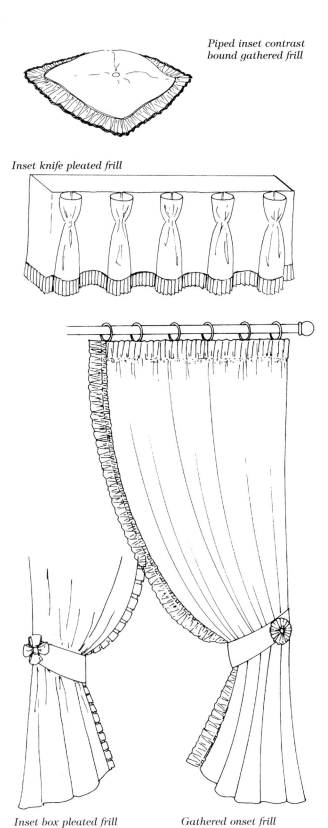

Piped inset contrast bound gathered frill

Inset knife pleated frill

Inset box pleated frill

Gathered onset frill

FABRIC QUANTITIES

As an example of the surprising amount of fabric you will need, the frill on three sides of an Austrian blind can take as much fabric as the blind itself. Never assume surplus fabric will be enough; always work out the quantity. Here are a few tips:

PATTERNED FABRIC

If pattern adjustment leaves you with a lot of wastage you may be able to use that. Work out how many drops you will have, and buy extra fabric if you need it.

PATTERN REPEATS

On small patterns you can cut the frill strips to the repeat so that all the seams match. However, on large patterns you would needlessly waste a lot of fabric. So cut your frill strips ignoring the repeat, and then colour match the strips together when you pin them into a longer strip. Make sure when you pleat or gather the strips that the mis-matched seams are hidden inside pleats or gathers.

To find the fabric quantity, you will need the following measurements:

1 Finished quantity of frill you need x fullness ratio. Divide the resulting figure by the usable width of fabric to give the number of widths (round up to a whole width).

2 Fullness ratio for gathered frills allow 2.5 x fullness, for pleated frills allow 3 x fullness.

3 Frill cut drop for contrast bound frills, see overleaf pp156-157.

Pinked frill - cut drop = the finished depth of frill. Double sided frill - cut drop is 2 x the finished depth + 2 seam allowances.

4 Multiply the number of widths you require by the cut drop of the frill, this will give you the frill fabric quantity.

Professional Tip

Even as experienced curtainmakers, we try out a piece of fabric the proposed depth and fullness; make a 'mock up' of the frill to see how it looks before making a final decision. Pin in place on the edge of the treatment, check the proportions, and alter if necessary.

GATHERING FRILLS

To pull up a large quantity of frilling evenly, work out the gathered measurement for each width of fabric. Divide the width of the fabric by the frill fullness ratio.

HAND GATHERING

Using strong thread, sew a running stitch within the seam allowance. Start by firmly securing the thread and sew evenly (the smaller the stitch, the smaller the gather). The gathers can be pulled up during the stitching process. The fullness should be evenly distributed; take care the gathers do not run along the thread and bunch up. Check the gathered measurement of each width. The running stitches can be removed once the frill has been sewn in place.

GATHERING BY MACHINE

Using the longest possible stitch length, sew a line just within the seam allowance, leaving 10cm (4in) thread ends at the start and finish of each width. Working on one width at a time, pull the threads from each side. Wind the threads in a figure of eight around a pin. The machine draw stitches can be removed after you have attached the frill.

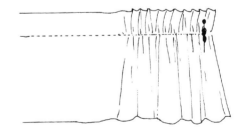

ALTERNATIVE MACHINE GATHERING

Put the fabric under the needle in line with the seam or gather line. Hold the frill either side of the stitch line, gather with a scissor-like action with your fingers. Simultaneously push the fabric forward and underneath the foot of the machine, a little at a time. The stitches will be left in the fabric, so sew just within the seam allowance.

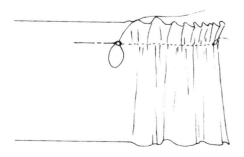

INSETTING FRILLS INTO SEAMS

1A DOUBLE SIDED FRILLS

The cut drop of the frill is 2 x the depth of the finished frill + 2 seam allowances. Cut out enough strips and join all the selvedges together; trim to 1cm (³⁄₈in) and press. Lightly fold the strip in half lengthways, right side out, and pin the raw edges at right angles.

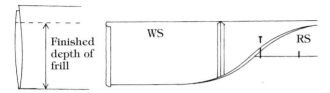

1B CONTRAST EDGED, DOUBLE SIDED FRILLS

Cut out the frill strips and the contrast strips. Join the selvedge seams separately. Trim the seam allowances and press open. Seam the fabric and contrast together lengthways, taking a 1cm (³⁄₈in) seam allowance. Press the seam open and fold the fabric in half, checking that the width of the contrast edge on the right side of the frill stays even. Pin the raw edges together, with the pins at right angles.

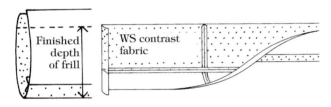

2 Gather or pleat up the frill. To insert, lay the right side down onto the fabric with the raw edges together. Machine in place. If piping is required, sew it onto the fabric at the same time as the frill.

3 Place the lining in position, turn the work over and machine the seam following the stitch line.

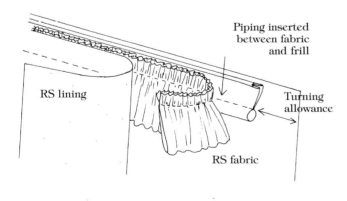

4 To neaten the end of the frill, unpick a few stitches and fold the raw edges inside. Sew across to secure.

SETTING FRILLS ONTO EDGES

1A FOLDED FRILL

Cut out and seam strips as opposite. With right sides together, fold in half lengthways and seam into a tube.

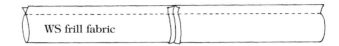

1B CONTRAST EDGED FRILLS

Cut out and seam strips as opposite. With right sides together, seam the fabric and contrast together lengthways to form a tube. Press the seams open.

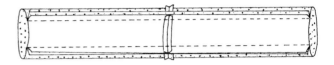

2 Use this quick method to turn the tube to the right side; seam across one edge. At this end, push the metre or yardstick into the tube, rolling the fabric down the stick. Remove the stick and press.

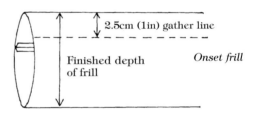

Onset frill

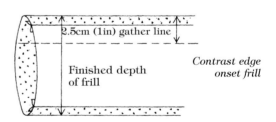

Contrast edge onset frill

3 Gather or pleat up 2.5cm (1in) down from the top edge. Set the frill onto the edge of the main fabric and either hand sew or machine in place.

Onset frill

4 To neaten the end of the frill, unpick a few stitches and fold the raw edges inside. Sew across to secure.

SINGLE OR DOUBLE PINKED FRILLS

1 With pinking scissors carefully cut strips of fabric to the finished depth of the frill. Seam the fabric along the selvedges with small French seams, see p120.

For a double frill, pink additional strips of contrast fabric – this must be 1.5cm (½in) wider than the inner frill. Seam the strips together as above. Lay the contrast behind the inner frill so that 0.5cm (¼in) shows at the top edge and 1cm (³⁄₈in) at the lower edge.

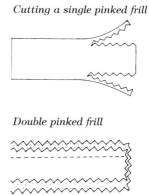

Cutting a single pinked frill

Double pinked frill

Professional Tip
For pinked frills use a tight woven fabric such as chintz or a crisp, light silk for the best effects. Do not use anything soft or thick. Pinked frills are usually onset to edges.

2 Gather with a line of stitching 2.5cm (1in) down from the top edge. Set the frill onto the edge of the main fabric and either hand sew or machine in place.

3 To neaten the end of the frill, fold the raw edges over twice and slip stitch.

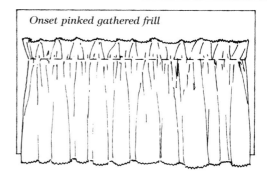

Onset pinked gathered frill

PLEATING FRILLS

Make cardboard copies of the appropriate pleat template, as below. Transfer the dot markings onto the seam or stitch line of the frill. Place the frill under the machine and fold dot to dot, to make either knife pleats or box pleats. Fold one or two pleats at a time and then machine in place. This row of stitching will not be removed so use a perfect thread match to the fabric.

You can vary the pleats by making your own template. Experiment by folding paper to the pleat size, and then make an accurate card template.

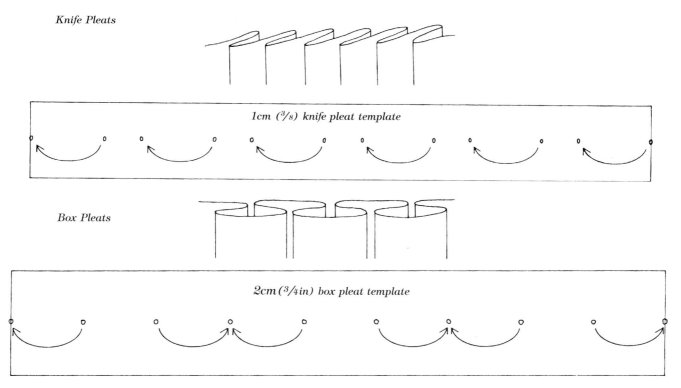

Knife Pleats

1cm (³⁄₈) knife pleat template

Box Pleats

2cm (³⁄₄in) box pleat template

Ribbon and braid sewn to the edges of curtains and valances is a simple but exceptionally striking design detail. For example, one or two rows of braid set in from the leading edges of plain curtains defines the line and adds texture and interest.

Petersham ribbon is ideal for soft furnishing as it has a matt finish with an attractive ribbed weave. It is reasonably firm, making it easy to use. For added interest, lay two different widths and colours of petersham on top of one another to make a striped effect, see p27 top left.

Braid hand sewn in scroll designs is an early form of period soft furnishing decoration. Some wonderful examples can be seen in the King's Bed Chamber at Hampton court. This type of decorative braiding is mainly used on flat fabric, such as pelmets and bed covers, see p45.

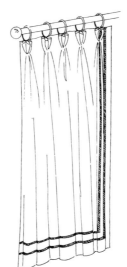
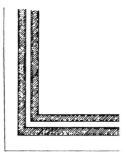

Left, a French headed curtain with a double ribbon border. Most ribbon decorations work well with two rows (see detail of corner above).

Right, ribbon or braid used with another trim, in this case with a deep fringe. The ribbon picks up the colour of the fringe.

MACHINING BRAID

Machine the braid onto the seamed panels of fabric, prior to folding up the hem and turning up the sides of the curtain or valance. Measure the required distance in from the edge of the fabric, including the turning allowance, and place a guide of masking or electrical tape onto the plate of the machine. Use a thread which matches the braid, and sew down each edge; if possible sink the machine lines into grooves in the braid. The machine tensions must be perfectly set to ensure the braid is not puckered.

To mitre the corners, simply fold a triangle underneath the braid and continue machining.

HAND SEWING CURVED BRAID

Sewing is easier when the fabric is held taut on a wooden frame like a tapestry. Back flimsy fabrics with an iron-on interfacing.

Use drawing pins to temporarily hold the top and the bottom of the fabric taut on the frame.

1 Mark out the design on the face of the fabric with a fabric marker pencil.

2 To make draw threads, use a long piece of thread and

sew small running stitches for approximately 30cm (12in) along one edge of the braid, leaving the needle in the work. Repeat with a second needle and thread on the other side.

3 Lay the braid onto the face of the fabric and gently pull up the draw threads to form the curves. Pin and stitch in place using a prick stitch on each edge.

4 Continue to sew the draw threads and braid to the fabric until the design is complete.

Step 1

Scroll design marked onto fabric and tacked onto braid.

Steps 2- 4

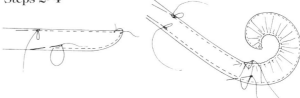

Fabric trims can be used to decorate virtually all curtains, valances, blinds and swags. But they should be used with a degree of subtlety. Too big or too bright, they will detract from the design rather than complement it.

You can guarantee success by making a paper mock-up of the trim. For a rosette, this could simply be cut out circles in one or two sizes; for trumpets, experiment with a paper pattern. Tables are given for suggested sizes. NOTE: Fabric trims have a small seam allowance of 1cm (³/₈in).

FABRIC QUANTITIES
Make a paper pattern of the trim to the required size and do a 'fabric lay'. Lay the paper patterns between two metre/yard sticks, spread apart to the usable width of the fabric. Check how much each trim requires and how many can be cut across one width, bearing in mind any pattern placements.

ROSETTES
These are very popular, and look best at the end of a decorative swag or the top of a tail. A single rosette is made from one piece of fabric. For a double, a second strip is cut, slightly narrower and in a contrasting fabric.

SUGGESTED ROSETTE SIZES AND FABRIC QUANTITIES	
Finished diameter	Fabric strips
SMALL 5cm (2in)	5cm wide x 36cm long (2in wide x 14in long)
MEDIUM 7.5cm (3in)	7.5cm wide x 68cm long (3in wide x 27in long)
LARGE 10cm (4in)	10cm wide x 96cm long (4in wide x 38in long)

Using rosettes

Double rosette

MAKING ROSETTES
MATERIALS
Fabric
Strong thread
Fabric covered button

1 Cut an appropriate sized strip of fabric. To form a ring, machine together the two shortest edges, taking a 1cm (³/₈in) seam allowance. Press the seam open. Fold in half lengthways.
NOTE: For a double rosette, repeat the process. Place the rings together.

2 Using strong thread with a large knot at the end, sew running stitches 0.5cm (¹/₄in) in from the raw edge. Running stitches are usually 1cm (³/₈in) in length, but you can increase the size for thicker fabrics, to make deeper folds. Pull up the thread to make a tight circle and secure.

3 Cut out a small circle of stiffening and cover it with fabric. Sew this onto the back of the rosette, making sure the gathers are evenly distributed. This neatens the back and provides an anchorage point for the button.

4 Cover a button with fabric and sew firmly in the centre of the rosette.

Front   *Back*   *Fabric covered button*

MAKING BOWS

One of the most popular trims, bows work in a hundred different ways, from tailored elegance to a pretty, feminine look. Experiment with a few paper bows, cut to the suggested sizes in the table opposite.

BOW FABRIC QUANTITIES

Width = 2 x finished width + 2 x seam allowance

Depth = 2 x finished depth + 2 x seam allowance

TAIL FABRIC QUANTITIES

Width = depth of bow + 2 x seam allowance

Length (optional)

MATERIALS

Fabric

Net

1 Cut out appropriate sized strips of fabric. Cut out two pieces of net for the bow to the required size. Place the layers of net onto the wrong side of the fabric. With right sides together, machine down the longest edge and press open the seam.

2 Turn through to the right side and with the seam in the centre, flatten out the tube. To form a ring, seam the ends of the tube with right sides together. Turn the seam to the inside of the ring. Pinch the centre of the bow together, to form an inverted pleat, and stitch to hold in place.

3 For the 'knot', cut a strip of fabric and fold the raw edges inwards to conceal. Wrap around the centre of the bow, trim away excess fabric, and stitch at the back of the bow to secure.

4 Cut out two strips of fabric for the tails. With right sides together, fold each strip in half lengthways. At the bottom of each strip, machine a line at a 45 degree angle, starting at the folded edge. Continue machining up the side.

SUGGESTED BOW SIZES AND FABRIC QUANTITIES		
Finished size	**Bow pattern dimensions**	**Tail pattern dimensions**
SMALL 7.5cm (3in) wide x 5cm (2in) deep	17cm wide x 12cm deep 6¾in wide x 4¾in deep	12cm wide length req. 4¾in wide x length req.
MEDIUM 15cm (6in) wide x 7.5cm (3in) deep	32cm wide x 17cm deep 12½in wide x 6¾in deep	17cm wide length req. 6¾in wide x length req.
LARGE 30cm (12in) wide x 15cm (6in) deep	62cm wide x 32cm deep 24½in wide x 12½in deep	32cm wide length req. 12½in wide x length req.

5 Trim away excess fabric at the points, turn the tails through to the right side and press. Put the two tails together, overlapping at the top, but with the tips facing inwards and slightly apart. Turn over 1.5cm (½in) at the top of the tails and stitch to the back of the bow.

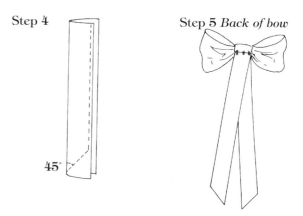

Step 4

45°

Step 5 *Back of bow*

6 Sew the bow firmly in place, or fix with Velcro fastening tape.

Using bows

Tie-back bow

Large tie-back bow

Pole ties

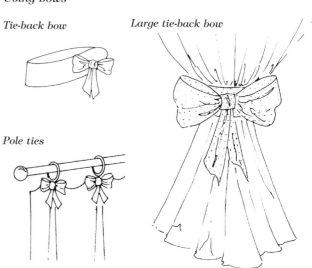

MAKING MALTESE CROSSES

In common with the trefoil Maltese crosses are upright tailored bows and particularly suit formal treatments. See opposite for suggested sizes. As with all trims, it helps to make a paper mock-up first in the various sizes and pin in place before you make your final decision.

FABRIC QUANTITIES

Width = 2 x width + 2 x seam allowance

Depth = 2 x depth + 2 x seam allowance

MATERIALS

Fabric

Net

Fabric covered button

1 Cut out appropriate sized strips of fabric for the horizontal and vertical bows, and two pieces of net per bow. To make up each bow, place the two layers of net onto the wrong side of the fabric and, with right sides together, machine down the longest edge and press open the seam.

2 Turn through to the right side and flatten out the tube with the seam in centre. To form a ring seam the ends of the tube, with right sides together. Turn the seam to the inside of the ring.

3 Take one ring, pinch the centre of the bow together to form an inverted pleat and stitch to hold in place. Place the bow inside and at right angles to the second ring. Pinch the front and the back of the bow separately and stitch through to secure.

4 Cover an appropriate sized button in fabric, and sew through the centre of the cross. Sew the cross firmly in place, or fix with Velcro fastening tape.

MAKING TREFOILS

A trefoil trim is made in the same way as a Maltese cross, but with the vertical bow cut in half and sandwiched inside the horizontal bow. It is combined with another trim, such as a tassel, or used with a trumpet below.

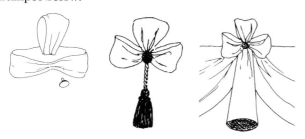

SUGGESTED FINISHED SIZES	
SMALL	10cm wide x 10cm deep (4in wide x 4in deep)
MEDIUM	15cm wide x 15cm deep (6in wide x 6in deep)
LARGE	20cm wide x 20cm deep (8in wide x 8in deep)

Steps 3 - 4

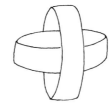

Striped Maltese crosses

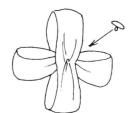

The different effects of stripes can be quite startling. The fabric can be cut on the cross, or along, or across the stripe. Ensure all the crosses on one treatment are cut the same way.

Using Maltese crosses

Trumpets can be set on to valances or fitted between swags. Trimmed with coronets and rope, trumpets can add a real kick to the effect. A favourite variation is the double trumpet, with its extra folds of fabric. Trumpets can be lined, either in self or contrast fabric, and a fringe can be sewn around the hem.

MAKING TRUMPET PATTERNS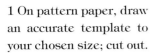

MATERIALS
Pattern paper
Fabric and lining

Decide on the size (see table). If you are unsure, sketch and cut out rough templates in the three sizes given, pin in place and choose which one suits your design best.

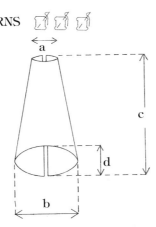

	SUGGESTED TRUMPET SIZES: FINISHED MEASUREMENTS FROM WHICH TO MAKE PAPER PATTERNS			
SIZE	a	b	c	d
SMALL	8cm (3in)	18cm (7in)	36cm (14in)	8cm (3in)
MEDIUM	10cm (4in)	23cm (9in)	50cm (20in)	10cm (4in)
LARGE	10cm (4in)	23cm (9in)	66cm (26in)	12cm (4in)

1 On pattern paper, draw an accurate template to your chosen size; cut out.

a Top width
b Bottom width
c Length
d Depth of hem shaping

Step 1

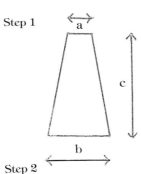

2 Fold a large piece of pattern paper in half. Fold the trumpet template in half and place on to the folded edge of the pattern paper. Draw round and remove template. Continue the pattern by first cutting only along the top and bottom lines, folding the doubled paper back along the slanted edge, which becomes the side fold line, then drawing around the extra panel. Finish cutting out the trumpet pattern.

Step 2

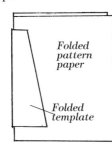

Folded pattern paper

Folded template

Side fold

3 Half open the pattern and mark d on the centre fold line, using the appropriate measurements given in the table. Measure half of d and mark it on the side fold line. To shape the hem, draw a gentle curve from d through the ¹/₂d point to the edge. Cut out the hem.

Step 3

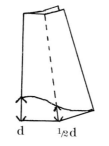

d   ¹/₂d

4 To hide the trumpet centre back seam, a separate lining pattern is needed. To make the lining pattern, take the trumpet pattern you have just made, fold in half and put the longest edge on the centre fold of a large piece of pattern paper. Trace round, draw on the side fold lines, and cut out the lining pattern.

5 Copy both the fabric and lining patterns onto new pieces of pattern paper, transferring all markings, including the side fold lines, and adding 2cm (³/4in) seam allowance all around both patterns.

Keep the original patterns and mark them "no seam allowance". They are useful for making other trumpet patterns and variations.

Step 4

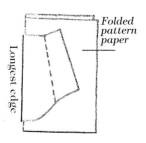

Folded pattern paper

Longest edge

Step 5

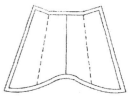

Fabric pattern with seam allowance

Lining pattern with seam allowance

MAKING TRUMPETS

1 Use the paper patterns to cut out the fabric and lining. If using a patterned fabric, place a suitable part of the pattern in the centre-front of the trumpet.

2 With right sides together, seam both the fabric and the lining into trumpet shapes. Press open the seams.

3 Turn the fabric trumpet through to the right side. Place it inside the lining trumpet, right sides together. Seam around the hem.

4 Turn the lining through to the right side, push it up inside the trumpet and press the hem seam.

5 At the top of the trumpet turn the seam allowances in, snipping them so that they lie flat. Slip stitch to neaten. Sew the trumpet firmly in place or fix with Velcro fastening tape.

Steps 1 - 2

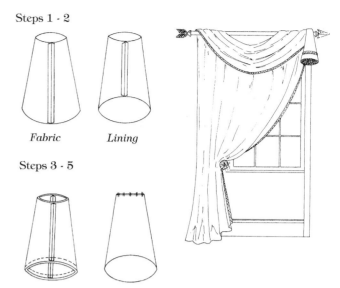

Fabric *Lining*

Steps 3 - 5

DOUBLE TRUMPETS

To make the paper pattern, decide on the following measurements.

a Top width of 1st trumpet
b Bottom width of 1st trumpet
c Length
d Depth of hem shaping
e Top width of 2nd trumpet
f Bottom width of 2nd trumpet

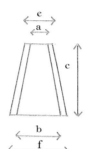

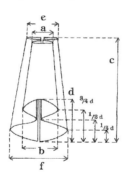

SUGGESTED DOUBLE TRUMPET SIZES FINISHED MEASUREMENTS FROM WHICH TO MAKE PAPER PATTERNS						
SIZE	a	b	c	d	e	f
SMALL	6cm (2¼in)	14cm (5¼in)	36cm (14in)	10cm (4in)	8cm (3in)	18cm (7in)
MEDIUM	8cm (3in)	18cm (7in)	50cm (20in)	15cm (6in)	10cm (4in)	20cm (8in)
LARGE	8cm (3in)	20cm (8in)	66cm (26in)	20cm (8in)	10cm (4in)	23cm (9in)

1 Make fabric and lining patterns as on p162, but mirror two more sections incorporating the extra ½e and ½f measurements. This will give an 8 segment trumpet. Fold in half. Mark d on the centre fold, ¾d, ½d and ¼d on the following fold lines. Draw a gentle curve.

2 Make up trumpet as above, Steps 1-4.

3 To pleat up, use the paper pattern and mark d and ½d with pins. Flatten the fabric trumpet to bring the centre fold lines together and machine along ½d 10cm (4in) down from the top. Open the seam and place it on top of the centre back seam, flattening the front trumpet.

4 Repeat Step 5 above.

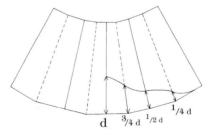

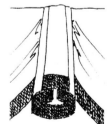

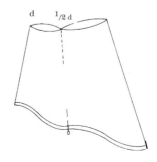

These are shorter than the longer side tails shown on p189, and are made in a similar way. They can be trimmed with coronets and rope. Used with swags, they look best when they are shorter than the swag.

To make the paper pattern, decide on the following measurements.

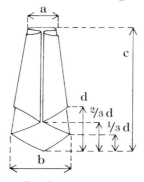

a Top width
b Bottom width
c Length
d Depth of hem shaping

Suggested Tail Sizes				
Size	a	b	c	d
Small	8cm (3in)	18cm (7in)	30cm (12in)	15cm (6in)
Medium	10cm (4in)	23cm (9in)	40cm (16in)	20cm (8in)
Large	10cm (4in)	23cm (9in)	50cm (20in)	25cm (10in)

MAKING PAPER PATTERNS

1 On pattern paper, draw a tail template the required size, following the measurements in the table.

2 Fold the tail template in half through the centre. Place its folded line onto the fold of a piece of pattern paper. Draw round, and remove template. To mirror the shape, cut along top and bottom lines on the paper, fold the shape over and draw round. Repeat again and cut out.

3 Fold the pattern in half along the centre-back line. Mark the d measurement you have chosen (see table above) on the right outside edge. Divide into 3 and mark down $\frac{1}{3}$ on each fold until the centre fold, which is the full length of the tail. Repeat from the centre up to the left edge, then join the marks - you should have a gently curved hem. Cut away the excess paper.

4 Copy the pattern onto a piece of pattern paper, transferring all markings, including the fold lines, adding a 2cm ($\frac{3}{4}$in) seam allowance.

MAKING TAILS

1 Use the paper pattern to cut out the fabric and lining. If using a patterned fabric, place a suitable part of the pattern on the front of the tail.

2 Place the lining and fabric right sides together, and machine around the sides and the hem.

3 Trim the seam allowance at the corners and turn through to the right side. Press the seams, ensuring that the edges of the fabric and lining and level. If required, sew fringe onto the hem.

4 To pleat up, place the paper pattern on top of the tail and mark the fold lines at the top and the bottom with pins. Fold the pleats and temporarily pin in place.

5 The raw edges at the top of the tail can be turned in and slip stitched prior to pleating, or they can be bound with fabric like a tail, see p190. Coronets or rope can be sewn to the top of the finished tail (see opposite). Secure the tail in place with tacks or Velcro.

Steps 1 - 2

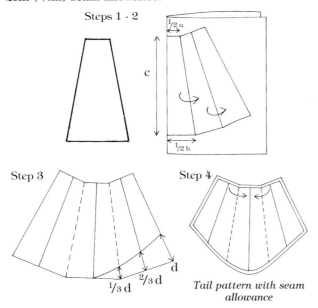

Step 3   Step 4

Tail pattern with seam allowance

Steps 1 - 2   Steps 3 - 5

WS fabric

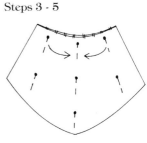

GOBLET CORONETS

A coronet sits above another trim, such as a trumpet or decorative tail, with rope or braid covering the join. They are stiffened to hold their shape. Amazingly, one size suits most windows, so a pattern is given on the right.

The inside of a goblet coronet will be visible, so it can either be lined in self or in a contrast fabric.

MAKING GOBLET CORONETS

Make a copy of the pattern. Trace around the shape, adding a seam allowance on 3 sides. Make a second stiffening pattern by simply tracing around the first shape.

MATERIALS
Fabric
Lining
Iron-on stiffening

1 Cut out the fabric and lining. If using a patterned fabric, place a suitable part of the pattern in the centre of the goblet.

2 Use the stiffening paper pattern to cut out the iron-on stiffening; iron it to the wrong side of the fabric.

3 With right sides together, seam both the fabric and the lining into goblet shapes. Press open the seams.

4 Turn the fabric goblet through to the right side and place it inside the lining goblet, right sides together. Machine around the top edge taking 1cm (³⁄₈in) seam.

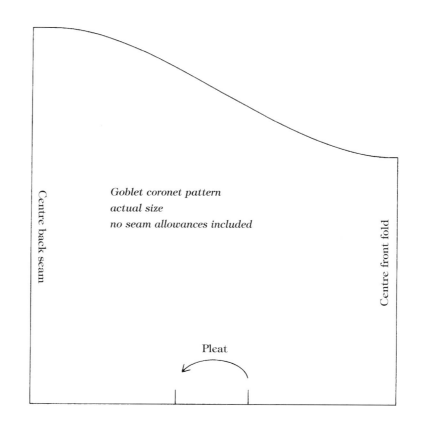

Goblet coronet pattern
actual size
no seam allowances included

Centre back seam

Centre front fold

Pleat

5 Turn the lining through to the right side and push it down inside the goblet; press the top.

6 Turn the seam allowance in at the bottom of the goblet and slip stitch. Place the paper pattern around the goblet and mark with pins the position of the two side pleats. Make the small side pleats and stitch along the base.

7 Stitch the goblet in position or fix onto the front edge of the pelmet board using 2cm (³⁄₄in) brass tacks.

TOPS 1: SCARF DRAPERY, PELMETS & VALANCES

Once the basic curtains are finished you can go on to create something wonderful to adorn the top. This section includes many ideas, from light scarf drapery, pelmets and valances occasionally decorated with short trumpets and tails, to the real knock-out magnificence of full swags and tails in TOPS 2. All have their place, all can be adjusted, changed, dressed up or dressed down as you prefer. Let your imagination roam!

SCARF DRAPERY

A delightful style for the ever-popular pole, but not quite as casual as it may seem. The wrapped fabric or 'scarf' has the curved shaping of swags, and yet appears to be informally draped from a single straight length, just thrown over the pole. Choose your design from our suggestions opposite.

The scarf should be lined with the same fabric, so that when it is wrapped alternately in front and behind the pole, the back becomes the front and it looks exactly like a single scarf.

When a scarf is paired with functional curtains, the pole is set out from the wall to allow adequate space for the curtain track behind; see p227 for fitting notes.

DRAPING SCARF SWAGS

Measure the length of the pole. If you are using more than one swag, add an extra 15cm (6in) per overlap allowance. (There is always one less overlap than the number of swags.) Divide this figure by the number of swags to find the width of each one.

If you have a pinboard cover it with pattern paper and mark a line the width of one swag, and a vertical line for the depth ($\frac{1}{5}$ of the curtain length). If you don't have a pinboard, tape paper onto a flat wall, or pin it onto the back of a long sofa.

You will need some chain, see p105 for what to buy. Take a length of the chain – enough to mock-up the bottom of the swag curve. Drape it to make an attractive shape, then pin or tape it down. Measure along the chain – this is the hem.

Drape another length of chain to mock-up the top of the swag. Start and finish the chain 15cm (6in) in from the sides and let it droop a little. When the swag is finished the pole will be seen in the centre of each swag.

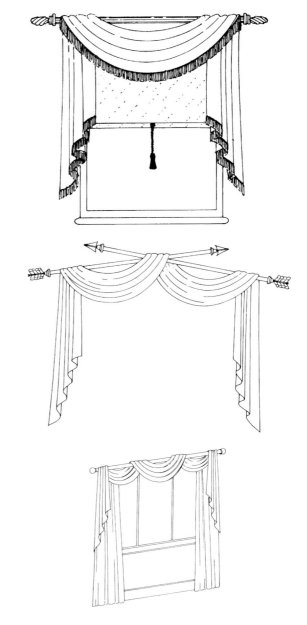

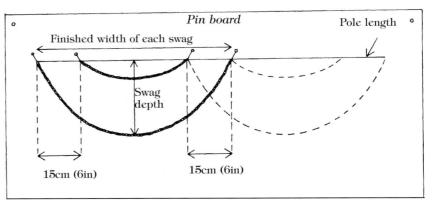

166

MAKING PAPER PATTERNS

Working on folded pattern paper, draw ½ the top and hem chain measurements, spaced 2 x the swag depth apart. Join these lines together to make the side lines. The hem line can be emphasised by adding a further 7.5cm (3in) to the depth at the centre and drawing a smooth curve up to the side of the swag. Add a seam allowance all round and cut out the swag pattern.

To make a pattern for the tail, allow 115cm (45in) for the width x the finished length of the tail and mark these measurements onto a piece of pattern paper.

To shape the hem, find the length of the short side edge. At the bottom of the short side edge draw a line 10cm (4in) long, at right angles to the side.

Repeat at the bottom of the long side edge. Join the lines together. Round the corners with a smooth, freehand curve. Add a seam allowance all round. Cut out the tail pattern.

You can use these patterns to lay on the fabric and see how much you will need for each swag and tail; by measuring all along the hem you can also find how much you will need of any trim.

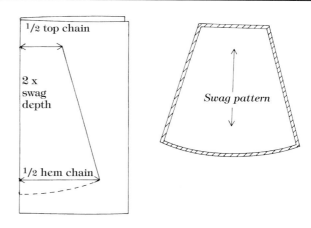

Making curves on a tail pattern

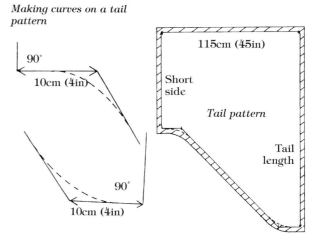

MAKING SCARF WRAPS

1 Cut out 2 pieces of fabric per swag and tail.

2 In the correct sequence, seam the first set right sides together. The top of one swag is seamed to the hem of its neighbour, and the tails are sewn onto the outer sides of the swag, with the short edge of the tail in line with the top of the swag. The width of the tail is likely to be wider than the side of the swag and so to make it fit, put two or three tucks into the top of the tail. Repeat for the second set.

3 Place the scarves right sides together and machine around, leaving a gap at the top of one of the swag sections. Clip and notch the seam allowance, turn through to the right side and press all round. Slip stitch or machine along the folds of the opening.

4 At each intersection, sew a row of gather stitches either by machine or by hand, sinking them into the seam. Pull up the gathers to 15cm (6in) and tie them off by sewing securely.

5 Wrap the scarf over the pole, placing the swags alternately in front and behind the pole, dressing the swags into even folds and the tails into even pleats.

Steps 1- 3

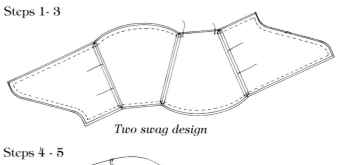

Two swag design

Steps 4 - 5

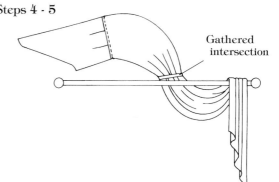

Gathered intersection

FIXING TO POLES

On wooden poles, tack or staple through the scarf to hold it in place. For metal poles, hand sew Velcro to the underside of the gathered intersection and glue the corresponding side to the top of the pole.

Pelmets and valances are light top finishes to the curtain, rounding off your design and adding their own touch of detail with matching or contrasting textures and colours. They can be as simple or as elaborate as you wish, adding height by covering wall space above the window, and creating a more elegant look.

FLAT PELMETS

A pelmet is a flat piece of fabric, sometimes with a shaped hemline, suspended from a pelmet board. A lambrequin is a shaped pelmet that extends down the side of the window.

The practical function of the pelmet is to cover the curtain track. However, the decorative potential is enormous, from a simple flat panel to a fringed tapestry pelmet hung from a gilded wood cornice box – and everything in between.

Fabrics with large distinctive patterns such as a Toile de Jouy are shown to their best advantage on a flat pelmet. Highly decorative fabrics on a flat pelmet can be complemented with a less expensive plain curtain.

There are two basic types; a stiffened pelmet made with either a buckram or a synthetic iron-on interfacing, or a plywood upholstered pelmet which needs strong support.

Quilted pelmets are a hybrid; the stitching emphasises a pattern or print, while geometric quilting on a plain fabric creates a feeling of depth, and creates a luxurious effect.

DESIGN VARIATIONS

A basic pelmet can be decorated with over-drapery and trims, such as trumpets with coronets, rosette and choux trims, as well as rope and tassels. They can also be embellished more simply with traditional swirls of braid. For a guide to basic proportions, see p99.

You can change the design by trying out shaped hems. The depth at the side of the pelmet – where it falls over the stack back area – can be deeper than in the middle.

A lambrequin can be shaped to fall right to the bottom of the window frame or even to the floor.

A stiffened pelmet can have a shaped hem which repeats motifs or shapes that are important to the room's scheme. You can design your own hemline based on the curtain fabric, the moulding of the window, or an architectural or design motif used in the decoration of the room.

MAKING STIFFENED PELMETS

1 Make a paper pattern of the pelmet shape you want.

2 Cut it out in buckram or stiffening. To add some padding, cut a piece of interlining (down the length of the fabric, to eliminate bulky seams). Place the interlining onto the buckram and machine round.

3 Cut out the fabric and lining widths you need, adding a 10cm (4in) allowance to the pattern. Seam fabric and lining together. Place a full width of fabric at the centre of the pelmet to avoid a seam.

4 Machine a strip of Velcro onto the right side of the lining, 2cm (3/4in) down from the raw edge. With right sides together, machine the fabric and the lining along the top just above the Velcro.

5 Place the stiffening between the fabric and lining. Ensure the centre of the stiffening is level with the centre of the fabric. Tack it in place along the top.

6 Lay the pelmet face down and trim the fabric to the shape of the hem, leaving a turning allowance.

7 Working from the centre outwards, wrap the fabric over the stiffening, pulling it taut. Pin to hold. It will be necessary to snip the turning allowance for convex curves and disperse the fullness around the concave curves. Tack along the base of the pelmet.

Points leave little turning allowance; to prevent fraying, dab some clear nail varnish on to the tip of the snipped fabric on the wrong side of the pelmet.

8 Fold in the fabric turning allowance at the sides and fold down the lining onto the back of the pelmet. Trim the lower edge leaving a 5cm (2in) turning allowance. Fold the lining under to within 1cm ($^3/_8$in) of the edge, again snipping the turning allowance where necessary and pin in place.

9 Slip stitch the lining to the fabric down both sides and along the base of the pelmet. It may be easier to use a curved needle. It's better than using fabric glue, which can dry out or dissolve when dry cleaned.

10 Hand sew any braid, fringe or trim to the lower edge of the pelmet. Use a curved needle if necessary.

NOTE: For some hems with sharp 'v's it may be easier to sew the lining onto the pelmet first. Bring the raw edges of the lining onto the front of the pelmet and sew in place. Pull the fabric taut on the front of the pelmet and sew in place. Trim and cover the stitches and raw edge with braid or fringe.

Another way of coping with 'v's and points is to line the pelmet with the main fabric, sewing around the shape. Cut out the exact shape of the pelmet in fabric adding a seam allowance all round. Presew Velcro to the top of the lining fabric if required. Place the two layers of fabric right sides together and sew around the hem. See professional tip on p170.

FIXING PELMETS

Attach Velcro to the front edge of the pelmet board. Fix the pelmet onto the board, creasing it at the corners to return the pelmet to the wall. Secure the returns with tacks.

To make a neater return, fix corner blocks to the underside of the board. Secure the returns firmly to the blocks with either Velcro or tacks.

Steps 1 - 10

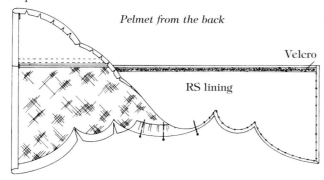

Pelmet from the back

Velcro

RS lining

Fixing a pelmet

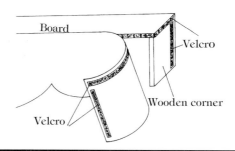

Board

Velcro

Wooden corner

Velcro

Professional Tip

MAKING PELMET PATTERNS WITH A CURVED LOWER EDGE

1 Decide on the shape you want. Draw a scale diagram on graph paper.

2 Take a large sheet of pattern paper, wide enough for half the finished width of the pelmet, and mark the lines for the top and bottom and the outside edge. Make a fold line at the return and centre.

3 Plot the vertical lines where the shaping changes direction. Either join the points with a ruler, or with a pair of compasses for a curved edge.

4 Having created the shaping, add a 5cm (2in) seam allowance all round and cut out the pattern which is half of the full pelmet.

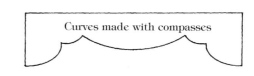

Curves made with compasses

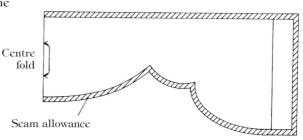

Centre fold

Seam allowance

MAKING UPHOLSTERED PELMETS

Pelmets can be covered, using upholstery techniques, for a padded finish. But be careful; they tend to be heavy and will need strong support.

1 Make a paper pattern of the pelmet shape, see p169.

2 Cut out the pelmet shape in composition board or plywood. You may need to ask a carpenter to do this for you. Cut out the sides separately and chamfer all the edges so they will fit at right angles to each other.

3 To make a hinge for the returns, lay them at each side of the pelmet and glue a strip of fabric 15cm (6in) wide over the join. Do this on both sides.

4 For the padding, cut a piece of wadding or foam and staple or glue it to the board. Trim away any excess at the edges.

5 Make up as for a stiffened pelmet, stapling rather than sewing the fabric.

A shaped pelmet with hand sewn braid

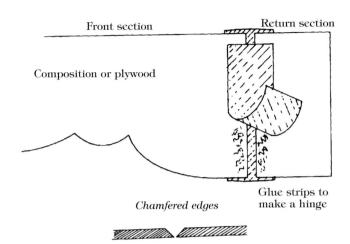

Front section   Return section

Composition or plywood

Chamfered edges   Glue strips to make a hinge

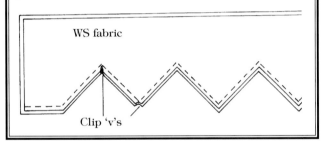

> **Professional Tip**
> To make a pelmet pattern with a pointed lower edge, follow instructions overleaf for a shaped pattern; see p169.
>
> WS fabric
>
> Clip 'v's

MAKING BRAIDED PELMETS

Cut out and seam the widths of fabric together as before.

Lay the pelmet shape on top of the fabric and draw around it with fabric marker pencil. Next, mark the position of the braid, see p158.

Sew the braid to the fabric and then make up the pelmet as before.

MAKING QUILTED PELMETS

When estimating fabric requirements, remember to add a generous 10% to both the width and the length measurements of the pelmet to allow for the 'take up' of the quilting.

Seam the lining and fabric widths, place wrong sides together with the wadding in between. Quilt your chosen pattern by hand or by machine.

Use the stiffened pelmet make-up method and do not attempt to pull the fabric too tight or you will reduce the effect of the quilting.

A quilted pelmet

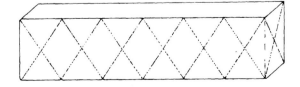

Valances are versatile top treatments; their headings are fixed because valances hang from a rail or from the front edge of a pelmet board, therefore any decorative heading with various details will work well. You can use machine taped or hand sewn headings.

The lower edge can be defined with either contrast bindings, frills or fringes, and can also be arched, serpentined or scalloped. A simple valance looks sophisticated when hung from a curved or scalloped board. Valances can be used with bed curtains as well, so there are other ideas in Beds and Everything Else. But all instructions for valances are given here.

VALANCE PROPORTIONS

Deciding the correct depth of the valance in relation to the curtain length is just as important as sewing it together beautifully.

The ideal proportions, when you have average ceilings and adequate wall space above the window, is $1/5$ of the curtain length.

Check that the depth of the valance will just cover the top of the glass. It should not hang over too much of the window, as this will block out light; an important consideration for small windows.

There are, however, one or two exceptions. Where the top of the window is close to the ceiling with little or no wall space above it, the depth of the valance can be shorter, $1/6$ of the curtain length.

In cottages, or rooms with extremely low ceilings and small windows, the valance can be as little as $1/6 - 1/8$ of the curtain length. In this case choose a simple style of valance in keeping with the architecture.

SHAPED VALANCES

Shaping the hem of the valance softens the horizontal lines of the window.

Professional Tip

If you have coving or cornices, and/or limited wall space above the window, where a normal valance will block out too much light, make a narrower than usual valance , so that it still just covers the frame, but add a stand up frill to the heading.

This gives the appearance of good proportions, as the frill stands above the fixing, but it will not block out any additional light.

ARCHED

These are particularly suited to tall windows. The deepest part of the valance falls over the curtain stack back area, so there shouldn't be any loss of light. An arched valance will work well on landscape windows, but the curve will look shallower, giving a less pronounced shape.

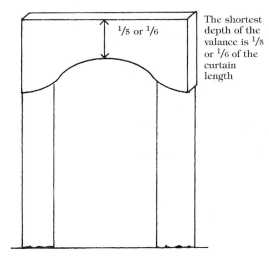

$1/5$ or $1/6$

The shortest depth of the valance is $1/5$ or $1/6$ of the curtain length

SERPENTINED

These are adaptable to any shape, effective in softening the harsh horizontal lines of wide picture and patio windows. The shaping can be quite subtle, as little as 5cm (2in) difference between the shortest and longest points of the valance (see p56).

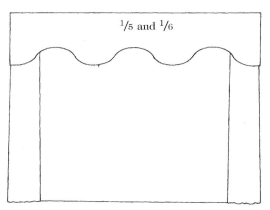

$1/5$ and $1/6$

The shortest depth of valance is $1/5$, the deepest $1/6$ of the curtain length

MAKING BASIC VALANCES

1 Measure the window and decide on the finished width and depth of the valance.

2 Work out how much fabric, lining and interlining you need, according to your style; see table on p116.

3 If you are going to use any of the following trims, refer to these pages:

Contrast bound edges, p151
Contrast piping, p121
Frills, pp154-5
Rope and fringe trims, p149

4 Cut out and seam the fabric, lining and interlining panels. If you wish, add any contrast edges now. You need to cut the main fabric to the finished depth of the valance, seam the contrast binding onto the top and bottom edge.

5 Place the seamed fabric and lining panels right sides together and machine along the lower edge (it is not essential for the fabric and lining seam lines to match).

6 Press the seams open. Fold the lining to the back of the valance and lightly press the hemline. Fold over the heading allowance. If you have a contrast edge, mark the depth of the contrast on the right side with pins, and fold the fabric over on this line.

7 Fold in the edges at the sides of the valance. Fold the lining in slightly further from the folded edge of the fabric so that it cannot be seen from the right side and pin in place.

Slip stitch to just below the heading.

8 Choose a decorative heading, see pp134-45. Make up following the instructions.

Valance

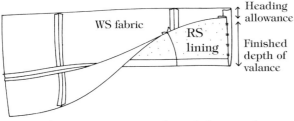

Seams: one centre panel, two halves at sides

Valance with contrast bound edges

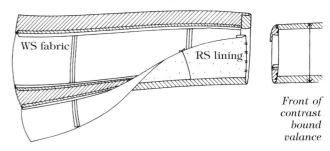

Front of contrast bound valance

Professional Tip

INTERLINING VALANCES
Interlining the complete valance gives a luxurious padded effect and is quick and easy to do. Simply cut the interlining to the exact finished depth of the valance and lay it between the fabric and lining. There is no need to interlock the interlining as with curtains because it is secured by the heading.

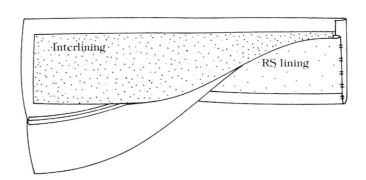

For arched or serpentined valances, cut the interlining to the exact shape of the hem line and to the finished depth of the valance. Sandwich the interlining between the fabric and the lining.

SHORT CUT TO PADDING OUT
To give the heading of lined valances a padded look, lay a strip of interlining slightly deeper than the heading in the top of the valance. This will make the heading more rounded, and it's a useful trick when you have had to save on fabric, and there is less fullness in the valance than you would have preferred.

GATHERED VALANCES

Gathered valances can be trimmed with a frill for a softer effect or with rope and fringes for a smart finish. Machine taped or gathered by hand, variations include puffed, smocked, pencil or frilled gathered headings. Allow an extra $1/2$ width of fabric for covering the returns of the pelmet board or valance rail. Follow instructions for the basic make-up, then turn to gathered headings, see pp134-9.

MAKING RUCHED VALANCES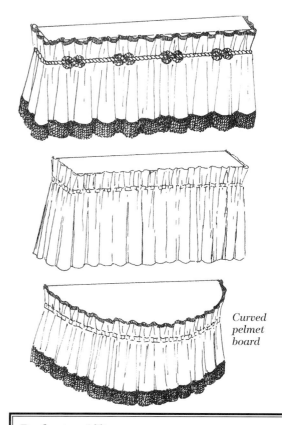
WITH PIPED FRILLS

A variation of the gathered valance - ruching has vertical and horizontal fullness like an Austrian blind. It is easy to make and the scalloped hemline resembles a pretty swagged effect. When working out the fabric you will need, make an allowance for vertical fullness as well; cut double the finished depth to allow for the gathering.

1 Cut out the fabric and make up the basic valance following Steps 1-4 opposite.

2 Make up the frill and the piping and machine into the fabric/lining seam at the lower edge, see p156.

3 Fold in the edges at the sides and fold down the heading allowance.

4 Machine gathering tape on the top or hand gather across the valance.

5 To make the ruching, first work out the spacing as shown in the next column, either hand sew small rings, or machine attach loop tapes (the kind used for Austrian blinds).

Pull up the heading tape or hand gathers to the required measurements and secure. Tie a piece of cord onto the lower ring or loop and thread through the remaining rings or loops. Tie the cord onto the top ring or loop so that the cord measures half the finished length of the valance.

Curved pelmet board

Professional Tip
WORKING OUT THE RUCHED SWAGS

Decide how many swags you want on your valance. The average window looks best with at least three swags, each around 46cm (18in) wide.

To find the flat width of the valance return, multiply the returns of the pelmet board or valance rail by the fullness ratio of the valance, see p116.

Sew the first row of rings or loop tape onto the outside edges of the valance. Measure the flat return to give the position of the next row of rings or tape.

Divide the remaining width by the number of swags required, and sew rings or loop tape at these intervals.

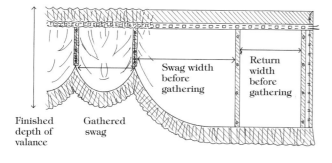

Finished depth of valance — Gathered swag — Swag width before gathering — Return width before gathering

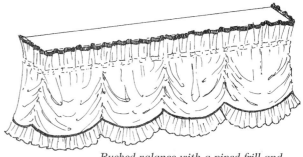

Ruched valance with a piped frill and contrast top

CURTAINS WITH ATTACHED VALANCES

The advantage of a valance attached to the top of the curtain is that it draws open with the curtains.

This is the ideal solution where there is no wall space above the window and a normal valance would block out too much light. It is normally hung from a pole or a fabric covered lath.

The valance proportions are calculated in the same way as a valance hung from a pelmet board.

FABRIC QUANTITIES

For the curtain and valance to be cut from a single length of fabric

Cut drop = finished curtain length + hem allowance + 2 x valance finished depth + heading allowance

To ensure that the fabric pattern is uninterrupted where the valance and the curtain meet, you may need to put in a lining insert (see below). Cut the top of the curtain off and seam in a piece of lining. If you are going to have a deep fringe or frill, then simply make sure that the valance shows one whole motif if possible.

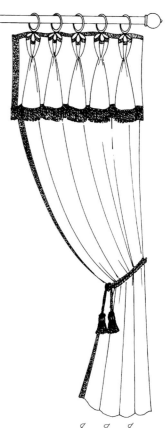

French headed contrast bound attached valance on a curtain with a contrast leading edge

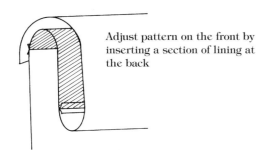

Adjust pattern on the front by inserting a section of lining at the back

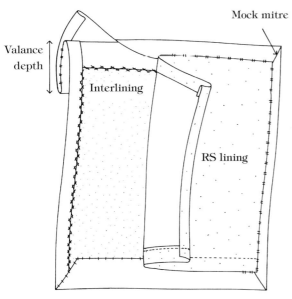

Valance depth

Interlining

Mock mitre

RS lining

MAKING ATTACHED VALANCES

Make up the curtain to the heading stage. Fold the valance fabric approximately in half, so that the raw edge finishes just below the top of the curtain. Turn under the raw edge of the lining and slip stitch.

Fold the valance onto the right side of the curtain and sew the chosen heading through all the layers of fabric.

NOTE: for a hand sewn buckram heading, insert the buckram at the top of the *valance* section.

Professional Tip

INTERLINING CURTAINS WITH ATTACHED VALANCES
On the curtain, cut the interlining to just below the position of buckram or heading. Herringbone stitch over the raw edge of the interlining, taking small stitches through the fabric.

To reduce bulk at the heading, use a lighter weight domette interlining in the valance section. Cut the interlining to the finished depth of the valance and lay it in between the two layers of fabric. For a hand sewn buckram heading, place the buckram in the valance section of the fabric level with the top of the valance interlining.

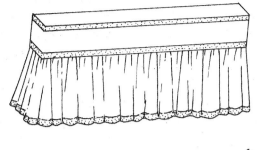

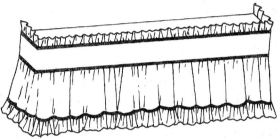

YOKED VALANCES

A flat yoke at the top of the valance looks attractive above a pleated or gathered skirt. The skirt can also be arched, scalloped or serpentined. The yoke is stiffened with a strip of pelmet buckram or stiffening. For a neat finish, pipe the top and bottom of the yoke.

PROPORTIONS

The yoke should be $1/3$ and the skirt below it $2/3$ of the finished valance depth. For a slightly lighter look, make the yoke $2/5$ and the skirt $3/5$.

FABRIC QUANTITIES

Take the finished measurement of the yoke and add a seam allowance all round. On patterned fabrics it will look much better if you position a whole or a contained part of the design on the yoke. Estimate the quantities for the skirt of the valance in the usual way.

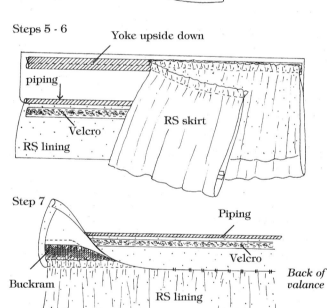

Steps 1 - 4

Contrast piping Seam

Finished depth of yoke

WS lining

Velcro

Steps 5 - 6

Yoke upside down

piping

Velcro

RS skirt

RS lining

Step 7

Piping

Velcro

Buckram

RS lining

Back of valance

MAKING YOKED VALANCES

1 Cut the necessary number of yoke fabric widths the finished depth of the yoke + two seam allowances. Seam them together into a long strip. Repeat for the lining.

2 Cut and sew piping to the top and bottom edges of the yoke fabric, see p121.

3 Sew Velcro onto the right side of the yoke lining just below the top seam allowance.

4 Place the fabric and lining right sides together and sew along the top edge.

5 Cut and make up the skirt of the valance. Gather or pleat up to the finished width of the valance.

6 Place the yoke and skirt right sides together and machine.

7 Cut a strip of stiffening the finished width and depth of the yoke. Insert it between the fabric and the lining. Fold under the raw edge of the lining, pin in place and hand stitch to neaten.

Professional Tip

INTERLINING YOKE VALANCES

To give the yoke a slightly padded finish, machine a strip of interlining to the buckram or stiffening in the same way as a tie-back (see p196).

To interline the skirt, use a lighter weight interlining, such as domette, to reduce the bulk at the top of the frill where it is either gathered or pleated onto the yoke.

HAND SEWN PLEATED BUCKRAM HEADINGS

Hand pleated valances have many design possibilities. As they are more structured than gathered valances, they have a neat, tailored appearance.

Basic instructions for buckram headings are given on pp140-2. Although they always require more preparation than tape headings, the results are rewarding.

FRENCH AND GOBLET PLEATS

These look particularly attractive with rope knotted at the base of the pleats, and fringe sewn onto the hem. Contrast edges can also define the shape of the pleats. Fringe and frills can be added to the lower edges; pleated headings combine well with box or knife pleated frills.

DOUBLE PLEATS

Double pleats are a sumptuous yet simple variation of French, goblet and box pleats. A double pleat has two lines of stitches to make two pleats which lie directly on top of one another. The two pleats are finished in different ways to make French, goblet or box pleats. The French pleat, when only partially stitched, makes an attractive fan-pleated effect.

To work out pleat and space sizes, use the same method as for single pleats on p140. However, the total pleat size is doubled, approximately 30-40cm (12-16in) which is divided between the first and second pleat. The space between the pleats can be from 20-40cm (8-16in). For patterns with a large horizontal repeat, a double pleat will easily accommodate the design of the fabric.

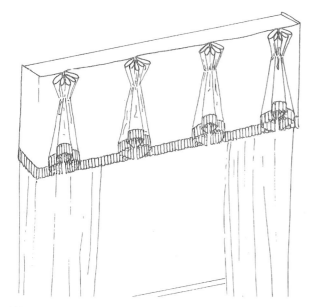

Pleated valances look attractive hung from curved pelmet boards

MAKING DOUBLE PLEATS

For French and goblet double pleats, the top and bottom pleats are of equal size. For a box pleat, the top should be 6-8cm (2½ - 3¼in) smaller than the bottom.

Mark the total width of the pleat with pins. Next, mark the centre pleat with two more pins. Sew the pleats 4cm (1½in) up from the lower edge of the buckram. For double goblets, sew the first pleat to the top of the buckram.

FRENCH DOUBLE PLEATS

Divide the first pleat into three folds and sew through the base. Flatten the second pleat and fold each 'wing' in half at the base of the pleat and secure. The top of the pleat will form a fan.

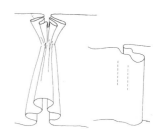

GOBLET DOUBLE PLEATS

Make the top pleat into a standard goblet. Finish the second pleat as described above.

DOUBLE BOX PLEATS

Flatten the pleats and put small stitches right through the side folds at the base of the buckram.

SCALLOPED SHAPED HEMS ON PLEATS

The hemline is shaped into scallops, rising up in the centre of the single or double pleat, falling into a curve in the space between.

For single pleated headings, the pleats should be generous in size, approximately 20cm (8in) in order to form the trumpet effect, and the spaces can be between 20-40cm (8-16in) wide to accommodate the scalloped hem shaping.

For single pleats, when working to these sizes the valance has 2 x or less fullness. A double pleat will increase the fullness of the valance.

On patterned fabrics the size of the pleats and spaces is dictated by the *horizontal* pattern repeat.

A repeat of 46cm (18in) for example, could have a single pleat of 20cm (8in) and a space of 26cm (10in). A larger repeat of 64cm (25in) could have a double pleat of 38cm (15in) and a space of 26cm (10in).

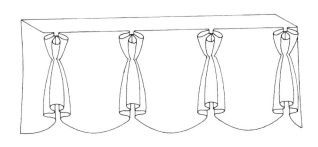

SCALLOPING OF PLEATED VALANCE HEMS

1 Seam up the widths of fabric and lining and work out the size of the pleats and the spaces. Mark these with pins along the top of the fabric.

2 Cut a piece of pattern paper, the width of the pleat, plus a space, by the depth of the valance, and fold in half. Mark a line $\frac{1}{3}$ of the distance up from the hem and draw a gentle curve to the lower side edge of the paper.

3 Make a second paper pattern adding a hem and heading allowance. Use this for the fabric.

4 Place the pattern onto the fabric, centring it over the first pleat and draw round, then continue along the whole valance. Note that the return is straight. Cut out the valance.

5 Use the fabric as a template, lay it over the lining and cut out to the same shape. If interlining the valance, cut the interlining to the exact shape of the valance, omitting the seam allowance at the hem and the heading.

6 Make up the basic valance. Instructions for hemming a shaped valance, see p181. Instructions for goblet and French pleats, see pp141-2.

Making a paper pattern

Step 2

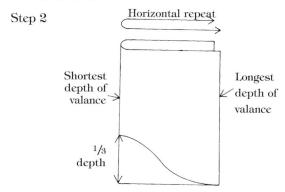

Horizontal repeat

Shortest depth of valance

Longest depth of valance

$\frac{1}{3}$ depth

Steps 3 - 4

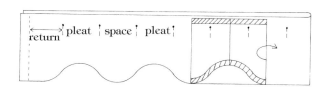

return | pleat | space | pleat

Double pleated valance

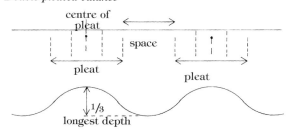

centre of pleat

space

pleat

pleat

$\frac{1}{3}$ longest depth

TRUMPET VALANCES

Trumpets are inserted between flat panels of fabric. The hemline can be straight, scalloped or arched. You can use double trumpets to make it more elaborate. A trumpet valance can hang from a pelmet board, or from a pole with the curtains set on a track behind. The hemline can be trimmed with braids, fringes, frills or contrast binding. The trumpets need to be contrast lined or lined in the main fabric, as the lining will show.

The number of trumpets is optional. Space them approximately 25-40cm (10-16in) apart. An odd number looks best, as you end up with one in the middle as a focal point for the window. To find the exact number, start with the length of the pelmet board or pole. Deduct 20cm (8in) then divide the remainder by the estimated number of flat sections. You should have one more trumpet than flat section. The return on either side will be the width of the pelmet board or the distance from the pole to the wall + 10cm (4in) which allows the end trumpets to sit on the front edge of the pelmet board or pole.

MAKING THE PATTERNS

To start with you will need two patterns, one for the valance and another for the trumpet. Although this takes time making the valance afterwards will be quite straightforward.

PROPORTIONS

The depth is calculated in the same manner as for a straight or arched valance.

1 Cut out a paper pattern, half the finished width by the finished depth of the valance. Draw vertical lines to mark the flat sections, the return, and if you wish, shape the hem into scallops. Cut out each section. These will be your templates.

2 To make the trumpet pattern see p162. The length of the trumpet must be the same as the side of the flat section.

> **Professional Tip**
>
> If the valance is to be hung from a pole, the lines look more fluid when the trumpet is tapered to approximately 2.5cm (1in) at the top. Adjust the pattern accordingly.

3 To make the fabric patterns, take the three paper pattern templates – the trumpet, the flat section and the return – and redraw adding a seam allowance around each one.

4 For the lining, seams should fall at the centre of the trumpets so they are not seen at the front. To make the lining pattern, layout the templates in the correct position on a large piece of paper (as illustrated in the diagram opposite). Add a seam allowance all round.

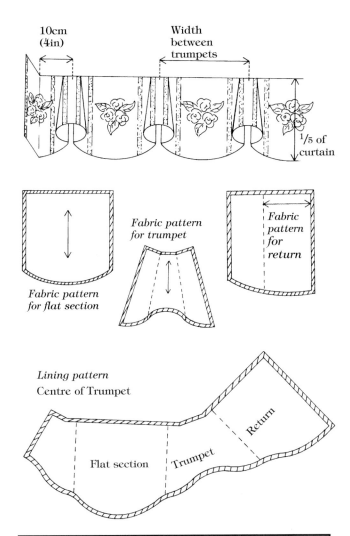

10cm (4in)   Width between trumpets

1/5 of curtain

Fabric pattern for flat section

Fabric pattern for trumpet

Fabric pattern for return

Lining pattern
Centre of Trumpet

Flat section   Trumpet   Return

> **Professional Tip**
>
> PATTERNED FABRICS
>
> For patterned fabrics, the individual trumpets and flat spaces will have to be cut carefully to centre the pattern. When seamed together, the seams will be concealed by the folds of the trumpets.

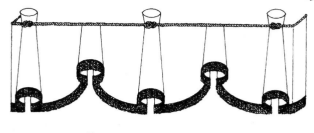

MAKING TRUMPET VALANCES
FABRIC QUANTITIES
Work out how many flat sections and trumpets can be cut out from a width of fabric, bearing in mind any pattern placements. Then add up the widths.

LINING QUANTITIES
Measure the lining pattern. The pattern can be cut with the centre seam placed on either the weft or the warp grain of the lining fabric. If extra seams are needed, place them through the centre of the trumpets where they cannot be seen from the right side.

Double trumpets

Steps 3 - 5

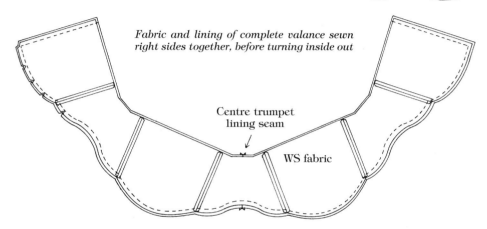

Fabric and lining of complete valance sewn right sides together, before turning inside out

Centre trumpet lining seam

WS fabric

1 Using the return flat section and trumpet patterns, cut out the appropriate number of each in the main fabric. On prints, place the pattern pieces with care.

2 Use the lining pattern to cut out the lining. If you also want interlining cut it from the same pattern and trim away the seam allowance. Remember, the lining will show on the right side. Use the main fabric as a lining or a contrast lining.

3 Seam the sections together alternately, remember to add the return section at each end; press the seams open. Join the lining together; press the seams open.

4 Lay the fabric and lining, right sides together, and machine down the sides and around the hem. The shaping of the hem is often quite gentle, so be careful to sew as accurately as you can.

5 Clip and notch the seam allowances around any curves, then turn through to the right side and press.

6 For a valance on a pelmet board, fold each trumpet in half to bring the seam lines together. Sew 5cm (2in) down the centre back to hold in place. Flatten the

Pleating up trumpets

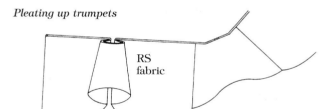

RS fabric

Binding the top

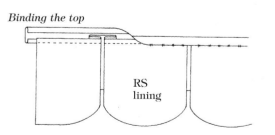

RS lining

sides, centring the trumpet over the back seam. Neaten the top of the valance with a 2cm (^{3}/4in) fabric binding, see p152. Secure the valance to the pelmet board with Velcro fastening tape or staples.

7 When hung from a pole, the raw edges are turned in at the top and slip stitched to neaten. Fold and seam down the trumpet as above. Hand sew the tops in place. Stab pin hooks or hand sew rings to the centre-back of each trumpet.

Shaping the hemline into either an arch or a serpentine requires a little planning. It is useful to draw a diagram of the finished valance, marking the various measurements and where you want the hem to rise and fall.

SHAPING VALANCES

THINGS YOU NEED TO DO BEFORE YOU START

1 Add the length and return measurements of the pelmet board together to find the finished width.

2 For fullness ratio, see p116. The actual fullness ratio is the seamed fabric width measurement, less side turning allowances, divided by the finished width of the valance.

3 The cut drop of the panels is the depth of the longest part of the valance + the heading and hem allowances.

Shortest point = $1/5$ or $1/6$ of the curtain length

Longest point = Optional: can be as much as 2 x the shortest point – the deeper the curve the more dramatic the effect. An allowance must be made for the return before the shaping starts at the front.

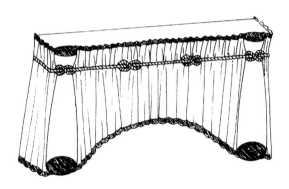

SHAPING ARCHED GATHERED VALANCES

1 Seam the fabric widths together and then seam the lining widths together. If necessary, trim the width of the lining to match that of the fabric.

The shaping is drawn onto the wrong side of the lining, this is then used as a template to cut out the fabric. Fold the lining in half through the centre of the valance, right sides together.

2 Multiply the return measurement by the fullness ratio to give the finished return measurement.

Allow 5cm (2in) for the side turning. Measure the flat return and, with a pin, mark this Point A.

3 To find Point B, measure halfway between Point A and the centre fold (Point C). Mark these points with pins.

A = Longest measurement + turning allowances
B = Midway measurement of A and C
C = Shortest measurement + turning allowances

4 Using a fabric marker pencil, join these points together. Draw a smooth curve between points A, B and C, starting and ending the line at 90° to the side edges.

For a deep arch, subdivide each section again to find more midway points to give further references. This saves guesswork and will give a smooth, even curve.

5 Cut out the lining along the curved line. The lining can now be used as a template to cut out the fabric. Remember interlining – if required – does not need seam allowances.

Marking a curve onto valance lining

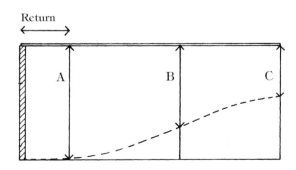

SHAPING GATHERED SERPENTINED VALANCES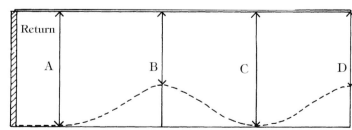

Draw a diagram of the valance shaping and mark it with all the measurements.

The hem snakes up and down between $\frac{1}{5}$ and $\frac{1}{6}$ of the curtain length.

There will be a high or a low point in the centre of the valance according to the number of scoops in the design. The width between the longest and shortest points is called a 'section'.

1 Fold the seamed widths of lining in half, right sides together. Work out the flat measurement of the valance return and with a pin mark Point A, see diagram below.

2 Divide the remaining width of the lining into the number of sections required.

3 Take a piece of pattern paper measuring the width of a section x the depth of the longest point + turning allowances. Mark the shortest point + turning allowances on one side of the paper.

Draw a smooth curve between the 2 points, starting and ending the line at 90˚ to the side edge of the paper. Cut out.

4 Place the paper pattern in line with the centre fold of the lining and mark the curved line with a fabric marker pencil. Turn the pattern over at each section to mirror the curves.

5 Cut out the lining along the curved line and use as a template to cut out the fabric.

6 Hem the valance, see Professional Tip opposite. Gather the valance, either using heading tape, see p125, or hand gather, see pp138-139.

Professional Tip

HEMMING SHAPED VALANCES

Due to the curved shaping of the valance, the lining is partially visible from the right side. On a pleated, scalloped shaped valance the inside of the pleat is visible on the right side of the valance. Therefore, the valance is either fully lined in the main or contrast fabric or, to save fabric, the lower half only can be lined in the main or contrast fabric.

Alternative decorative hem finishes that conceal the lining of the valances are frills inset into the hem seam, see p156, and contrast bound edges cut on the true cross of the grain, see p153.

FABRIC QUANTITIES

Allow for self fabric or contrast lining.
To half line the valance, allow 50% more fabric and 50% less lining.

1 Lay the shaped fabric and self or contrast lining right sides together and machine down each side and along the hem. Clip and notch the hem seam allowance, see p121.

2 Turn the valance through to the right side and press along the hem with both edges level.

3 Head the valance as required.

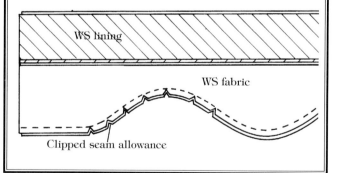

WS lining

WS fabric

Clipped seam allowance

Shaped valance lining

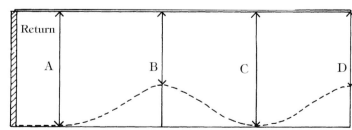

Side turning allowance | Return | A | B | C | D

TOPS 2: TRADITIONAL SWAGS & TAILS

Swags and tails are the ultimate way to dress a window; a classic treatment for a classic room. Fitted onto a pelmet board or draped over a pole, swags and tails – like informal scarf drapery – give the illusion of continuous fabric, although they are made up and fitted separately. Even though they can be set fairly high above the window and even if they are made up properly with correct proportions, they will always block out some light.

This formal style can be made even more luxurious with braid, fringes or pleated frills. Knotted rope and tassels add a three dimensional look. Good pattern cutting is the key, and be aware that it takes a considerable amount of fabric, time and patience. But for those with a hankering for something really out of the ordinary, this is a rewarding project.

SWAGS AND TAILS

PROPORTIONS

Swag Depth = $\frac{1}{5}$ of the curtain length

Tail length = 2 or 3 x swag depth, depending on whether you want short or long tails

Swag width when *butted together* = length of pelmet board divided by the number of swags

Swag width when *overlapped* = length of pelmet board divided by the number of swags + 5-10cm (2-4in) per overlap

FABRIC QUANTITIES

The only really accurate way of working out exact quantities is to make the patterns and measure them. However, if you have to buy the fabric before you begin, here are some guidelines:

One width of fabric will make a swag up to approximately 1m (39in) wide. Allow two widths for wider swags.

For the cut drop: allow approximately 2.25 x swag length. The exact amount of vertical fullness depends on the number and size of the pleats in the swag.

Straight tails: cut drop per tail = 1 width x length of tail + 10cm (4in) seam allowance

Curved shaped tails: you will have to make a paper pattern first to work out the fabric requirement.

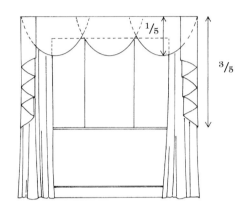

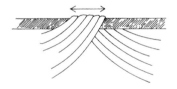

Swags overlapped

FRINGE QUANTITIES

For swags, pin a length of chain to a pinboard, the width and depth of the swag. Measure the chain and add 15cm (6in) ease and turning allowance per swag. Multiply by the number of swags.

For tails, make your pattern first if you can: a double pleated tail may only require 1.2m (47in) but a longer, triple pleated tail could take up to 2m (79in), which is quite a difference. Measuring the hemline will establish the exact quantity needed. Multiply by the number of tails.

If you have to buy the fringe first, be generous. You can use any leftovers for cushions or tablecloths.

FABRIC TRIMS

Remember to allow extra fabric for any trims such as rosettes, trumpets, choux, etc., see pp159-65.

Professional Tip

SWAG WIDTH

Swags are normally between 60cm (23$\frac{1}{2}$in) to 100cm (39in) wide. For a single swag design, the swag width can be over 2m (2yd); but they will be difficult to drape.

SWAG VARIATIONS

Should you cut the swag on the true cross or on the straight grain of the fabric? It is easier to drape on the true cross, but this is only suitable for plain fabrics. The size of the swag is also limited by the fabric width.

Cutting swags on the straight grain is totally versatile, accommodating patterns, stripes, slubbed weaves and fabric with texture or pile, like velvet. There is also no limit to the width of the swag, as equal panels of fabric seamed to the sides are barely noticeable.

The technique for cutting swags on the straight grain is given below. It can be adapted for swags cut on the true cross if you wish.

The swag pleats can either radiate from one point at the outer edge, or be staggered along the top. Pleats that radiate from a single point are easier to make and tend to look more graceful, and the make-up notes follow this method.

The technique for staggering pleats is explained in Making Asymmetric Swags on p188.

DRAPING PATTERNS

Making swag patterns is a two stage process. Firstly you drape a 'shape' to the finished size. Then you make the pattern by drawing around the shape and adding turning/seam allowances.

Where as all other shapes are made in paper first, swag shapes are always draped in fabric first, and then transferred to paper for the actual pattern.

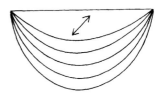

Radiating pleats, fabric cut on the true cross

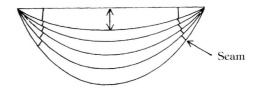

Radiating pleats, fabric cut on the straight grain, seams on each side

Seam

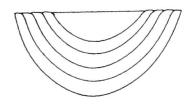

Staggered pleats

You may be able to use up old waste fabric - odd pieces of lining are ideal. With a big window, or a set of windows, buy 5-6m (6yd) of cheap lining fabric. It is worth the small cost to make perfect swag patterns - then you can cut into good fabric with confidence. You'll also need somewhere to work, such as a large pinboard or the back of a sofa. This is the only way to make draped swags that will hang perfectly.

Professional Tip

When cutting two pairs of straight tails in plain fabric, you can dovetail the pattern to save material.

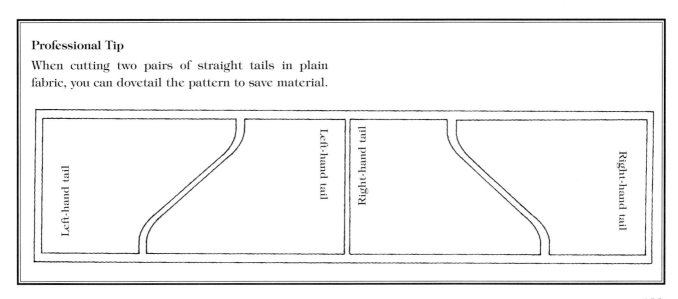

DRAPING SWAG PATTERNS

1 Pin a large piece of pattern paper on the pinboard and mark a line for the top of the swag. Pin a length of chain to fall in an arc to the finished depth of the swag.

2 Fold a piece of lining fabric in half across the width and press the fold. Straighten the top edge and cut off a wedge at either side to make the basic shape.

Pin the lining fabric to the line on the paper, placing the fold of the fabric in the centre. Measure down divisions of approximately 12cm (5in) for the pleats on each side.

3 Starting at one side, take the first pleat mark below the top edge; hold it loosely with the fold of the pleat held over the fixing point. With the other hand, lift and gently encourage the fabric to fall into an arc towards the centre of the swag.

Pin the fold to the fixing point; the pins will need to be at a steep angle to hold the weight. Repeat on the other side of the swag to complete the pleat.

Moving down the fabric, make four more pleats. All the folds must go up into the same fixing point on each side.

At this stage do not worry if the pleats are not perfect, just carry on and complete the swag. Then stand back and look to see where it can be improved – some pleats may be fatter than others, some may not be evenly spaced. Unpin and start again.

Check the centre crease. It should hang straight – if it is being pulled to one side, the pleats are uneven. Unpin and try to make it straight.

The bottom pleat has a tendency to be too thick. Stand against the wall and check that the pleats look even from the side.

4 When you have a pleasing shape, look at the left and right-hand sides and choose the best one. Working on this side, trim the fabric to the arc of the chain, including the layers at the side of the pleats.

5 Unpin the lining from the board and fold it in half. Trim away the excess fabric at the other side of the swag. Re-pin to check that the hem shape follows the arc of the chain. If necessary, trim at the hem. Unpin and check both sides are the same.

Step 1

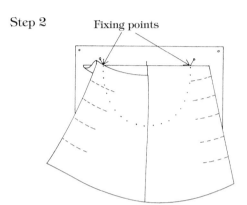

Swag width

Depth

Chain

Step 2

Fixing points

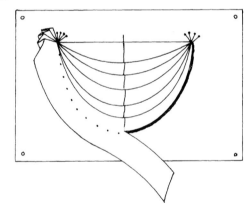

Steps 3 - 5

6 To make the paper pattern, lay the folded swag on a large piece of pattern paper. Draw around it, adding 1.5cm (³/₄in) seam allowance.

Mark the centre fold line and pierce holes at the outer and inner points of the pleats to mark the sewing line.

Write the dimensions onto the swag pattern for future use.

Step 6

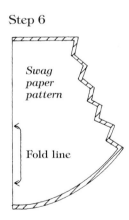

Swag paper pattern

Fold line

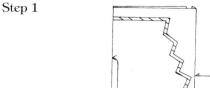

MAKING BASIC LINED SWAGS

<small>MATERIALS</small>
Fabric
Lining
Fringe (optional)

Step 1

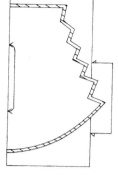

1 Place the paper pattern onto the fold of the fabric. Mark the cutting and sewing lines with a fabric marker pencil. Cut out. Repeat for the lining.

If using patterned fabric, centralise the pattern. For swags that are wider than the width of the fabric, seam extra panels to the sides, matching the pattern as necessary.

Steps 2 - 3

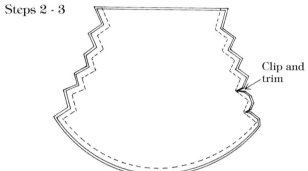

Clip and trim

2 Place the fabric and lining right sides together. Machine accurately down the sides of the swag and along the curved hem. Leave the top open.

3 Trim the seam allowance to 1cm (^{3}/$_8$in), snipping into the 'v's and clipping the corners.

Step 4

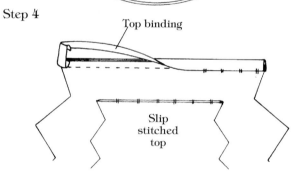

Top binding

Slip stitched top

4 Turn the swag through to the right side and press. It is important to pull out the side points fully, otherwise the swag pleats will be distorted. The raw edges at the top can either be bound or turned in.

For swags to be fitted to a pelmet board, neaten the top with a 2cm (^{3}/$_4$in) fabric binding, see p152. If required, sew Velcro to the back of the binding.

For swags draped over a pole, fold in the fabric and lining and slip stitch in place.

Step 5

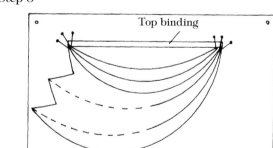

Top binding

5 Pin the swag onto the board over the chain, and pleat it up. Make sure that the last tip covers the other pleats, and then hand sew through all the tips to hold firmly in place. Lift up the last pleat and spot tack through the rest of the pleats.

6 To fit the swag to the pelmet board or pole, see pp230-1.

Professional Tip

<small>INTERLINING SWAGS</small>

Use a medium to lightweight interlining to encourage the pleats to drape into rounded folds. Cut out the interlining from the paper pattern; to avoid unnecessary bulk trim away the sides. Place the interlining onto the wrong side of the fabric and interlock in place, spacing the rows 20cm (8in) apart. Make up as above.

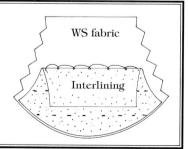

WS fabric

Interlining

MAKING ARCHED SHAPED SWAGS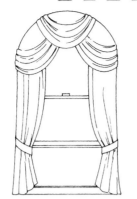

1 Make a paper template of the window, see p113 and mark on the central vertical line and a horizontal line at the widest point. Pin the finished template onto the pinboard. Make a note of the depth and proportions of the swags in your chosen design.

2 To make a centre swag with staggered pleats and a shaped top, pin up the chain on your template to give the required width and depth of the swag. Mark the staggered fixing points at each side of the swag on the curved line.

3 Fold your lining fabric in half and press the centre fold. Measure out the basic shape and cut away the excess fabric.

4 Pin the lining over the template, centring the fold on the centre of the arch. With a pencil, copy the top line of the arch onto the fabric up to the first fixing point.

5 Drape the fabric into folds, staggering the pleats to the fixing points marked on the paper template. Make sure the pleats are generous, as on this type of swag they have a tendency to look rather shallow.

6 Complete all the folds. At one side of the swag trim the hemline to the arc of the chain and to the arch at the top. Mark the staggered pleats on their fold lines and number each one. Also mark and number the position at which each fold is pinned, so that fold number 1 is pinned to position number 1 and so on.

7 Unpin the fabric from the board and fold it in half along its crease line. Trim away the excess fabric at the other side of the swag.

8 Draw around the lining on pattern paper, adding 1.5cm (^{1}/$_2$in) seam allowance all round. Transfer all the pattern markings.

9 Make up the shaped swag as for a plain swag. In this case, place the fabric and lining right sides together and only machine round the curve of the hem. Turn through to the right side and press. Pleat the swag and neaten the top arch with a 2cm (^{3}/$_4$in) binding, see p152.

186

Steps 1 - 2

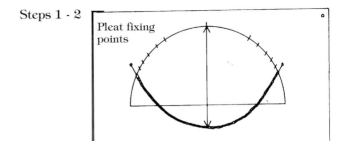

Pleat fixing points

Step 3

2 x swag depth

←——— ^{1}/$_2$ chain + 10cm (4in) ———→

Steps 4 - 5

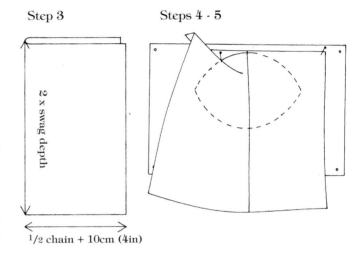

Step 6

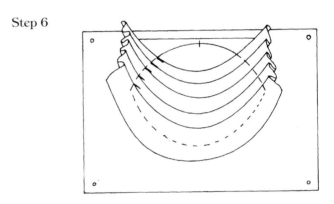

Steps 7 - 8

Staggered pleats

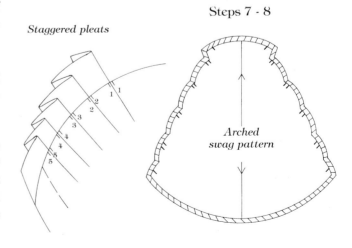

Arched swag pattern

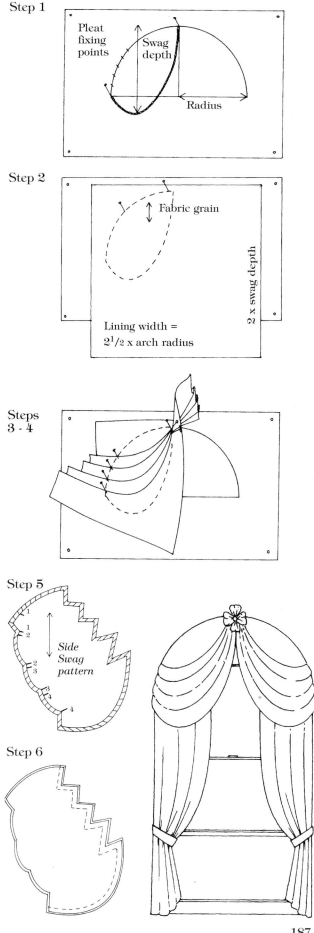

MAKING ARCHED SIDE SWAGS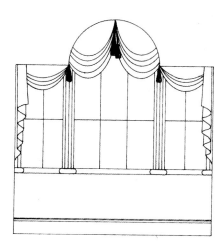

This is an asymmetric swag with staggered pleats and a shaped top. Make a paper template of the window as before.

1 Pin up the chain to the top centre point of the arch, bringing it out to the side in a graceful arc to the required depth. Mark the staggered fixing points at the side of the swag on the curved line. The pleats at the top of the swag can also be slightly staggered.

2 Pin the lining fabric over the template, centring the fold of the fabric over the centre of the arch. With a pencil, copy the line of the arch onto the fabric up to the first fixing point at the top and side of the swag.

3 Drape the fabric into folds, staggering the side pleats to the marks made on the paper template.

4 Having completed all the folds, trim the fabric at the hemline to the arc of the chain, and at the top to the shape of the arched template.

Mark the staggered pleats on their fold lines and number each one. Also mark and number the place to which each fold is pinned, so that fold number 1 is pinned to position number 1 and so on. Draw the grain line of the fabric onto the swag.

5 Unpin the fabric from the board and make a paper pattern in the same way as the centre swag.

6 Make up the swag as before. Place the fabric and lining right sides together, machine round the hem and the side where the pleats radiate from one point.

Pleat up the swag, then neaten the raw edges at the top with a 2cm (³/₄in) binding, see p152.

Step 1

Pleat fixing points

Swag depth

Radius

Step 2

Fabric grain

2 x swag depth

Lining width = 2¹/₂ x arch radius

Steps 3 - 4

Step 5

Side Swag pattern

Step 6

MAKING ASYMMETRIC SWAGS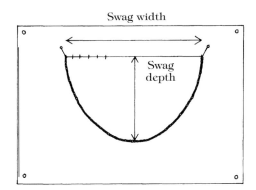

Asymmetric swags are also draped to the arc of a chain, but the pleats are spaced differently at the sides. They look particularly dramatic when draped over poles.

Combine asymmetric swags with decorative trims, such as decorative tails and trumpets – the effect is soft and graceful without being fussy.

1 Place a large piece of pattern paper over the pinboard and mark a horizontal line for the top of the swag. Mark the centre line and pin the chain up to the finished depth of the swag.

At the appropriate side of the swag mark the staggered fixing points of the pleats on the horizontal line. The distance between the pleats is optional, but they should be evenly spaced.

2 Use lining fabric to make the pattern. Pin the lining up to the top horizontal line, placing the fold of the lining over the centre point.

3 Drape the swag as instructed on p187. However, on one side of the swag take all the pleats to the top edge fixing point and at the other side stagger the pleats along the top edge.

4 Having created an attractive shape and still working on the pinboard, trim the lining to the *entire* arc of the chain and along the top of the staggered pleats.

Before unpinning, mark the staggered pleats on their fold lines and number each one. Mark and number the position to which each fold is pinned, so that fold number 1 is pinned to position number 1 and so on.

5 Draw around the lining on a piece of pattern paper, adding a seam allowance all round and transfer all the markings.

6 Make up the swag; place the fabric and lining right sides together and machine round the hem and the side where the pleats radiate from one point.

7 Neaten the raw edges at the top with a 2cm (³/₄in) binding, see p152. Stitch the tips together.

Step 1

Swag width

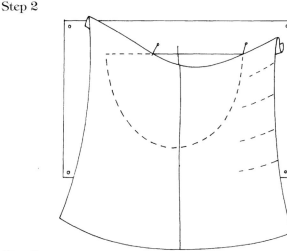

Swag depth

Step 2

Step 3

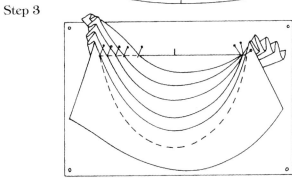

Step 5

Step 6

Asymmetric swag pattern

WS fabric of swag

Step 7   *Bind staggered pleats*

Slip stitched top

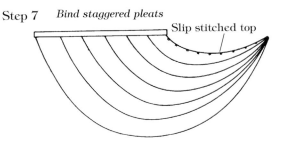

TAILS

Tail patterns can be a simple oblong shape, concertinaed into folds, with the hemline cut at an angle. The number of folds is optional, but even for long tails it is unnecessary to have more than three pleats. Too many pleats tends to look too busy.

For graceful tails, the pleats should be layered one on top of the other. This does create several thicknesses of fabric, but this is manageable with only three pleats. If the pleats are spread out or staggered, making the tail wide at the top, this will reduce the thickness. However the hemline will have a stepped effect which means losing the fluid curves. There are two basic tail shapes, a straight shape and a cone shape.

MAKING STRAIGHT TAIL PAPER PATTERNS

1 Decide on the length of the tail and the point at which the shaping begins. The length of the tail is 2-3 x the swag depth. The shaping usually begins level with the base of the swag.

2 Fold a piece of paper, the finished length of the tail, into a concertina of pleats. The width of the pleats should be between 10-14cm (4-5½in) wide. For short tails that are only 2 x the depth of the swag, 2 pleats are enough. Tails that are 3 x the depth of the swag need 3 pleats.

3 Open the paper out; at the front edge of the tail mark the shortest point and at the other edge, the longest point.

4 At the shortest point, draw a line 10cm (4in) long at right angles to the side edge. At the other edge, draw a line 10cm (4in) long at right angles to the side edge.

Join the lines together with a straight line. Draw smooth, freehand curves to round off the angle of the 2 lines at the top and bottom of the tail. Cut along the hemline of the tail.

5 Make a second pattern; at the longest edge add a return allowance the width of the pelmet board. Add a seam allowance all round and cut out.

Professional Tip

Add a 5cm (2in) flap to the short edge of the tail; this can be tucked around to the back of the tail to make a rounded edge.

Steps 1 - 4

7 sections in a triple pleated tail.

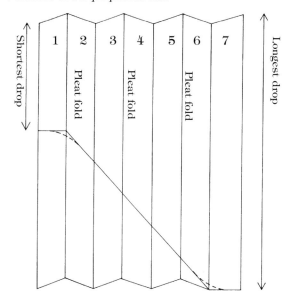

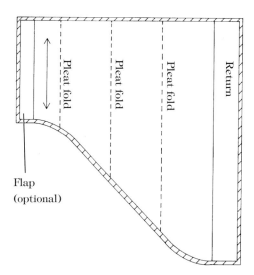

MAKING LINED STRAIGHT TAILS

1 Cut out the required number of tails in both fabric and contrast lining. Remember if you need a *pair* of tails cut out a left and a right tail by reversing the pattern.

If using patterned fabric, centre a suitable section of the pattern on the top pleat of the tail.

2 Place the fabric and lining right sides together and machine down the two sides and along the hemline. Clip and notch the seam allowance where needed.

3 Turn the tail through to the right side and press the edges of the fabric and lining level at the seam.

4 To pleat up the tail, place the paper pattern on top of the tail and mark the fold lines with pins. Following the pin marks, concertina the folds to make the required number of pleats.

Temporarily pin the pleats in position. Do not iron the pleats, as soft rounded folds are preferable to hard creased edges.

5 The raw edges at the top of the tail are neatened with a 2cm (³/₄in) binding in the same way as a swag, see p152. As there are several thicknesses of fabric to be sewn, it may be easier to sew the binding by hand.

Velcro sewn to the binding will hold lightweight tails. But for long, heavy tails, extra tacks or staples will be required to hold them in place on the pelmet board.

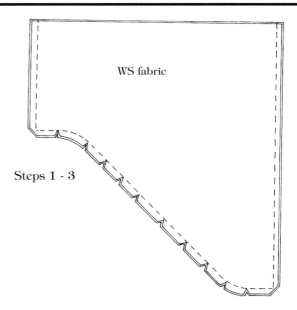

WS fabric

Steps 1 - 3

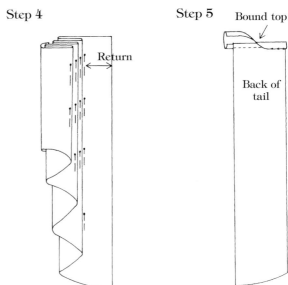

Step 4

Return

Step 5

Bound top

Back of tail

Professional Tip

INTERLINING TAILS

For most fabrics a lightweight interlining, such as domette, will help the fabric to make soft rounded folds. However, for thick, bulky fabrics such as velvet, it is unnecessary to interline.

Cut out the interlining using the paper pattern. Trim away at the top as illustrated right. Lay it onto the wrong side of the fabric, and stitch in place with vertical rows of interlocking spaced 20cm (8in) apart.

Herringbone stitch across the top, taking small stitches on the right side of the fabric. Place the fabric and lining right sides together and proceed as for a lined tail.

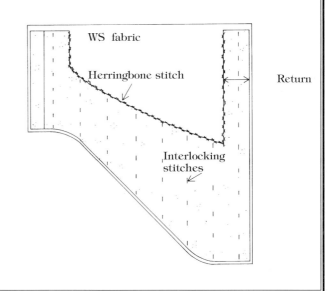

WS fabric

Herringbone stitch

Return

Interlocking stitches

MAKING CONE SHAPED TAILS

Cone shaped tails are tapered, and are made in the same way as straight tails.

The shaping of the tail usually begins level with the base of the swag. The finished length of the tail should be 2-3 x the depth of the swag.

NOTE: this pattern can only be used for plain fabrics as only the outer section of the tail falls on the straight grain of the fabric.

1 Decide on the length of the tail and the point where the shaping begins.

2 On a large piece of pattern paper draw a full tail section. To do this, draw a line the width of the top of the tail, usually 10-14cm (4-5^1/$_2$in). At the centre of that line, draw a vertical line the finished length of the tail. At the bottom of the vertical line, centre a line the width of the bottom of the tail - this is usually 20-30cm (8-12in). At the corners, join the top and bottom lines to form a tail section.

3 Cut along the top and bottom and the outside edge. Fold the pattern over, draw around the new outline. Again, cut the top and bottom edges and repeat until you have the required number of sections. A triple pleated tail has 7 sections, and a double pleated tail has 5 sections.

4 To shape the lower edge: measure from the point at which the shaping begins to the finished length of the tail, and divide this measure by the number of sections. This figure is the amount by which the shaping line steps down each section.

5 Mark these points onto the pattern. Start to draw the line at right angles at the front edge and the long side edge. and then join all the points with a smooth freehand curve.

6 Make a second pattern, adding a return allowance (i.e. the width of the pelmet board) to the long side edge of the tail. Add a seam allowance all round and cut out. The grain line is parallel to the return.

Steps 1-5

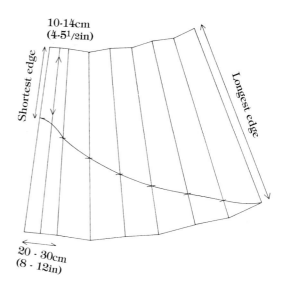

Step 6

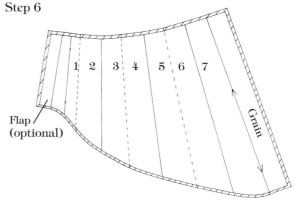

Professional Tip
For printed fabrics cut the tail pattern in two at a pleat fold. Add a seam allowance to both patterns at the cut fold line. The grain line of the long section is parallel to the return and the shorter section is parallel to the front section.

A swag valance is made by seaming trumpets in between swags to form a continuous design. It employs all the skills of draping and making a swag, plus some extra pattern cutting expertise - and patience!

PROPORTIONS
Swag depth = $1/5$ of the curtain length
Trumpet depth = $2/3$ of the swag depth

The minimum swag width should be approximately 50cm (20in) and the maximum approximately 100cm (39in) or it will lose its pretty, scalloped hem shaping.

Make an allowance for the first and last trumpets on the front of the pelmet board. Deduct 20cm (8in) from the length of the board, and divide the remaining figure by the number of swags. This gives you the width of each swag. The finished valance will be the pelmet board length + the returns.

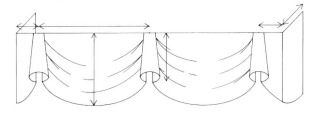

DRAPING SWAGGED VALANCE PATTERNS

1 Drape a swag pattern made up in lining as per the instructions on p184, Steps 1-3.

2 At the top right-hand corner, draw a vertical line the depth of the trumpet. Draw a smooth curve from the centre of the chain up to it. Trim away the excess fabric along the hemline and at the top.

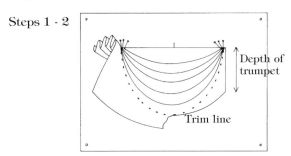

Steps 1 - 2

Depth of trumpet

Trim line

3 Unpin the lining from the board, fold it in half and trim the fabric at the other side to the same shape. Re-pin the swag onto the pinboard.

4 For the trumpet, make a paper pattern as described on p 162, without a seam allowance. Pin it up and centre over the vertical line. Check its dimensions.

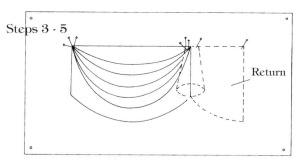

Steps 3 - 5

Return

5 To make the valance return, cut a piece of paper the finished depth of the valance x the width of the pelmet board + 10cm (4in). Pin it to the side of the swag, underneath the trumpet pattern. Draw a smooth curve from the trumpet to the outer edge of the return.

MAKING PAPER PATTERNS

Lay the lining swag onto a large piece of pattern paper and draw around it. Mark the centre fold line and add a seam allowance to the top and the hem. Add a seam allowance at the side of the swag (where the trumpet is positioned) but not at the side of the pleats.

Make the final trumpet paper pattern, adding a seam allowance all round and cut out.

Make the final return paper pattern, adding a seam allowance all round and cut out.

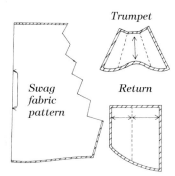

Trumpet

Swag fabric pattern

Return

To make the swag lining pattern, trace around the lining swag and lay the trumpet pattern (without seam allowances) at the side and trace around half of it. Add a seam allowance to the trumpet, along the hem, up the side and along the top, and cut out.

To make the lining return paper pattern, trace around the return (without seam allowances) and place the trumpet at the side. Draw around half of the trumpet. Add a seam allowance all round.

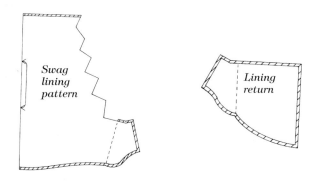

Swag lining pattern

Lining return

MAKING LINED SWAGGED VALANCES

1 Using the correct patterns, cut out the required number of swags, trumpets and one pair of returns in fabric and lining.

2 Beginning with the fabric pieces, seam the trumpets to the sides of the swags. This will create a stepped effect at the top of the trumpet. Seam the returns onto the outermost trumpets. Press all the seams open.

3 To make the lining, seam the lower side sections together through the centre of the trumpet. Seam the lining returns to the outermost sections. Press all the seams open.

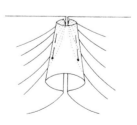

Steps 1 - 5

4 To hem the valance, place the fabric and lining right sides together and machine down each side and along the hem.
NOTE: the seams of the lining do not match those on the fabric.

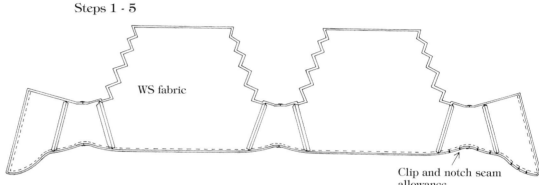

WS fabric

Clip and notch seam allowance

5 Clip and notch the seam allowance. Turn the valance through to the right side and press the sides and hem. Tack along the top and down the sides of the swags.

Step 6

Spot tack

Step

6 Pleat up the swags (the last pleat will be formed when the trumpet is placed in position). To hold firmly in place, hand sew through all the layers. Repeat for all the swags.

Step 7

7 Pin all the swags onto the pinboard, butting them together. Centre the trumpet over the junction of the swags and pin in place, bringing the top edges of the swag and the trumpet level. Smooth the last pleat into a rounded fold, and check that the trumpet hangs straight.

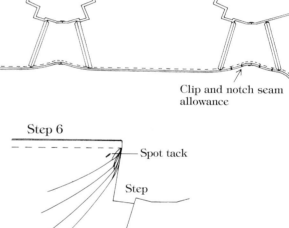

8 Having pleated up the valance, check that both the swags and trumpets match, and that the valance is the correct width.

Steps 8 - 9

Bound edge

9 Remove the valance from the pinboard. At the back, neaten the raw edges at the sides of the pleats and also the top with a 2cm (³⁄₄in) binding, see p152. Velcro can be sewn onto the back of the top binding if you wish.

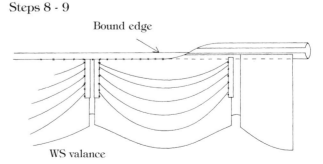

WS valance

10 Top fix the valance to a pelmet board, see p230.

Tie-backs hold curtains away from the glass to let in the light. They add a finishing touch. Tassel tie-backs introduce a different texture, while brass ombras and curtain bands add sophistication. You can sometimes buy antique ombras and bands in gilded bronze or carved wood. Fabric tie-backs can either be soft or stiffened; their design should be in keeping with the curtains. Stiffened tie-backs need to be slightly bow-shaped so that they will not stand away from the curtain at the leading edge.

Perhaps the only disadvantage is that tie-backs can cause a certain amount of creasing; this will not matter with dress curtains which are always held back. For curtains with fixed headings, tie-backs are essential to hold them open; an attractive alternative is Italian Stringing, described in detail on p197.

FIXED TIE-BACKS
OMBRAS AND CURTAIN BANDS
These look effective when coordinated with decorative curtain hardware, such as poles; see pp28-29.

An advantage is that the curtain can be quickly tucked into the band or behind the ombra. Check that there is a suitable place to fix them so that the outer side edges will not bow when the curtain is tucked in.

ROPE TIE-BACKS
Barrier rope tie-backs and tasselled rope tie-backs look rich and sumptuous, particularly when teamed with full length curtains. Barrier rope tie-backs are less formal, they are usually a single 2.5cm (1in) diameter piece of rope with small loops at each end.

Single and double tassel tie-backs are hugely versatile and available in a rainbow of colours, although you may have to order more exotic hues.

When you use tassels or rope, remember to use tie-back hooks with a large 'cup' which will hold two loops of rope.

Some styles of tassel tie-backs with centre knots can be made shorter or longer by adjusting the drop of the tassel. Rope tie-backs can be lengthened by using a second tie-back hook which is placed behind the stack back area.

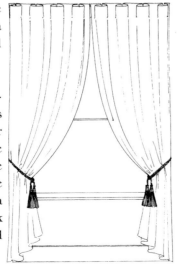

FABRIC TIE-BACKS
These should be designed to complement the curtains. Simpler is usually better; bright trim details and sharply contrasting fabrics should not overwhelm the effect of the curtain.

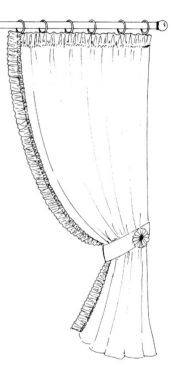

Soft padded tie-backs include ruched and plaited designs. A ruched tie-back is quick to make, and the ruching adds a light touch.

Stiffened tie-backs are all based on a 'banana' shape that sits neatly around the curtain. They also provide an opportunity to echo piping, bindings, frills and trims used elsewhere on the window treatment.

FINDING THE LENGTH OF THE EMBRACE
Too tight will pinch the curtain and look unattractive, too loose and it looks sloppy. The correct length is called the 'embrace'.

Try not to make the tie-backs until the curtains are fitted. Loop a tape around one curtain, hold it against the wall where the tie-back hook will be fixed, and adjust the length until the curtain hangs attractively. Note the measurement – this is the embrace.

MAKING RUCHED TIE-BACKS

MATERIALS

Fabric: 50cm (20in) per pair

Interlining or wadding: 2 x 15cm (6in) strips x length of embrace

Brass rings: 4 x 2cm (³/4in) per pair

1 Roll up a piece of wadding or interlining to 4cm (1 ¹/2in) in diameter. Stitch along the roll to secure.

2 Cut a piece of fabric 2¹/2 times the embrace measurement x 15cm (6in) deep. Fold in half lengthways and machine into a tube. Turn the fabric through to the right side.

3 To insert the wadding into the fabric tube, sew a piece of cotton tape 15cm (6in) long onto one end of the roll. Fasten the other end of the tape to a safety pin and thread it up inside the tube.

When the edge of the fabric covers the end of the wadding, pin them together and then ruche up the excess fabric evenly along the roll.

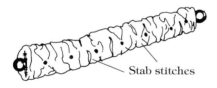

Stab stitches

4 Turn in the raw edges of the fabric at each end of the tube and slip stitch, catching the wadding.

Again, disperse the fullness evenly along the roll and sew invisible stab stitches to hold the fabric in place.

5 Sew either rings or small fabric loops onto each end of the tie-back.

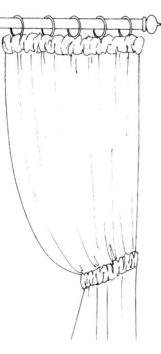

MAKING PLAITED TIE-BACKS

Keep the diameter of each tube quite small, approximately 2.5cm (1in), otherwise the plait will be too chunky.

Plaited tie-backs look attractive when made in three colours, one of the curtain fabric, one of the trimming fabric and one coordinating plain colour.

MATERIALS

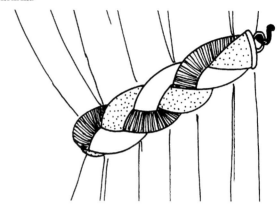

Fabric: 6 widths, cut 13cm (5in) deep, per pair

Wadding: 6 widths, cut 10cm (4in) deep, per pair

Brass rings: 4 x 2cm (³/4in) per pair

1 Lay a strip of wadding onto the wrong side of a fabric strip. Turn under the raw edge to make a tube approximately 2.5cm (1in) in diameter. Pin and then slip stitch along the tube. Make 3 tubes per tie-back.

Making a tube

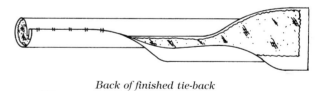

Back of finished tie-back

2 Pin the ends of the 3 tubes together and make a plait the length of the tie-back embrace. Pin the tubes together at the ends and cut away any excess fabric.

3 Bind the raw edges at each end with fabric. As it is quite bulky, sew this by hand. Make the binding as narrow as possible, approximately 1.5cm (¹/2in) wide. Sew either rings or matching fabric loops to each end of the tie-backs to finish.

STIFFENED TIE-BACKS

A curved bow shape ensures that the tie-back fits neatly round the curtain. A bowed shape with straight ends is a plain tie-back; a banana has curved ends.

MAKING THE PAPER PATTERN

1 Fold a piece of pattern paper in half and draw a horizontal box ½ the embrace x 20cm (8in) deep.

2 At the bottom of the fold, draw a line up 10-15cm (4-6in). On the opposite side at the top, draw a line down 5-7.5cm (2-3in). Draw smooth curves between the lines to form the tie-back. Adjust the depth to suit the length of the curtains – shorter curtains should have narrower tie-backs. For a banana shape, draw a curve at the outside edge.

3 Cut out the paper pattern and mark it stiffening. Make a copy, adding a seam allowance; cut it out and and mark this one fabric.
NOTE: Use a 2.5cm (1in) seam allowance for a plain tie-back and 1.5cm (½in) for a piped or banana one.

Lay the patterns on the fabric to work out quantities for fabric, lining and stiffening. See Buckrams p89, for various kinds of stiffening.

Professional Tip

Using the stiffening pattern, cut out the tie-back shape. Grey or orange buckram needs to be interlined so that the weave does not show through the fabric. Cut out a piece of interlining, and lay it underneath the buckram. Machine round, 1cm (⅜in) in from the edge. Trim off if necessary. The interlined side is on the front. Cut out the fabric and the lining. For patterned fabric, use a suitable part of the design. You need a left and a right for a pair, so adjust the pattern accordingly.

MAKING PLAIN TIE-BACKS

1 Place fabric and lining right sides together and machine around, leaving a gap at the bottom. Trim the seam, turn through to the right side and press. Insert the stiffened shape through the gap, turn in the seam allowance at the bottom edge, and slip stitch.

2 Sew rings securely onto the back; the front ring should be level with the edge, the back ring should be halfway over the edge.

MAKING PIPED BANANA TIE-BACKS

1 Cut and make up the piping; see p 121. Place it on the right side of fabric tie-back with the raw edges level and attach. Snip the piping seam allowance up to the stitch line to let it lie flat around the curves.

2 To join lengths of piping, cut the cord so that it butts together. On one side, trim the fabric up to the cord and on the other leave 4cm (1½in) of fabric. Fold in the raw edge, overlap by 2cm (¾in); machine across.

3 Lay the lining underneath the fabric, right sides together, and machine round following the stitch line. Leave a gap at the bottom large enough to insert the stiffening.

4 Clip and notch the seam allowance, turn through to the right side and press. Insert the stiffening. Turn in the seam allowances at the gap, and slip stitch to neaten.

5 Sew rings as for Plain Tie-Backs.

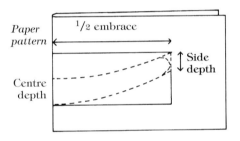

Paper pattern — ¹/₂ embrace — Side depth — Centre depth

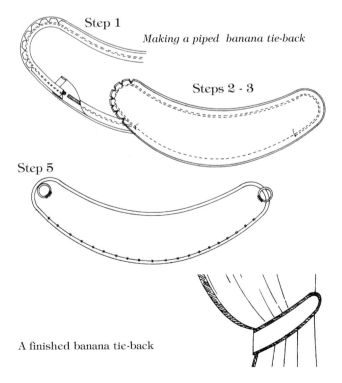

Step 1

Making a piped banana tie-back

Steps 2 - 3

Step 5

A finished banana tie-back

This is an unusual and very decorative method of opening fixed headed curtains which are hung from a pelmet board - see p68. The most elegant lines are created with tall windows and full-length curtains, hung from a straight or a curved pelmet board. If the window is wider than it is high, the 'swag' effect will be lost.

With its high take up point, Italian Stringing allows more light into the room than you will get with tie-backs set in the usual, fairly low position. But the folds of the curtains will need to be arranged, or 'dressed', whenever the stringing is pulled up, so they need a little extra attention.

ITALIAN STRUNG CURTAINS

MATERIALS

Length of chain and a paperclip

16 or more plastic/brass rings, 12mm (1/2in) diameter

Blind cord

Cleat hook and wooden acorn

NOTE: You must have a pelmet board for this style.

To see how it will look, fix one end of the chain to the centre of the pelmet board, and pull the chain out to the edge of the window glass, allowing it to fall into an attractive arc. The take up point will be approximately 1/3 of the distance down from the top of the pelmet board to the floor. Mark this point of the chain with a paperclip and measure see below.

1 Make up the curtains to the heading stage. The hem allowance is turned up and herringbone stitched to the fabric. Mock mitre the corners. Turn under the lining and slip stitch in place.

2 Position and sew the rings onto the back of the curtain, taking neat stitches through to the right side. Place the first ring at the take up point, set in 7.5cm (3in). It will take the weight of the curtain when it is open. On very light or old, fragile fabrics, sew a small clear button on the right side of the curtain to take the pressure of the stitches.

Sew the remaining 7 rings approximately 15cm (6in) apart in an arc, moving up 5cm (2in) every ring. If the fabric has a distinctive vertical pattern, where possible space the rings in line with the pattern.

3 Join the curtains together at the centre and cover with a rope or fabric trim. For pleated curtains, sew a patch of fabric over the join before positioning the trim.

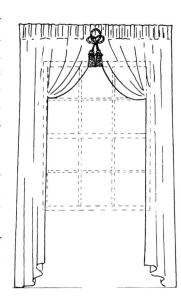

Steps 1 - 2   Back of Italian strung curtain

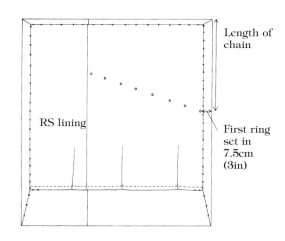

Length of chain

RS lining

First ring set in 7.5cm (3in)

4 Hang the curtains with either hooks and screw eyes or Velcro. To guide the cords along the underside of the pelmet board, fix two screw eyes directly in line with the edge of the window glass and a third screw eye at one edge of the board for either a left-hand or a right-hand pull.

5 Tie a length of cord onto the first ring, and thread through all the rings up to the screw eye on the pelmet board, along to the outer screw eye and down to waist level. Repeat for the other curtain.

6 Be prepared to adjust the position of the rings, or the screw eyes, to achieve a graceful arc.

7 Tie the ends of the cords into the acorn and wrap around a cleat fixed to the wall. Unwind to close the curtains.

A transparent view of a curtain showing the cords running along the pelmet board down to the cleat hook

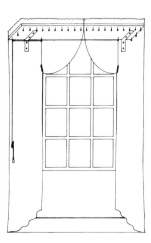

BLINDS OF ALL KINDS

The three main types of blinds are roller, Roman, and gathered. A blind requires little or no space around the window, and can be fitted either inside or outside the recess. They are ideal for windows in restricted spaces. Roller and Roman blinds are also useful for skylights.

Roller and Roman blinds are economical on fabric; patterns and weaves are shown to advantage by the flat surfaces. The most suitable fabrics are tightly woven light to mediumweight.

A gathered or a Roman blind is useful when there are dissimilar windows in the same or adjoining rooms. For example, with an elaborate curtain treatment on a large window, hang a gathered blind on the smaller window, using the same fabric and decorative heading. Blinds are also convenient when teamed with full curtains. They control light and ensure privacy during the day.

ROLLER BLINDS

A simple and inexpensive window covering. A flat piece of fabric with a wooden lath at the base is wound round a wooden or metal roller. The fabric is usually stiffened to keep it flat and to prevent the edges from fraying. The hem can be shaped and/or trimmed with fringe below the lath.

HOLLAND BLINDS

Traditionally made out of plain, woven 'Holland' fabric and used specifically as a sun screen, often in conjunction with curtains. The cream or pale colour allows light into a room even when pulled down. Holland blinds protect soft furnishings and furniture from fading.

The linen or cotton fabric has a limited life, as it becomes weakened, brittle, and easily torn with age. (Polyester fabrics are not affected as badly.)

LAMINATED ROLLER BLINDS

Fabric is laminated onto a backing fabric to make it stronger, more durable and waterproof. This needs to be done professionally; you can then continue to make the blind in the usual way.

Bear in mind the combined thickness of two fabrics; a long laminated blind will make a large roll, and take up more space. This will be even more evident if you use a blackout backing fabric, often requested in bedrooms or dark rooms where the exclusion of light is important.

A spring mechanism in the end of the roller with a pull cord in the centre of the hem is the standard. Occasionally it may need to be re-tensioned; pull down the blind, lift off from the brackets, re-roll by hand and replace. Repeat if necessary.

Another mechanism is a side-winder, with a loop of cord at one side. This is less conspicuous and especially useful for places like kitchens, where a centre pull would easily become soiled.

WHERE TO FIX THE BLIND

Inside the reveal of the window: hanging next to the glass – roller blinds have some light insulating qualities.

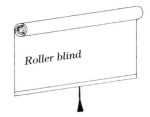

Roller blind

Without a recess: either face fix to the wall or fix to the underside of a pelmet board. Increase the depth of the pelmet board by an extra 5cm (2in) to accommodate the blind.

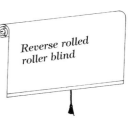

Reverse rolled roller blind

For a smart finish, the blind can be 'reverse rolled' so that the fabric is rolled down over the front of the roller (see above).

For particularly wide windows, hanging two or more roller blinds next to each other is better than attempting to cover the whole width with one blind.

MAKING ROLLER BLINDS

Firstly decide if the blind is to be fitted inside or outside the window recess and take the necessary measurements: see p111.

For a fitting outside the reveal, extend the measurement 5-10cm (2-4in) at both sides, above and below the window, to exclude light and draughts.

MATERIALS

A roller blind kit – this will contain:
a roller with a self-adhesive strip, universal brackets, end cap and pin, bottom lath, cord, knot holder, acorn and screws.

Fabric
Fabric stiffener, a spray or liquid (optional)

In general, follow the kit intructions – they are usually quite easy. But here are some extra tips:

Brackets can be top fixed, face fixed or end fixed, according to the space available. Fit the bracket with the round hole on the right-hand side of the window. When fitting brackets, allow for the diameter of the retracted blind.

On a standard blind the roller is in front. To make a 'reverse rolled' blind, follow the intructions, but with the wrong side of the fabric uppermost. Then turn the whole blind around and fit as usual, so that the fabric rolls out and down in front of the roller.

FABRIC QUANTITIES

After you have worked out the finished width and length, add 30cm (12in) to the length to allow for a 5cm (2in) hem allowance; the remaining fabric is wound onto the roller. You also need a stiffening and cutting allowance added all round. When fabric is treated with a stiffening spray or solution, it may shrink. Generally allow 5-10cm (2-4in) on all sides for this. It is worth stiffening a small piece of the fabric first to see how it reacts and how much it shrinks, then adjust your measurements accordingly.

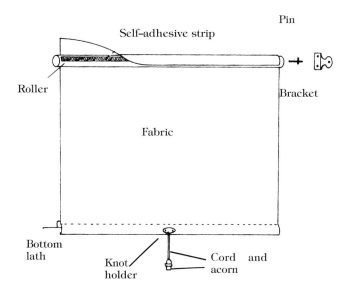

Professional Tip

If the blind will not roll up evenly check the following points:

Are the brackets level?

Has the top edge of the fabric been fixed onto the roller absolutely level?

Have the sides of the fabric been cut parallel?
This will be impossible to rectify without making the blind smaller, so you may have to start again.

ROMAN BLINDS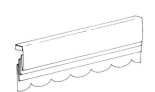

These elegant blinds are flat panels when down, but pleat up into even, horizontal folds when raised. To keep the folds straight, wooden laths or metal or plastic rods are inserted into pockets at the back. The top is fixed to a special track or to a narrow wooden batten, and the blind is pulled up by draw cords. Accurate make-up and fitting is all-important.

A Roman blind provides a tailored window dressing, suitable for modern as well as traditional rooms, and they look particularly elegant with inset borders or with a narrow strip of contrast fabric along the lower edge. Block fringe can be sewn along the hem for added texture and interest.

Roman blinds look better when they are longer than they are wide. Hang two or more blinds next to each other if necessary. A bay window can have a blind hung at each section.

Roman blinds can be unlined, lined or lined and interlined with domette. If required, they can be lined with blackout lining.

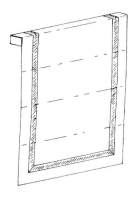

A scalloped hem and an inset braid

ROMAN BLIND FITTINGS

There are special tracks that have Velcro pre-fixed to the face. They also have integral cord guides, and a ratchet device to hold the cords.

Another option is a fabric covered wooden batten with screw eyes or cord guides fixed to the underside to carry the draw cords. The length is determined by the width of the window, the other measurements are usually 2.5-5cm (1-2in) wide x 2.5cm (1in) deep.

Small, flat wooden laths or dowels for the back of the blind are readily available from most DIY stores. These are more bulky than metal or plastic rods and could warp over a period of time. Metal rods, from specialist curtain shops, will hold their shape.

Plastic rods can be rolled up, like a hose, to take home. They are easy to use and very easy to cut, but may not be strong enough for big or heavy blinds.

WHERE TO FIX THE BLIND

Used with curtains, a Roman blind can sit inside the recess, but on its own, it looks far more attractive fitted outside. When the blind is pulled up it needs space above the glass – the depth of the folded pleat + the depth of the track or batten. For small windows a blind inside the recess may block out too much light – another reason for moving it.

If the blind is to be fixed outside the window recess, extend the width of the blind 5-10cm (2-4in) at both sides and at the base, and 10-20cm (4-8in) above the window.

FABRIC QUANTITIES

Allow 6cm (2 1/4in) for each side turning to the finished width.

Cut drop = finished length + 30cm (12in). This allows 6cm (2 1/4in) heading and hem allowance + extra fabric to cover the batten.

For an unlined blind, allow extra fabric to make the separate rod pockets, approximately 4-7.5cms (1-3in) per pocket.

For a lined blind, the pockets are made by sewing folds in the lining. Add 4-7.5cm (1 1/2in-3in) per pocket to the length of the lining for a comfortable fit.

Professional Tip

If you are using a wooden batten to fix the blind, extend the finished length of the blind by the width of the batten, then you can fix the Velcro out of sight on top of the batten. The fabric will turn over and cover it, giving a neat finish.

WORKING OUT THE SPACING FOR THE LATHS OR ROD POCKETS

The pockets should be spaced approximately 20-30cm (8-12in) apart. The fold lines are between the pockets.

1 Take the finished length of the blind and deduct a 5cm (2in) allowance for the track or batten.

2 Divide this by between 10-15cm (4-6in) – depending on how deep you want the folds to be to give an *odd* whole number. This gives you the number of folds in the completed blind and the size of each one.

3 Draw a diagram. Mark on the distances between the folds. There is a pocket on every other fold line. The bottom only has one fold + a pocket for the bottom lath. Add 5cm (2in) to the top fold for the batten.

MAKING LINED ROMAN BLINDS

MATERIALS

Fabric

Lining

Laths or rods: 1 per pocket + 1 for the hem

Batten: 5cm x 2.5cm (2x1in) x blind width

Screw eyes: 1 for each draw cord + 1 more

Blind cord

Small angle brackets

Wooden acorn and cleat hook

1 Cut out the fabric to the finished width and length + a 6cm (2¼in) turning allowance all round. Use a set square to make sure the corners are right angles.

2 Mitre the lower corners, fold up the hem and turn in the side allowance. Place a lath or rod, cut to the finished width of the blind, into the fold of the hem. Slip stitch the mitres and pin up the hem and sides.

3 Cut out the lining to the finished width and length + the additional pocket allowances. At each side turn under 2cm (³/₄in) and press.

Mark the pockets by lightly creasing folds across the fabric with an iron. Make sure that the lines are precisely at right angles to the side, and machine a row of stitching to make each pocket.

4 Position the lining onto the back of the blind, placing the first pocket the required distance up from the hem and turn under the raw edge. Slip stitch to the fabric, down each side and along the hem.

Step 3

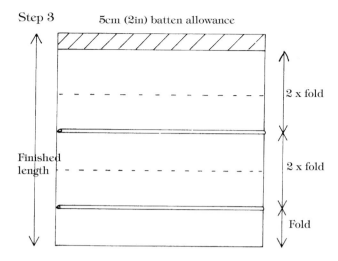

5cm (2in) batten allowance

Finished length

2 x fold

2 x fold

Fold

5 Measure the finished length of the blind, trim the turning allowance to 1.5cm (¹/₂in) and sew Velcro to the back of the blind, covering the raw edge.

6 Cut the laths or rods to the width of the lining and slot into the pockets; sew up the ends. Sew rings onto the edge of the pockets in rows up each side. Set the rings 7.5cm (3in) in from the side edge. The first ring on the lowest pocket will take the weight of the blind and must therefore be secure. For blinds over 100cm (39in) wide, sew extra rows of rings.

7 To hold the fabric and lining together, sew small spot tacks through the fabrics just below the pockets, wherever a ring has been sewn. These will be hardly visible from the right side of the blind and are less obtrusive than rows of machine stitching.

Steps 4 - 7

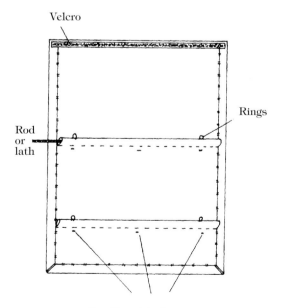

Velcro

Rings

Rod or lath

Small spot tacks

MAKING BATTENS AND FITTING BLINDS

Using a staple gun, cover the batten with fabric. Staple Velcro either to the top, or the face of the batten as required. Fix screw eyes to the underside of the batten, directly in line with the rings and draw cords. Use small brackets to fix to the wall.

To hang the blind, align the Velcro; tie a length of blind cord to each ring on the lowest rod pocket and thread through all the rings, up to the screw eyes, along the batten and down the side.

Lower the blind and apply a little tension to each cord to take out any slack, cut the ends level and thread through the acorn. Tie the cords into a knot and hide the ends inside the acorn.

Fix the cleat hook onto the wall at a suitable height. Pull up the blind, helping it into its folds. The fabric needs time to 'dress' into folds. After one or two days it should pleat up easily.

NOTE: If the blind does not hang level and swings to one side, check that it sits correctly on the track or batten and that the draw cords are even.

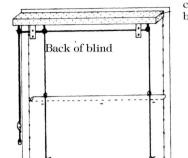

Fabric covered batten

Back of blind

Cleat hook

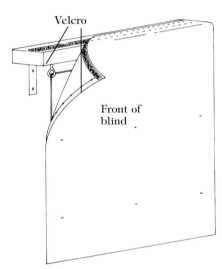

Velcro

Front of blind

Professional Tip

INTERLINING ROMAN BLINDS

Cut the interlining to the size of the fabric, lay them together and make up in the same way as for a lined blind. Use a lightweight interlining.

WATERFALL OR CASCADE BLINDS

For a waterfall or cascade, the pockets are stepped so that when the blind is pulled up, each fold makes a 'step', one on top of another.

To calculate the pocket spacing, work out the measurements as for a Roman blind. Find the middle pocket, then alter the pocket measurements below and above by adding or subtracting 5cm (2in) respectively. When the blind is pulled up the difference between the pleats will be 2.5cm (1in), creating the waterfall effect.

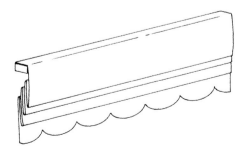

FAN-TAIL BLINDS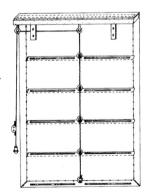

This style is only suitable for small, narrow windows, as the blind is pulled up by a single, central cord.

The pockets are spaced approximately 15cm (6in) apart, and the first ring is sewn at the hem of the blind.

All the laths or rods are cut in the middle; when the blind is pulled up they drop into a fan shape. Fan-tails look best when only half drawn up so that the fan is left hanging. Made up in thin material, they are useful for letting in light whilst blocking out an unwanted view.

Simple gathered blinds were one of the first forms of functional drapery and were hung at the tall, elegant windows of early Georgian houses. They were in fact 'pull up' floor length curtains corded and hung from a wooden batten. Some fine examples of this type of treatment can be seen in the refurbished King's Apartments at Hampton Court. When made with very little fullness and hung from a cornice box, this traditional blind is not fussy.

There are three main types of gathered blinds, an Austrian blind, a festoon or ruched blind, and a pull up curtain. They have varying degrees of fullness to achieve different effects.

AUSTRIAN BLINDS

There are a variety of headings which can be used for Austrian blinds, including puffed, smocked, French pleated, goblet and box pleated. They can be made with either scooped up or dropped down sides.

The hem and the side edges of the blind look smart with a contrast binding or a frill, see pp152-7 to define the pretty scoops. Fringe along the hem also emphasises the swagged effect.

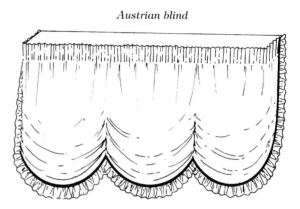

Austrian blind

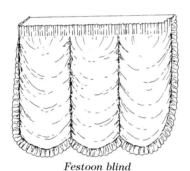

Festoon blind

FESTOON BLINDS

A festoon, or ruched blind has a gathered heading, 2 x fullness. It also has vertical gathers, again with up to 2 x fullness. The fabric is gathered along the lines of the draw cords. This type of blind is unlined and usually made up in a sheer fabric or a light silk. The heading works well with a simple gather tape, and the hem and edges look attractive when finished with a frill. A festoon is normally strung into continuous scoops.

PULL UP CURTAINS

This traditional style has less than $1^1/_2$ x fullness creating a more tailored look. The most suitable heading is a gather, either with tape or by hand. A pull up looks stunning hung from a cornice box which conceals the heading altogether. Make your own simple box using a piece of door architrave, see p48.

The edges look attractive when contrast bound or defined with an inset braid. The shaping of the hem looks even richer when trimmed with bullion fringe.

The wider the window, the more scallops there will be, but too many scoops will look fussy. The depth of the scoop depends on the fullness of the heading and the spacing of the rings.

DROP DOWN SIDES

The first scoop can be set in from the side edges. The further the first cord is moved in from the side, the longer the drop down side will be. As a general rule, the sides should be half the width of the scoop.

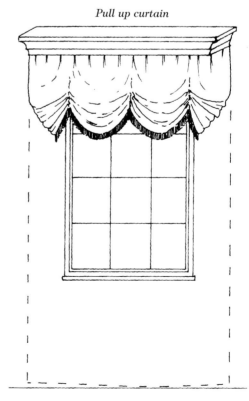

Pull up curtain

FABRIC QUANTITIES

Estimate the fabric quantities in the same way as for a curtain, using the blind fullness ratios below. The finished width of the blind is the length of the track or batten plus 2 x the return measurement.

Austrian and festoon: 2 - 2.5 x fullness
Pull up curtain: 1.5 - 1.75 x fullness

The finished length of the blind is measured from the top of the track or batten (+ any decorative heading allowance) to the required length + 30-50cm (12-20in) overlong measurement. This allows the blind to retain the decorative scoops even when let down.

For a pull up curtain which lets down to the floor, omit the overlong allowance.
For a festoon, allow extra vertical fullness 1.5 - 2 x the finished length + overlong allowance.
Allow for frills and trims as necessary.

MAKING AN AUSTRIAN BLIND WITH A FRILL

MATERIALS
Fabric
Lining
Loop tape
Tape for the heading (optional)
Lead-weight tape
Blind cord

1 Seam up fabric and lining widths.

2 If you are including piping and frills sew them onto the sides and hem of the fabric (see p121 and pp154-6).

3 Lay the fabric and lining right sides together and machine down each side and along the hem.

4 Place lead-weight tape into the hem and sew it onto the seam allowance with a quick interlocking stitch. Trim the seam allowance at the corners, turn the blind through to the right side and press.

5 Machine loop tape in vertical lines, the required, spacing apart.

6 Measure the finished length of the blind. Fold over the fabric and trim as necessary. Complete the heading. Use the Velcro heading tape or sew Velcro onto the back.

7 Make up the batten and thread the cord through the rings, as on p202.

AUSTRIAN BLIND FITTINGS

Gathered blinds can be fixed to a special blind track which has Velcro pre-fixed to the face. An alternative is a 7.5cm (3in) wooden batten which should allow space for brackets large enough to take the weight of the blind.

A gathered blind requires stacking space above the window, so fit the blind track or batten well above the window, 15-30cm (6-12in), to avoid blocking out light.

DRAW CORD SPACING

Establish the number of scoops required. Make a diagram of the blind, noting the length of the track or batten and the number and finished width of each scoop. Multiply the width of the scoop by the fullness ratio to give the distance between the cords. Remember, for drop down sides set the cords in half the width of the scoop at each side.

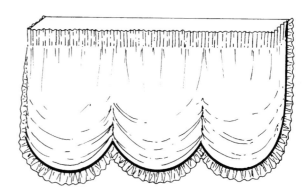

Austrian blind with three scoops and machine tape heading

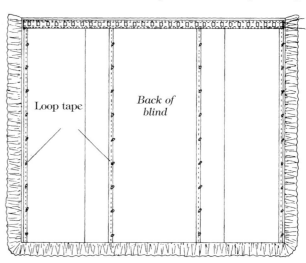

Professional Tip
To make a festoon blind, make as an Austrian using a festoon tape that gathers the blind vertically.

MAKING A HAND SEWN LINED BLIND WITH DROP DOWN SIDES

MATERIALS

Fabric

Lining

Small brass or plastic rings

Heading tape

Lead-weight tape

Blind cord

FABRIC QUANTITIES

To work out fabric requirements, see previous page.

1 Seam up the fabric and lining widths.

2 Lay the fabric face down onto the table. At the sides and along the hem, fold and press a 6cm (2³/₄in) turning allowance. Sew lead-weight tape in the fold line of the hem using an interlocking stitch. Mitre the lower corners and slip stitch.

3 Place the lining on top of the fabric, right side uppermost, matching the seams where possible at each side. At the hem of the lining, turn under the raw edge and slip stitch to neaten.

4 Hand sew rings, spaced 15cm (6in) apart, in vertical lines down the blind. See Draw Cord Spacing, previous page.

5 Measure the finished length. Fold over the fabric and

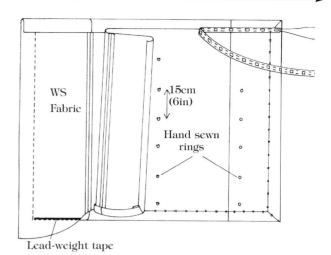

WS Fabric   15cm (6in)   Hand sewn rings

Lead-weight tape

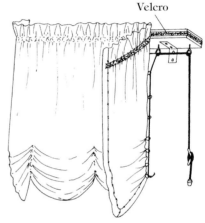

Velcro

trim as necessary. Complete the heading. Use Velcro heading tape or sew Velcro onto the back.

6 Make up the batten and thread the cord through the rings, as on p202.

LONDON OR SOFT PLEATED BLINDS

The inverted pleats at each side give a little fullness, this allows the hem to fall into a shallow scoop with small drop down sides. If the width of the blind increases, add a central inverted pleat.

To estimate the fabric quantity, allow approximately 30cm (12in) for each pleat + finished width of the blind, + 2 x the return measurement + turning allowance. It is imperative that the seam lines are hidden inside the pleat, so allow extra width to give you manoeuvrability.

Make up as above. Fold the inverted pleats in position and machine down from the top 15cm (6in) to hold them in place. Sew rings at the centre back of the pleats through both fabric and lining to hold them together. Sew Velcro to the top edge.

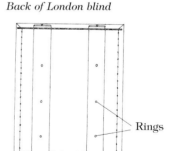

Vertical pleats from back

Back of London blind

Rings

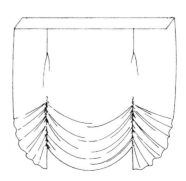

ANTIQUE CURTAINS

Curtains made from 'Antique' textiles have a homely charm and a faded elegance all of their own. In rooms full of old furniture they will look as if they have been part of the furnishings for years.

Some wonderful antique textiles can be seen at Waddesdon Manor in Oxfordshire. Some of the fabrics used to make the curtain for the house in the 1870's were over a hundred years old at the time.

Apart from the value of old fabrics, another reason for remaking curtains could be to reuse an old 1950's print that is no longer available. Or perhaps when moving house the curtain fabric coordinates with other furniture.

The design of the window treatment often has to be ingenious with the 'just enough' fabric factor in mind. Finding a design to suit the scale of the window and the amount of fabric or trim available is a bit of a juggling act but inevitably produces stunning results.

DESIGN IDEAS

Remaking curtains to fit smaller windows does not present a problem but when they are not quite long enough the style has to be redesigned to make them fit the new dimensions. This often results in a unique curtain design.

A simple way to visually lengthen the curtains is to fix the curtain track on the wall, just above the window. The pelmet or valance can not only be lengthened with contrast fabric borders, but can also be hung from a pelmet board fitted well above the track.

Adding contrast borders to curtains is not only an effective method of gaining extra length but also a valid design feature. Take care to choose a sympathetic colour for the contrast so that it complements the fabric. A poor colour match gives the game away.

REMAKING CURTAINS

Remaking old curtains can often involve more work than making up new ones. If the curtains are reasonably new then they should be professionally dry cleaned, to remove as much dirt as possible, before they are re-made.

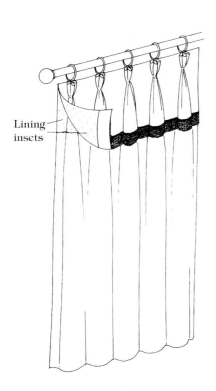

Lining insets

You can use frills or wide borders sewn onto the curtain on any or all edges to make it wider as well as longer

Attach a valance to the top of a curtain to hide seams when you need a longer drop

To lengthen curtains just a little, you can lower the track and make a deeper valance

The main concern about remaking curtains is where the fabric is starting to deteriorate.

If the fabric is old and fragile it is not a good idea to submit it to a chemical cleaning process where a tiny hole could develop into a larger one. To remove as much dust as possible, temporarily hang the curtain and lightly vacuum clean them. Place a piece of muslin over the nozzle to prevent loose threads from pulling.

For reasonably new fabrics, it is only necessary to unpick the areas that are to be resewn. However, when working on old fragile fabrics extra precautions have to be taken. Sunlight weakens fabrics, so you must first assess the stability of the fabric. Some silks will literally shred in your hands. Old cotton sewing thread may rot so each seam must be carefully be unpicked to be resewn.

If the curtains are faded at the leading edges and starting to shred, and there is ample fabric, it can be cut away. If however, every last morsel is needed, fuse strips of lightweight interfacing onto the back of the fabric over the affected areas. If possible when rehanging, put the old leading edges to the outside where they will encounter less wear.

REPLACING LININGS

Unless the curtains are relatively new, it is better to replace old linings. The old lining, having being constantly exposed to the sun will have been weakened and so it is false economy to keep it if it will only last for a short period.

Old interlinings can be reused if they have been well protected by the lining. If however, they have absorbed a lot of dirt and dust, you may prefer to replace them.

A curtain tied onto a pole only needs a 1.5 fullness ratio, so it's useful for occasions when you have a minimum quantity. Blinds are an alternative solution when you are short of fabric; see p53.

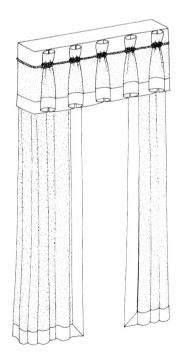

Rope knotted over goblets will hide the seams of an additional top border.

With a beautiful pattern, use your length of fabric for swags and tails, and a plain, coordinating fabric for the tail lining and the curtains underneath.

207

PART FOUR: BEDS AND EVERYTHING ELSE

The bed is the focal point of the bedroom, but whether simply covered with a throw or lavishly dressed with bed curtains, the design should tie in with that of the window treatment.

Bed curtains range from simple muslin hung on the wall behind the bed, to pretty corona and half-tester dressings, to the ultimate romance – a four-poster bed.

BEDS

BED SIZES

These are the most common sizes, but they do vary between manufacturers, so always check.

Single   100cm x 190cm (3ft x 6ft 3in)
Double   140cm x 200cm (4ft 6in x 6ft 6in)
King size   180cm x 200cm (6ft x 6ft 6in)

As a guide, mattresses are normally 15-20cm (6-8in) in depth. The base of the bed to the floor, i.e. valance depth, varies from 30-60cm (12-24in), but a standard depth is 33-36cm (13-14in).

NOTE: Upholstered headboards have not been included here; upholstery requires different skills and equipment to obtain a really professional finish.

MEASURING

Do take time as there are a lot of measurements to be taken. If you have an old bed frame there may be extra details, such as bed posts etc. Listed below are the specific measurements you will need for bed valances, covers and curtains.

BED VALANCES

1 Width of bed

2 Length of bed

3 Depth of bed base to floor

For beds with posts, measure around each one, and then make up the valance with slits so that the skirt can fall to either side.

BEDCOVERS OR QUILTS

1 Width of bed taken over the normal bedclothes + an allowance for dropping down at each side. Covers can be three quarter length to show some of the bed valance or full length down to the floor.

2 Length of bed over the normal bedclothes. At the foot measure to the required length. At the head, allow an extra 30cm (12in) to fold over the pillow; for a pillow tuck you'll need a further 30cm (12in).

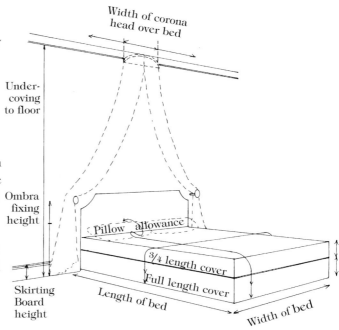

BED CURTAINS HUNG FROM CORONAS AND HALF-TESTERS

1 Width of bed.

2 Under coving or ceiling to floor. This measurement is used to determine the height at which to fix the corona board or half-tester pelmet board.

Check the windows and mouldings for a suitable height.

3 The depth of the skirting board behind the bed.

If a back curtain is required, the hem is slotted onto a wooden dowel and secured to the wall above the skirting board.

4 The height at which to fix either the ombras or tie-backs which hold curtains to the wall at each side. Ombras or tie-backs are usually positioned at about the same height as the headboard.

BED VALANCES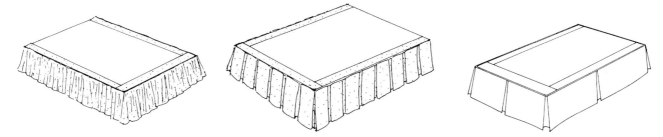

Bed valances are placed beneath the mattress on top of the base, and have a skirt or frill on three edges to conceal the divan or sides of the bed. The valance base is made out of lining, edged with strips of the main fabric.

For a smart finish, pipe the seam joining the skirt to the base. Skirts are usually gathered, pleated or straight with kick pleats at the corners.

FABRIC QUANTITIES FOR THE SKIRT
Gathered skirt = 2.25 - 2.5 x fullness
Box pleated skirt = 3 x fullness
Straight skirt with kick pleats = 40cm (16in) per pleat + 2 x length + 1 x width + extra fabric to hide seams in the pleats

Cut drop = finished depth of skirt + 10cm (4in) seam and hem allowance. Adjust the cut drop for pattern repeats if necessary.

FABRIC QUANTITIES FOR THE BASE
2 strips: 15cm (6in) deep x bed length
1 strip: 15cm (6in) deep x bed width
Allow for piping all round.

LINING QUANTITIES
For the base of the valance, allow the length of the bed + 10cm (4in). For the skirt, allow the same number of lining widths as fabric. Cut drop = finished depth of the skirt.

MAKING GATHERED OR PLEATED BED VALANCES
1 Make the lining base up to the finished size + a seam allowance all round. Seam the fabric strips on to the sides and base. If the bed has rounded corners, shape the corners to the curve of the bed.

2 Cut and make up the piping, see p121. Seam down the sides and the bottom edge of the lining base.

3 Cut out the fabric and lining widths for the skirt. Make up as for a valance, see p172, and gather or pleat as required. The finished amount of skirt you will need is 2 x length + bed width + an extra 10cm (4in).

4 Pin and seam the skirt onto the base, starting and finishing the skirt 5cm (2in) in on each side at the bedhead end.

NOTE: For box pleated skirts, position a pleat in the centre of the valance at the end of the bed.

5 Neaten the piped edge at the top of the valance with a 10cm (4in) flap of fabric binding, see p152.

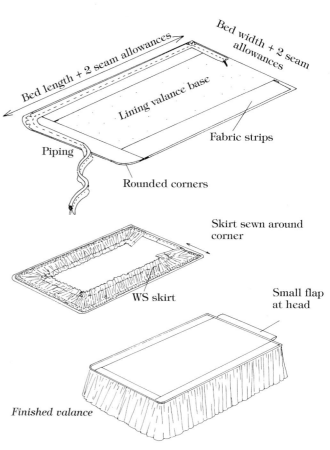

Bed length + 2 seam allowances

Bed width + 2 seam allowances

Lining valance base

Fabric strips

Piping

Rounded corners

Skirt sewn around corner

WS skirt

Small flap at head

Finished valance

COVERS

Bedcovers can be lined, interlined or quilted. Interlining and quilting acts like a blanket, providing extra warmth, but it also makes it heavy. Quilted bedcovers must be dry cleaned. The greatest advantage is that they will not crease. They are either three quarter length or full length, and hems can be contrast bound or wadded. Here are a few design ideas:

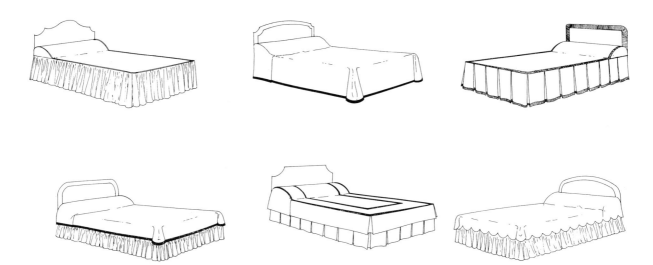

1 Cut and seam up the fabric and lining. Trim to the finished size + 5cm (2in) seam allowance all round.

2 Round the corners at the base, see Professional Tip on opposite page.

3 Place the fabric and lining right sides together and machine round, leaving a 50cm (20in) gap at the top. At the corners, clip and notch the seam allowance.

4 Turn the cover through to the right side and press. Sew fringe or onset frills onto the edge if the design includes them.

5 Neatly spot tack the lining to the main fabric at intervals down the seams.

Steps 1 - 3   Steps 4 - 5

WS fabric & lining before turning inside out

Notched corners

Professional Tip

INTERLINING BED COVERS

Make up like an interlined curtain and finish with a decorative edge if you wish.

1 Follow Steps 1 - 2 opposite.

2 Cut out, seam up and trim the interlining to the same size as the fabric.

3 Lay the interlining onto the wrong side of the fabric and interlock in place (see p129). Space the rows 30cm (12in) apart down the length of the cover.

4 Fold over the 5cm (2in) turning allowance and herringbone stitch all round. At the corners, evenly distribute the excess fabric around the curves.

5 Lay the lining, right side up, onto the interlining and interlock in place. Trim and turn under all the raw edges of the lining, leaving 2.5cm (1in) of fabric showing. Slip stitch in place.

QUILTED BEDCOVERS

Quilting can be used on bedspreads in numerous ways. The entire bedspread can be quilted, or just the top or a border. There are a variety of stitch designs for quilting from variations of square and diamond shapes to shell designs and outline quilting. Choose a stitch design to complement the pattern of the fabric. A check or geometric pattern is easy to follow using either square or diamond rows of stitching. A pretty floral design will come to life when it is outline quilted, making a raised effect out of the flowers.

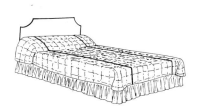  

FABRIC QUANTITIES

Add an extra 10% to the width and length for the 'take up' of the quilting.

Choose a polyester wadding:
Lightweight - 60g (2oz)
Mediumweight - 120g (4oz)
Heavyweight - 180g (6oz)

QUILTING BEDCOVERS

Specialist companies will quilt large areas of fabric for for you if you prefer. You can then finish the edge to complete the cover. Here are some guidlines if you want to do the quilting yourself:

PREPARING FABRIC FOR QUILTING

Lay the fabric on top of the wadding with the lining underneath, and tack together. It is important to sew several rows of stitches, approximately 15cm (6in) apart, to hold the layers together.

MACHINE QUILTING

A large area is difficult to quilt because of the bulk of the fabric and wadding. To machine in the centre, the bulk on one side of the work has to be rolled up and tucked under the arm of the machine. Try quilting a width at a time and then join the widths, perhaps adding a contrast piping into the seams to make it a design feature.

Having quilted and seamed together the total area required, trim the cover to the size you need, leaving a turning allowance.

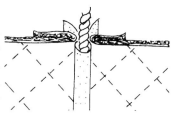

> **Professional Tip**
> Mattresses have curved corners; to curve the corners at the foot of the bedcovers, work out the length of the bedcover that overhangs the side including the hem allowance. Follow the shape of the mattress to work out the hem curve.
> Mark the curve with tailor's chalk and cut round and hem as usual.
>
>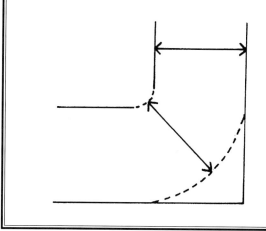

A simple hem finish is to overlock or swing needle the raw edge and turn up a 2.5-5cm (1-2in) hem. Hand sew or machine in place. For more decorative edges, see pp150-151.

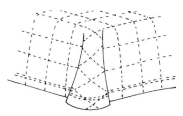

NOTE: If the lining has not been quilted on the back, finish as for an interlined bedspread.

BED CURTAINS

Bed curtains range from unlined plain muslin dressings to four-posters fitted with silk curtains, swags, side curtains and tented ceiling. A simple decoration can be made by hanging curtains from a pole behind the bed, or a pretty piece of fabric draped informally into swags.

For a more formal look, a corona track or pelmet board can be fixed above the bed with dress curtains hung from it. Valances or swags can also be hung from the front edge of the board, see p62. A half-tester is a rectangular pelmet board fitted above the bed, from which the curtains and valance hang. Four-poster beds often have a fabric covered ceiling and curtains at each post, see pp 66-7. Four-posters can be hung with light fabrics such as muslin or sumptuously swagged and fringed. Here are a few design ideas:

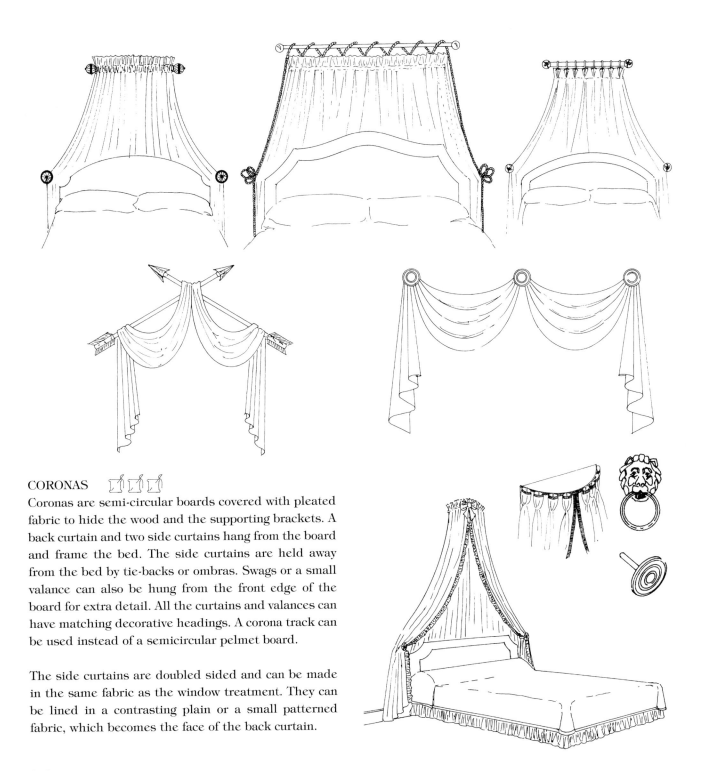

CORONAS

Coronas are semi-circular boards covered with pleated fabric to hide the wood and the supporting brackets. A back curtain and two side curtains hang from the board and frame the bed. The side curtains are held away from the bed by tie-backs or ombras. Swags or a small valance can also be hung from the front edge of the board for extra detail. All the curtains and valances can have matching decorative headings. A corona track can be used instead of a semicircular pelmet board.

The side curtains are doubled sided and can be made in the same fabric as the window treatment. They can be lined in a contrasting plain or a small patterned fabric, which becomes the face of the back curtain.

FABRIC QUANTITIES

Work out the fabric requirement as for curtains. If the window curtains have been interlined the side curtains should also be interlined to give the same padded look. For side curtains add 20cm (8in) overlong measurement to the finished length. The extra is required to accommodate the 'take up' of the leading edge as the curtains are held in tie-backs.

BACK CURTAINS

Allow 2 widths for a single bed and 3 widths for a double bed. This curtain can either be lined or unlined, so allow for it if required.

Finished length = pelmet board to skirting board + 20cm (8in) heading and hem channel allowance

SIDE CURTAINS

Allow $1^1/_2$ widths per curtain i.e. 3 widths per pair. A single width at each side of the bed looks skimpy. These are double sided curtains; contrast line to match the back curtain.

FOUR-POSTERS

Can also have a set of curtains at the foot of the bed, one at each pole.

TOP TREATMENTS

Allow fabric for these by measuring as you would for a valance. Use contrast lining to match the back and side curtains to link all the elements in the design.

PLEATED CORONAS, HALF-TESTER AND FOUR-POSTER CEILINGS

Measure the outside edges. For a corona, measure around the curve of the front. Multiply this figure by 2.5 x fullness and divide by the width of the fabric to establish the number of widths required.

For the cut drop, measure from the centre of the board to a corner + 10cm (4in) handling allowance. For a corona, measure from the centre back to the outer edge. Allow extra fabric or contrast lining to cover the top of the board and to make a rosette trim.

Professional Tip

SIZE SUGGESTIONS FOR CORONA BOARDS

Make a paper pattern of the corona shape, then cut it out in 22mm (¾ in) plywood. The size of the corona is optional, but here are some suggestions:

Small = 30cm (12in) long x 20cm (8in) deep
Medium = 50cm (20in) long x 30cm (12in) deep
Large = 70cm (28in) long x 35cm (14in) deep

Use a small to medium size corona for a single bed and a medium to large for a double bed.

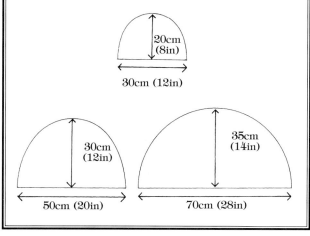

COVERING CORONA BOARDS
MATERIALS
2 angle brackets
Screw eyes
Velcro
Fabric to pleat onto board
2cm (¾in) tacks

1 Cover the top of the board with fabric and staple it to the front edge. Trim away the excess fabric.

2 Screw the brackets to the underside of the board.

3 For a small board, cut one width of fabric 20cm (8in) deep. For a medium or large board, cut two widths 30cm (12in) and 40cm (16in) deep respectively.

4 Join the widths together if necessary. Sew a row of large stitches, approximately 2cm (¾in) in length, along one of the long edges. Pull up the stitches into a tight concertina and secure the thread.

5 Place the gathered fabric in the centre of the board and fan out the fullness. Staple the fabric onto the back edge of the board. Use small tacks to secure the fabric in the centre of the board, hiding them in the folds.

6 Pull the fabric taut around the curve and staple to the front edge, ensuring that the gathers or pleats are even. Trim away the excess fabric and cover the raw edges by stapling Velcro around the curved edge.

7 Make a rosette, see p159. Tack it in place to cover the gather stitches.

Step 1   Step 2

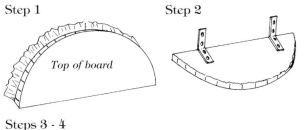

Top of board

Steps 3 - 4

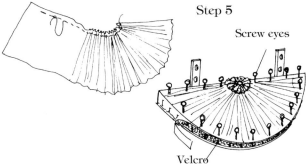

Step 5

Screw eyes

Velcro

8 Fix screw eyes to the underside of the board, spaced approximately 5cm (2in) apart and set 1cm (⅜in) in from the edge.

NOTE: If the heading of the side curtain is to sit on the front edge of the board without a valance, omit the screw eyes.

9 Fix the corona board to the wall at the required height above the bed in the same way as a pelmet board. See Fitting on p225.

MAKING BED CURTAINS
MATERIALS
Curtain fabric
Contrast lining fabric
Ombras or tie-back hooks
Wood dowel 22-25mm (¾-1in) x bed width
2 large cup hooks for the wood dowel

They can be unlined, lined or even interlined. Make them up in the same way as window curtains (see pp127-30), with the following amendments.

When you make up the side curtains, sew the leading edges and hem, but leave the inside edges open.

When you make up the back curtain, seam the two or three widths of fabric together, then machine a channel at the hem large enough for the wood dowel.

JOINING THE BACK CURTAIN TO THE SIDE CURTAINS
1 With the right sides of the lining fabric together, sew the side curtains to each side of the back curtain. Leave the lower 100cm (39in) of the seams open.

2 Turn in the raw edges at the lower section of the side curtains and slip stitch to neaten. Also neaten the side edges of the back curtain.

3 To head the curtains, machine gathering tape onto the right side of the main fabric, continuing round to the wrong side of the back curtain, and finishing on the right side of the other curtain.

4 Pull up the tape to the measurement of the corona board, insert the hooks and hook onto the screw eyes.

NOTE: There is a lot of fullness to be gathered into a small area, which may be too much for some machine tapes. The alternative is to hand gather around the curtain see p138.

5 Thread the wood dowel into the hem channel of the back curtain. To hold the dowel, fix large cup hooks into the wall just above the skirting board.

6 Fix the tie-back hooks or ombras into the wall at each side of the bed to hold the side curtains. Dress them, allowing the leading edge to 'bow' attractively.

7 Make up the contrast lined valance, pelmet or swags as required. Fit to the front edge of the corona with Velcro.

Steps 1 - 5

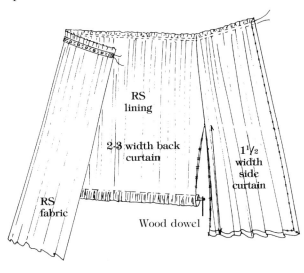

Hanging curtains from screw eyes

Design variation:
When the side curtains also form the decorative heading around the corona board, they are 'stepped' above the back curtain.

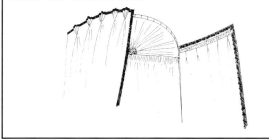

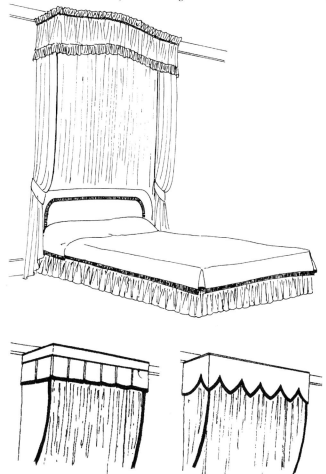

Half-Tester design variations

MAKING AND DRESSING HALF-TESTERS

A half-tester is the same as a corona, but the shape of the board is oblong rather than a small semicircle.

Half-tester curtains are hung from a pelmet board that is placed above the bed. Like a corona board, it is covered in fabric and supports a back and side curtains. The front edge of the board will be covered by a valance, pelmet or swags.

The tester or pelmet board is cut out of 22mm (³⁄₄in) plywood. As it should be 30-50cm (12-20in) wide, it will be quite heavy, and needs large shelf brackets to fix it to the wall. To reduce the weight, cut out two oblong shapes in the middle of the board but leave a centre support.

The board is covered in fabric, stapled or tacked on in a sunburst design, see p217.

Tracks or screw eyes can be fitted for the dress curtains, and the valance or pelmet hung from the front edge of the board using Velcro.

FOUR-POSTER BEDS

Four-poster bed dressings will largely depend on the design of the framework. However, it is important that any tracks or fittings are concealed, which sometimes means having a second valance or pelmet inside the framework.

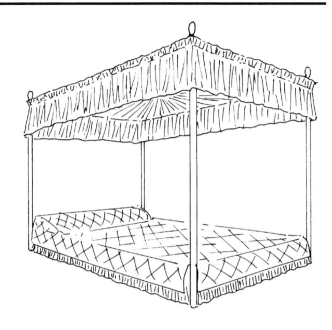

A four-poster bed should be dressed in a style to suit the frame. For example, unlined curtains can be simply tied to a wrought iron frame.

More traditional beds can be dressed in the same way as a half-tester, with a back and side curtain and a valance, pelmet or swag arrangement around the top. Further curtains can also be hung at the foot posts.

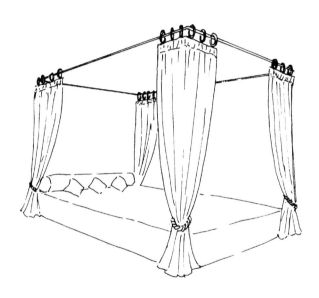

Due to the tester being supported by four posts, the side curtains cannot be joined onto the back curtain and are made up separately. Adjust the make-up notes according to your bed frame and individual fittings.

An added challenge is to 'tent' the ceiling; for an example, see pp66-67.

HANGING THE CURTAINS

The tester, or frame above the bed, is effectively a large pelmet board from which curtains are hung. Some four-posters have light frames and no ceiling.

Depending on the weight and the thickness of the curtains, they can hang from net wires, thin brass rods, or tracks fixed firmly to the bed frame.

MAKING TENTED CEILINGS

A fabric sunburst is fixed onto a wooden frame or stretcher which is then supported by the bed posts.

Measure between the posts and build a frame to those measurements. If necessary, you can support it by fixing small wooden blocks or brackets onto the posts. Brace the frame with horizontal and vertical cross stretchers, cutting out a hole in the centre.

Wooden frame for tented ceiling

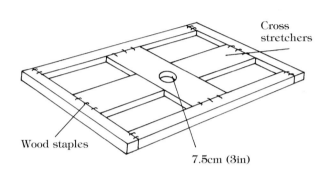

A quick and easy sunburst has occasional tucks of fabric around the edge of the frame. The fabric is then gathered into the centre. Because there is so much fullness at the centre, it is better to use a lightweight fabric such as fine cotton or silk.

FABRIC QUANTITIES
For most beds, the fabric quantities will be approximately 8-10m (8-10yds), see p213.

1 Cut and seam up the widths of fabric. Seam together the first and last widths to form a circle, whose circumference measures the same as the length around the outside edges of the frame.

2 Staple the right side of the fabric onto the outside edge of the frame. Ease the fabric round the corners, making tucks as necessary. Trim away any excess.

Fabric covered frame

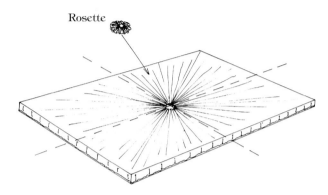

3 Working on one quarter of the ceiling at a time, pull the fabric to the centre of the frame. Make sure the fabric is evenly gathered, and taut. Staple each fold in place, close to the centre.

4 Check that the sunburst is pleated evenly. Only then can you trim away the excess fabric at the back of the wooden frame.

5 Make a rosette for the centre of the sunburst. It must be large enough to cover the staples around the central hole, see p159. Tack in place, hiding the heads of the tacks in the folds.

6 If you want to neaten the top of the frame, staple lining fabric onto it.

TABLECLOTHS

Tablecloths provide an opportunity to introduce different textures and to accent or complement colours in a room. A printed chintz trimmed with a frill will enhance a bedroom, while a heavier, cotton dobby woven fabric trimmed with a bullion fringe will look elegant in a sitting room.

FABRIC QUANTITIES

1 Finished cloth diameter = table diameter + 2 x table height + optional overlong allowance (this can be between 2.5-5cm (1-2in)

2 Cut diameter:

Lined cloth = finished diameter + 2 x 1.5cm (³⁄4in) hem allowance

Interlined cloth = finished diameter + 2 x 5cm (2in) hem allowance

Adjust for pattern repeat if necessary.

3 To find the number of widths of fabric you need, divide the cut diameter by the width of the fabric.

MAKING LINED ROUND TABLECLOTHS

MATERIALS

Fabric

Lining

Hem trims (optional)

1 Seam up the fabric and lining.

2 Fold the fabric in half, matching the seams. Fold in half again.

3 The radius is half the cut diameter. Put the tape measure on the absolute centre of the fabric, and repeatedly measure and mark off the radius. Join these marks together to form a curve.

4 Cut along the curve, and unfold. Use the circle as a template for cutting out the lining.

5 Lay the fabric and lining right sides together and machine round, leaving a gap for turning it through. Trim all the seam allowances, turn the cloth to the right side and press. Slip stitch the opening.

HEM TRIM QUANTITIES

Measure the hem circumference of the cloth to find the amount of trim you will need. For contrast binding, wadded hems, and frill quantities, see pp150-57.

NOTE: If you are using a 10cm (4in) deep bullion fringe, take the circumference measurement of the cloth at the point at which the fringe will be sewn.

Professional Tip

INTERLINING TABLECLOTHS

MATERIALS

Fabric

Lining and interlining

Hem trims as required

1 Lay fabric, wrong side up, and place the interlining on top; check that the seams line up. Sew rows of interlocking stitches 30cm (12in) apart, see p122.

2 Turn up and pin the 5cm (2in) hem allowance, dispersing the fullness evenly, and herringbone stitch over the raw edges.

3 Lay lining, right side up, onto the cloth, and interlock to the interlining in rows 30cm (12in) apart.

4 Fold under and pin the raw edge of the lining 2.5cm (1in) in from the edge of the cloth and slip stitch.

Hand sew fringe or frills around the hem.

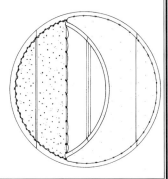

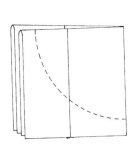 

WS fabric

TV TABLECLOTHS

A TV tablecloth is made up in two pieces. A gathered skirt is hung from a track fitted to the underside of the table top. A round cloth with an overhanging frill fits on top of the table. Make sure your TV will fit inside the table.

FABRIC QUANTITIES

1 Measure the top of the table to find the diameter and circumference.

Measure from the track to the floor to find the length of the skirt.

2 For the top cloth fabric and lining, the cut diameter = diameter + 2 x seam allowance. The finished piping and frill quantities are the same as the circumference, see pp121 and 155.

3 For the skirt, find the number of widths you will need by multiplying the circumference by 2.5 x fullness, and divide by the width of the fabric. Round up to the nearest whole number.

Steps 1 - 5

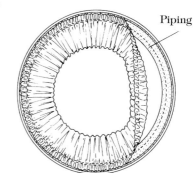
Piping

Skirt cut drop = finished length + 10cm (4in) heading and hem allowance. Multiply this number by the number of widths for the total skirt fabric quantity.

4 For the total fabric quantity, add the top cloth, frill and skirt quantities together. The lining quantity is the fabric quantity, minus the frill.

Steps 6 - 7

MAKING LINED TV TABLECLOTHS

1 Make a paper pattern of the table top. Add 2cm (¾in) all round and cut out. Cut out the fabric and lining using the paper pattern.

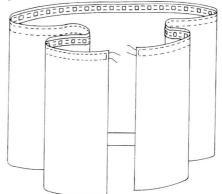

2 Lay the fabric and lining wrong sides together.

3 Make up the piping, see p121. Start at the back of the cloth and seam on the piping, taking a 1.5cm (½in) seam allowance. Join the piping as you would for a piped tie-back, see p196.

4 To make the frill, see p156. Join the widths of frill fabric together into a circle. Gather or pleat up to the circumference of the tabletop. With right sides together, sew onto the top cloth following the row of stitching made when attaching the piping.

5 Trim and swing needle or overlock the seam allowance.

6 The skirt is made in the same way as a straight valance, see p172. Machine attach a gathering tape.

7 Pull the tape up to the measurement of the track, including the overlap allowance. Slip in the hooks and hang on to the track.

Lay the round cloth on top of the table and cover with the protective glass.

CUSHIONS

Cushions are not only cosy and comforting, adding a touch of colour and pattern, but also a good soft furnishing project to start on. As cushion covers use a relatively small amount of fabric, it's an economical way of introducing luxurious fabrics such as silk, lace or tapestry weaves. There is a wide variety of trimmings for cushions. Piping gives a smart, clean finish, frills and fan edging add a pretty feminine touch, ties are perfect for kitchens and country furnishing, while cord, fringe or braid are more tailored.

SCATTER CUSHIONS

It is usual to have an uneven number of scatter cushions on a sofa i.e. three or five. A cushion arrangement on a sofa will look more interesting if the covers are made up in two or three different types of fabric, rather than all matching. The impact of scatter cushions is in the choice of fabric and the different types of frill and passementerie edgings.

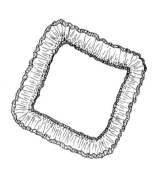

For scatter cushions, square and round shaped pads are most commonly available. An average size for a square scatter cushion is 45cm (18in). However, cushions can range from very small to large floor cushions.

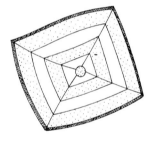

CUSHION PAD FILLINGS

Goose and duck down is the softest filling (and most expensive) and curled feather is the standard. Polyester and other synthetic fillings are an alternative, especially for people who are allergic to feathers or suffer from asthma. They are not as soft as feathers but they are easy to wash.

Foam is mainly used for squab and window seat pads, and gives firm support. It is is available in sheets 2.5, 5, 7.5 and 10cm (1, 2, 3 and 4in) in depth.

Specialist suppliers will cut the foam for you if you supply them with dimensions or a paper template. They can also cover the foam in a thin stockinette cover to make it easier to insert into the fabric cover.

BOXED SQUAB OR CHAIR CUSHIONS

A squab cushion is shaped to the seat of the chair. It usually has a gusset and some form of tie. The pads are usually made of feathers or foam, to a depth of 5cm (2in). Check that the extra height will not make it difficult to sit at the table.

BOLSTER CUSHIONS

These are cylindrical shaped, feather filled cushions which are used on sofas and beds to support the back or arm. They were traditionally used at the ends of period upright settees.

The circular ends of the cover look attractive when finished with a huge, fabric covered button or key tassel. The diameter is usually 20-25cm (8-10in), while the length is tailored to the depth of the chair or sofa.

NOTE: Covers for feather filled scatter cushions are made 2.5cm (1in) smaller than the pad. This ensures a snug fit and a pleasingly plump finished cushion.

Covers for boxed cushions are made to the exact size. This is important for foam pads. If the cover is too small it will buckle the foam and bend. It should either be an exact fit or fractionally too big as the fabric is likely to shrink when washed.

Cushion covers can easily be removed for cleaning if they are made with a zip or Velcro opening. For some cushion covers, where rope is hand sewn to the edge, it may be easier to hand sewn the opening together. Frills on cushions should always be generous for a pleasing finish. Allow 2.5 x fullness for square cushion covers and 3 x fullness for round cushions.

FABRIC QUANTITIES

Make a paper pattern to the finished size and shape of the pad; only box and squab cushions need a seam allowance all round.

PLAIN FABRICS

Use the paper pattern to calculate the amount of fabric for the front and back. Allow extra for gussets and self or contrast coloured piping if you need it.

PATTERNED FABRICS

Divide the cut length of the cushion by the pattern repeat and round up; this ensures that the pattern can be carefully positioned on the cover. This is especially important if the same pattern repeat is required on several cushions.

To establish the quantity of piping needed, measure around the edge of the paper pattern. For boxed or squab cushions, double the amount of piping.

For one or two cushion covers 50cm (20in) is the minimum amount of piping fabric to use to avoid having too many joins. 75cm (30in) will make at least 15m (15yd) of piping, with the joins a metre/yard apart.

To calculate the fabric for frills, see pp154-157. You will need more fabric for the frill than the cover itself, so never assume wastage will be enough.

MAKING PIPED AND ZIPPED COVERS

MATERIALS

Fabric

Piping cord

Zip (slightly smaller than the seam length)

1 Place the paper pattern on the fabric, centring it over the part of the design you want to feature. Mark round it and cut out. Cut out the back of the cushion; this does not have to be the same part of the pattern repeat or even in the same fabric, although if you want to turn the cushions over regularly it should be.

2 Cut and make the piping, see p121. With raw edges together, seam onto the right side of the front of the cushion cover. To allow it to curve around the corners, snip the piping seam allowance. For round cushions, snip every 2.5cm (1in). To join piping, see p196.

Step 1

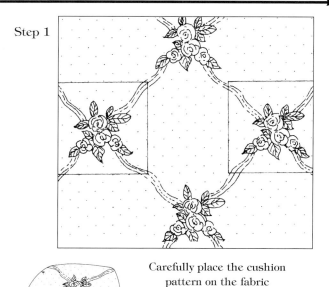

Carefully place the cushion pattern on the fabric

Steps 2 - 3

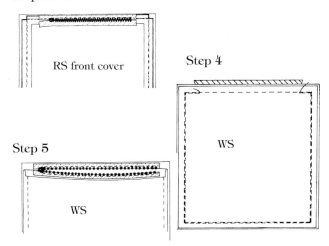

RS front cover

Step 4

WS

Step 5

WS

3 Place the zip, face down, on the right side of the front of the cover (at the lower edge of a patterned cover).

Using a zip foot, machine down the right-hand side only, close to the teeth.

4 With right sides together, sew the back cover to the front, beginning and ending at the zip and following the piping stitch line.

5 Machine as close to the teeth of the zip as possible. Stop within 5cm (2in) of the top of the zip leaving the needle in the work. Lift the machine foot and open the zipper below it. Continue to sew the zip to the top ensuring that the locking teeth are level.

6 Turn the cover through to the right side and press. Insert cushion pad, and plump into shape.

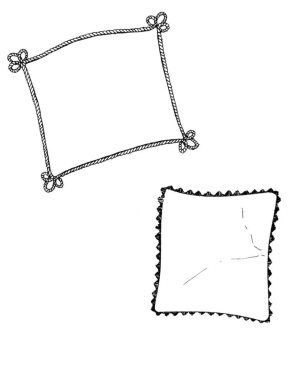

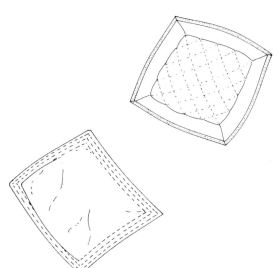

EDGINGS

For inset edgings follow instructions given on p121, substituting fringe or fan edging for the piping.

Flanged rope is attached to a tape so it can be inserted just like piping. Machine as close to the rope as possible, using a zip foot, so that the tape cannot be seen on the right side. To make a join, overlap the rope taking the cut edges down into the seam allowance.

Another way of attaching rope is to make up the cover (minus the piping) and then hand sew rope around the edge. It can be knotted or looped at the corners for a decorative effect.

MAKING QUILTED CUSHION COVERS

Cut out a piece of fabric, backing fabric and wadding 20% larger than the finished cover. On the face fabric, mark out the design of the quilt stitching with a fabric marker pencil.

Sandwich the wadding between the fabric and the backing, tack together, and quilt as required. Some machines have guides for standard diamond quilting.

Trim to the size of the cover plus seam allowances and make-up.

MAKING BOLSTER CUSHION COVERS

A bolster cushion cover is simply made up with a tube of fabric and two circular ends. This basic bolster cushion design can be enlivened in a number of ways. Sew a fabric tube, gather it at the ends, and cover the join with either a fabric covered button or a bolster tassel. Alternatively, make a slightly longer tube and bunch up the excess fabric at the ends for a 'cracker' effect.

Professional Tip

MAKING A TAPESTRY INTO A CUSHION COVER

Tapestries made up into cushion covers look delightful when piped and backed in velvet. To give a small tapestry more emphasis, or simply to make a larger cushion, sew a fabric border around it, rather like a picture mount.

To prepare the canvas:
If the tapestry needs to be reshaped, pin it onto a large wooden board with drawing pins, pulling it into its original shape. Hover a steaming iron above the tapestry, without touching it, to set it into its new shape. Allow the fabric to cool and repeat if necessary.

Remove from the board and trim the canvas to within 4cm ($1^1/_2$in) of the embroidery. If you wish, sew strips of fabric around the edge to make a border and mitre each corner. Continue to make up as a piped cushion, see p221.

MAKING BOXED CUSHION COVERS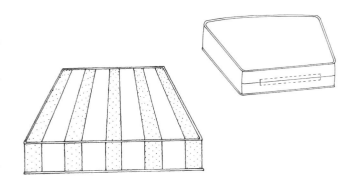

Although a piped cover can be made quite quickly, making a boxed cover takes a little more time. The extra work is involved in making the additional piping, and inserting the gusset. Most boxed cushions can have a zip at the back see right.

For large window seat covers, the zip opening needs to be generous in size, otherwise it is nearly impossible to insert the pad. The opening can be hidden at the back of the pad, and be as long as the pad itself. You will need a very long zip or a strip of Velcro. It can be sewn into a seam at the back, or into the centre of the gusset, with a short vertical seam at each end.

1 Make a paper pattern the exact size of the pad and add a 1.5cm (^{3}/$_4$in) seam allowance all round.

2 Cut out the top and bottom covers. For a very long cushion you may need seams on either side.

Cut and seam strips of fabric for the gusset. Allow for the depth + 2 x 1.5cm (^{3}/$_4$in) seam allowances.

Ensure that the pattern on the front of the gusset matches up with the pattern on the top of the cover. You can match the sides by cutting out the gussets individually and seaming them at the corners. Stripes can only be matched one way, usually on the front of the gusset.

3 Cut and make up the piping. With raw edges together, seam onto the right side of the top and also the bottom cover. Seam onto both the top and bottom covers. Snip the piping seam allowance to allow it to curve around the corners.

4 Measure around the cover to find the exact length of the gusset and then seam it together. For squab covers with ties, make vertical seams in the gusset where the chair legs are and inset a tie into each one.

5 With right sides together, seam the gusset onto the front cover, following the piping stitch line. On patterned fabrics start machining at the front to ensure that the pattern matches.

6 Sew the zip onto the lower edge of the gusset and bottom cover seam in the same way as for a piped cover, see p221.

7 Sew the gusset to the bottom cover. Turn cover through to the right side and press.

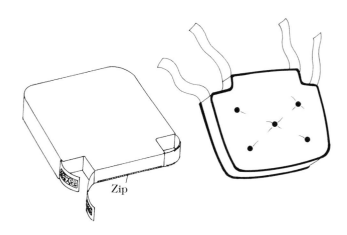
Zip

MAKING CUSHION BUTTONS

A pair of buttons or button tufts can be sewn on to the top and the bottom of the pad with an extra long buttoning needle. Use a generous length of doubled button hole thread or linen twine making a single stitch to hold them in place. Pull the thread taut to make a dimpled effect and tie securely. Cut the threads and hide the ends underneath the button.

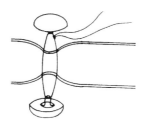

Professional Tip

MAKING BUTTON TUFTS

You will need 50cm (20in) of embroidery silk or fine wool. Make a peg board by hammering two nails, 3cm (1^1/$_4$in) apart, through a piece of wood. Leave a short length of thread, and wrap around the nails in a figure of eight several times, to make an attractive bow. Tie the ends together, wrap one thread around the middle several times, and then tie off with the other thread. Remove from the nails, and sew the tuft in place, see p32 for use with goblet headings.

PART FIVE: INSTALLATION & FITTING

Fitting the hardware and hanging curtains and top treatments requires the same patience and high standards as curtain making. The overall design determines the type of fixtures required. If the heading is to be visible, curtains should be hung from a fabric covered lath or a decorative pole. However, if the heading is covered by a pelmet, valance or swags and tails, the curtains can be hung from a track on a pelmet board or a valance rail and track. See Choosing Tracks, Poles and Other Fittings on p91.

Follow the manufacturer's installation instructions and advice when fitting tracks and poles. Fitting hardware can be heavy work, so it makes sense to have someone with you to help; in most cases, you will definitely need another pair of strong hands. Ideally, curtain fixtures should be fixed into place before the curtains are made so that accurate measurements can be taken.

TOOLBOX
Electric drill and drill bits
Pipe and cable detector
Retractable steel tape measure
Spirit level
Hammer and tacks
Staple gun and staples
Pliers (a really strong pair)
Galvanised steel No.8 wood screws, 20-50mm (³/4-2in)
Wallplugs for No.8 wood screws
Screwdrivers

Step ladder
Extension lead
Wood doweling or plastic spacers
Brackets for pelmet board
Tie-back hooks
Ess hooks
Screw eyes
Small tenon saw
Plaster filler
Silicone spray
Bradawl

Professional Tip
DRILLING
Establish the type of surface that you will be drilling into and check carefully for any pipes or cables with a detector. When you start drilling, have someone hold a dustpan directly under the drill to stop dust getting into the air and falling onto your brand new curtains.

To prevent *Wood* from splitting, make a pilot hole with a bradawl or small drill bit. Do not drill too closely to the edge of a window, because that can also cause splitting.

Brick does not usually present any problems. Watch out for red brick dust because it can stain curtains. If the bricks are soft you could go up to a No.12 screw, 50mm (2in), provided it fits through the bracket holes.

Breeze blocks are softer than bricks; to ensure a snug fit use a drill bit smaller than the required size.

Plaster board requires special plugs for hollow walls. Hollow wall plugs expand behind the plaster board to give a secure fixing for the screw. There are a wide range of hollow wall plugs on the market, so if you are unsure ask for assistance when purchasing.

Concrete lintel is an exceptionally hard surface to drill into; you will need a powerful hammer-action drill. Replace drill bits frequently, as they quickly become blunt and ineffective.

TRACKS

You can hang lightweight curtains from plastic tracks, but always use metal corded tracks, for heavier, interlined curtains.

Tracks are either top fixed to the underside of the pelmet board or face fixed to the wall. When tracks are corded, the cords can be fitted into a tensioner which is screwed into the wall or onto the skirting board. Alternatively, the cords can be cut and have brass acorn weights tied onto each end, but this can only be done when the track length is less than the track to floor measurement.

Tracks should be sprayed with a silicone spray to ensure that they run smoothly.

Most track brackets convert to either top or face fixing, but double check when you purchase them.

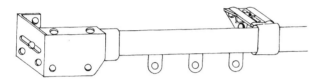

There are so many kinds of track that it is very important to make sure you understand the instructions. Call the manufacturers if you are in any doubt or difficulty.

FITING PELMET BOARDS

These are made from 20mm (3/4in) PSE timber and are either painted or covered with matching fabric. The length of the board should be approximately 5cm (2in) longer than the track, to allow space for the curtain to be returned to the wall. The width of the board is usually in the range of 15-23cm (6-9in). The width is dictated by the number of layers used in the window treatment and also any protrusions, such as radiators, that could affect the hang of the curtain.

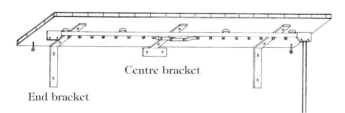

Centre bracket

End bracket

When pelmets, valances, swags and tails are fixed to the front edge of a pelmet board the curtain track should be set back 6-8cm (2½-3in) to allow the curtains free movement. A similar distance is required between the track and the wall or window, hence the depth of a pelmet board is usually 12-18cm (5-7in).

End brackets should be approximately 2.5cm (1in) shorter than the width of the board to give maximum support. A centre bracket is required for pelmet boards over 170cm (67in) long. These have a short back plate so that they are unobtrusive. To position the boards, see pp114-5.

At one side of the window, measure up from the top of the window to the bottom of where you want the pelmet board to be. Mark with a pencil, then repeat on the other side. Using a flat piece of wood or a metre stick, draw a line between the two points.

If this line looks level to the eye, mark the position of the brackets. Hold one bracket against the wall and mark the wall through the screw holes with a pencil. Repeat for the second bracket and any other brackets.

Drill holes about 44mm (1¾in) into the wall. Insert plugs into the wall and fix the brackets securely to the wall with No. 8 44mm (1¾in) screws.

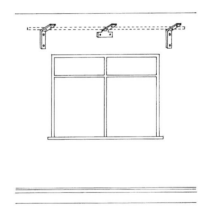

Lay the pelmet board across the brackets and centre it over the window. On the underside of the pelmet board, mark through the screw holes with a bradawl. Using No.8 25mm (1in) screws, secure the pelmet board into position.

> **Professional Tip**
> If necessary, use wood doweling or plastic spacers to create a gap between the board and the track for the arms of the brackets to slip through.
>
> Spacer

SHAPED PELMET BOARDS

Curved and shaped pelmet boards are a simple and inexpensive way of elevating valances and fixed headed curtains treatments. They work well on classic, portrait shaped windows up to 2m (2yd) wide.

Curved boards should have a minimum central depth of 23-30cm (9-12in). They can be cut out of timber or plywood. There should be sufficient depth left at the sides of the board for small brackets.

Scalloped boards are made up in the same way as curved boards but with additional scallop shaping. They can be up to 35cm (14in) deep at the centre.

If you want to fix a valance to the board, stick or staple Velcro to the front edge. Track specialists can bend tracks to the shape of the board from a template. Tracks should be fitted about 7.5cm (3in) in from the front edge of the board.

If the curtains are permanently secured in the centre, fix 20mm (3/4in) screw eyes onto the lower edge of the board 1cm (1/2in) in from the front edge. You will always need some method of holding the curtains back when the top is fixed.

A tiara board has a 'tiara' shaped piece of wood screwed to the pelmet board, flush with the front.

BAY WINDOW FITTINGS

Plastic tracks curve around bays quite easily, but use metal for heavy interlined curtains. These will need to be custom-curved to fit around your bay, see p112 for details. Pelmet boards are fitted as for a straight run, but are mitred at the angles with brackets screwed each side of the mitres.

Poles can be fitted in the same way. Hang a curtain at each angle, either side of the supporting bracket.

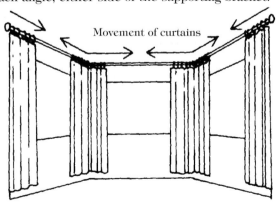

Movement of curtains

Shaped boards for valances

Scalloped board

Curved board

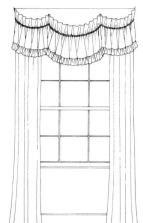

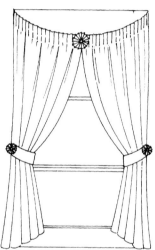

Fixed headed curtains

ARCHED FITTINGS

Either fit a pliable plastic track, or bend a metal track to the correct shape. The tracks can be bent and fitted to the architrave of the arch, or onto a plywood frame.

If swags are going to be fitted in front of the curtains, make a 7.5cm (3in) deep plywood frame for them. Cover the plywood with a band of fabric.

Covering frame with fabric band

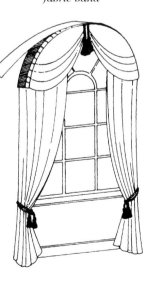

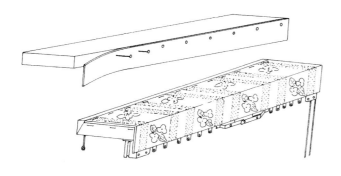

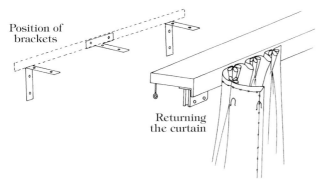

Position of brackets

Returning the curtain

MAKING FABRIC COVERED LATHS

The track is fitted to the underside of a narrow 10cm (4in) pelmet board and concealed by a fabric or wall paper covered fascia. The fascia can be made from either hardboard or pelmet buckram to a depth that allows the hooks and overlap arms free movement.

To make a lath, tack a hardboard fascia approximately 4.5cm (1¾in) deep to the front of a narrow pelmet board. Cover it using glue or a staple gun.

Fix the track directly behind the fascia, with the runners and arms hanging below.

Position screw eyes and hooks at the ends of the lath for the curtain return.

You can screw the pelmet board into the ceiling if there is no space on the wall for fixing brackets.

FITTING POLES

Work out the distance between the brackets; this must be 5-15cm (2-6in) less than the pole length (calculated without the finials). Measure the height up from the floor, mark the position of the bracket screw holes with a pencil. Drill and plug holes and screw the bracket into position.

Rest the pole in the bracket and move to the other side of the window. Check that the pole is level to the eye; remove the pole and fix the second bracket.

Poles over 150cm (59in) will need a centre bracket. Put the correct number of rings on the pole. Gathered headings usually have a hook every 15cm (6in). Hand pleated curtains generally have one hook per pleat.

Screw the finials into place at each end of the pole. Centre the pole on the brackets. Make sure there is one ring between the bracket and the finial on each side. There should be equal numbers of rings on either side of the centre bracket.

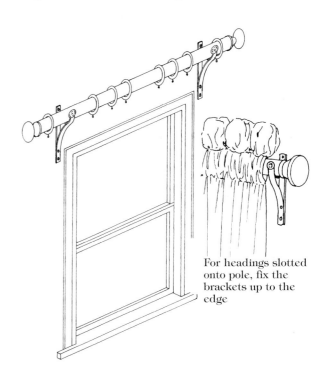

For headings slotted onto pole, fix the brackets up to the edge

---

Professional Tip

For poles used with swags or valances with curtains hung behind, fix the pole brackets onto painted wooden blocks, 5-7.5cm (2-3in) deep. Fix the curtain track to the wall behind and just below the pole. It is important to note, when combining tracks and poles, ensure that the track is shorter than the pole.

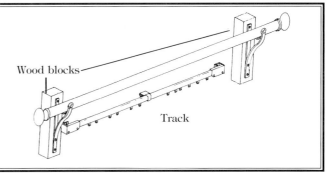

Wood blocks

Track

HANGING CURTAINS

For tape headed curtains, work from the outside edges and pull up the draw cords. Allow enough width for the curtains to be returned at the outside edges. The surplus cord can be wound into a skein and tucked into a small pocket sewn at the top of the curtain.

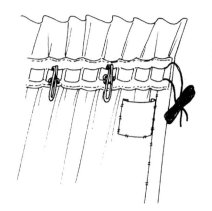

Pulling up tape headed curtains

Insert hooks into the tape pockets every 15cm (6in). For hand pleated curtains, hooks should be pinned in or sewn at each pleat and on the returns and overlaps.

For a multilayered treatment, start by hanging the layer nearest to the window glass and work outwards.

Set the ladder so that you have the least stretching to do. Put the curtains over one shoulder to take the weight. Start hanging the curtains from the centre of the track. Never start by hooking them onto the overlap arm, as the weight will bend it, or worse still, snap it off completely. The outside edges of the curtains should be hooked onto a screw eye so that the curtains are returned to the wall.

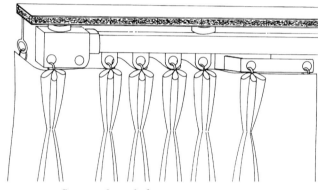

Curtains hung before top treatment

If the curtains are short you could lengthen them using spacers and/or Ess hooks, see opposite. If you are using pin hooks, they can be adjusted up or down to raise or lower the curtains.

DRESSING CURTAINS

When curtains are first hung they should be dressed to encourage them to fall into rounded, even folds. Interlined curtains respond especially well to this process.

To dress the curtains, draw them into their stack back position and, starting from the outside edge, work from the top downwards and run your hands firmly down the length of each pleat or fold.

For goblet or French pleats hung from a pole, or a track where the top of the curtain hangs below it, push the spaces to the back. Where curtains are hung from a lath with a fascia, or where the heading hangs in front of the track, pull the spaces between the hooks forward.

TO STEAM CURTAINS

Ideally, creases should be allowed to hang out naturally. Steamers can be used, but the combination of heat and moisture can cause shrinkage. They are however, good for raising the pile on velvet. Special fabric anti-crease sprays are also available, check the manufacturers' instructions and use with care.

TO BANDAGE CURTAINS

Tie three strips of waste lining or fabric, and bandage around each curtain. They should hold the folds in position but they should not be so tight that they leave indentation marks.

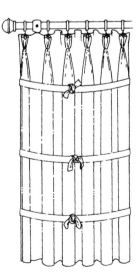

Leave for 2 or 3 days. Remove the ties and draw the curtains. They should then hang in the set folds.

ADJUSTING THE CURTAIN LENGTH

If the curtain track is covered by a valance or pelmet, it is possible to adjust the length of the curtains to compensate for uneven floors, or for curtains which have shrunk during cleaning.

You can use metal Ess hooks, opened up with pliers, to hang between the gliders and the curtain hooks.

To lower a track underneath a pelmet board, place one or two small spacers between the track and the pelmet board. Replace track with longer screws to compensate.

If needed, use both methods together.

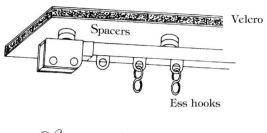

Velcro
Spacers

Ess hooks

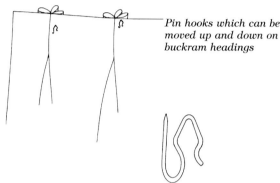

Pin hooks which can be moved up and down on buckram headings

FITTING TIE-BACK HOOKS

Tie-backs need to be positioned with care in order to maintain the best proportions. For full length curtains, the hooks are usually fixed around 95cm (38in) up from the floor.

For tassel tie-backs however, hooks need to be fitted slightly higher, approximately 100cm (39in) up from the floor.

Do not fit the tie-back hooks until after the curtains have been hung, so that you can check that the outside edges of the curtains hang straight.

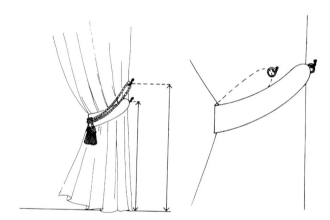

HANGING VALANCES AND PELMETS

Valances are either hooked onto a valance rail or, when hung from a pelmet board, fitted to the front with Velcro fastening tape.

Using Velco ensures that the valance is taut against the front edge, and gives a neat finish. When fitting valances always start from the centre of the valance and the board, and work outwards to each side.

Dress the valance into its folds and also smooth any fringing or frill. Fine fringing can be straightened by using a soft bristle brush to comb it out.

Flat pelmets are also hung using Velcro. Again, start at the centre of the board and work outwards. For both valances and pelmets, see that the returns are smoothed neatly onto the Velcro as you turn the corner.

FITTING BLINDS

For specific information on the fitting of each type of blind, see pp198-205.

It is especially important to make sure that all recessed blinds are level. Not just because they will not pull up and down easily, but because inside the hard lines of the window recess, any tilt to one side will be much more obvious.

Flat Roman blinds hanging outside the recess should be fixed as close to the wall as possible; otherwise the gap at the sides will let in a great deal of light and make the whole fitting look clumsy. There are strong metal tracks with pulley systems available for large or heavy Roman blinds.

All gathered or Roman blinds should be dressed after they are hung.

HANGING SWAGS AND TAILS

Hung from a pelmet board, swags and tails are finished at the top with a simple fabric binding. This should be sewn securely as it will hold the entire weight of the swag. Either tack or staple the binding onto the top of the board, or face fix with Velcro onto the front edge.

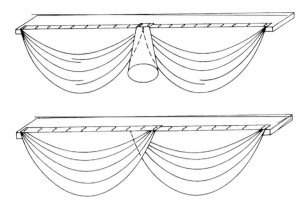

It is easier to fit swags onto the board before you put it up. Fix the brackets to the wall, as on p225. Lay the board on the edge of a table so that the swags can hang freely. Tack, staple, or Velcro each swag in order, following the design. Start at the centre as usual. Pull the tops taut as you work to prevent any puckering.

Now place the whole pelmet board onto its brackets and screw firmly in place. This is usually a two-person job, especially for a wide window.

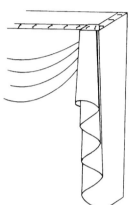

Lastly, tack any trims or rope in place, and smooth out the swags and tails until they hang in perfect folds.

Once the pelmet board is in place, you can fit the tails, making sure they hang straight. Tack, staple or Velcro them in place, with the binding folded onto the top edge of the board. Take care to fix the corners neatly.

Professional Tip
HANGING SWAGGED VALANCES

Staple the binding at the top of the valance onto the top of the pelmet board. Start at the centre and work outwards.

If it is a short valance, you can fit it with the pelmet board in place. If it is wide or deep, it is better to fit the valance in place before you lift the board onto its brackets.

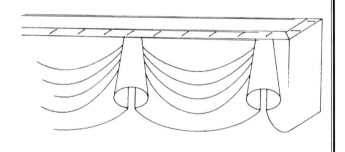

DECORATIVE ROPE AND TRIMS

Once the basic valance or pelmet is in position you can add any rope and/or small trims. Fix them to the front edge of the board with 22mm (³/₄ in) brass tacks.

If your design includes coronets, tack them into place before you add the rope trim in front.

Make knots or rope clovers, see p149. Work from the centre out to each side. Tack either side of each knot or clover and continue tacking every 20cm (8in).

At the ends, cut the rope and wrap sticky tape around the end to stop it unravelling. Tuck the end under at the very back of the return and tack firmly in place.

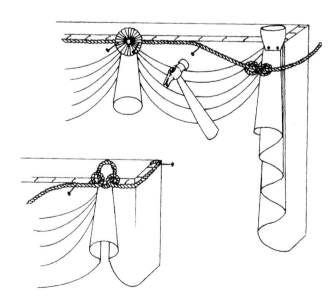

DRAPING SWAGS OVER POLES

The curtains are hung from a track on the wall, set behind and below the pole. The pole should be slightly longer than the track and should be extended by screwing onto wooden blocks, see Professional Tip p227.

The top of the swag is self neatened, see p185. Put up the pole, and then drape the swags over it, one at a time, adjusting the drop to suit your design. Then tack the swag in place. If you have a metal pole, glue Velcro to the pole in the appropriate places, and sew the other side of the Velcro to the swag.

Now fit the tails. If the design shows they fall over in front of the pole, tack the binding to the top. Screw in the finial and make sure the tail side return folds flat.

If the tail falls behind the pole, you will have to cut a tiny slit at the side of the return so that the finial can be screwed to the pole.

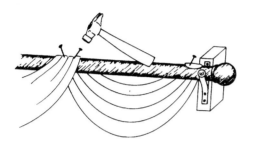

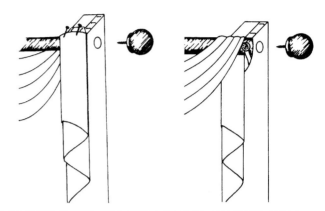

CARE AND CLEANING

Check fabric manufacturers' instructions before cleaning. Unlined curtains and blinds may be washed, but shrinkage, fading and losing finish and body can all occur. Remove hooks and loosen tapes before washing.
Man-made sheers fabrics need washing regularly to keep them bright. Cotton muslins also need to be washed regularly, but they may shrink.
Lined and interlined curtains and tops should not be washed. Vacuum them regularly to remove dust and grime. Put gauze over the nozzle to stop excessive pulling to avoid threads being dislodged.

DRY CLEANING

Some cleaners will take the curtains and pelmets down and also re-hang them after cleaning. Any brown water marks or sunfade will be more pronounced after the cleaning process.

STAIN PROTECTION

Curtains exposed to excessive dust and dirt should be coated with stain protector. It can either be applied before they are made up or simply sprayed onto the finished curtains. Specialist companies will apply stain protection for you if you prefer.

FIRE PROOFING

Curtains in commercial properties may need fire proofing. Buy treated fabric, or have it done professionally.

REPAIRING CURTAINS

Dust, direct sunlight and handling weakens curtain fabric. The leading edges are the areas usually most in need of repair. These can either be cut off and have a contrast leading edge sewn on in a new fabric, or if there is plenty of fullness, they can simply be turned in.

You may be able to swop them round so that the faded leading edges become the outside edges.

Faded and weak linings can also be replaced. See Remaking Curtains. Rare or valuable antique fabrics should be restored by specialist professionals. Always handle delicate fabrics with extreme care when making, hanging and cleaning.

DYEING CURTAINS

If curtains are still in good condition but have faded, or they no longer match your colour scheme, have then professionally dyed to give them a new lease of life.

STORAGE

Curtains are very bulky items, the only way to keep them safe before they are fitted is to hang them on temporary tracks or poles in the workroom.

You can also lay them out on a spare bed. Cover with a clean sheet to keep them dust-free. Or carefully fold them lengthways, and pack in polythene.

The selected companies listed in this Suppliers Directory offer a wealth of products and relevant information. Where the company states that it sells retail products, everybody is welcome to buy from their showroom or shop. The term 'trade' means that they offer a service to Soft Furnishing shops and Interior Decorators who hold accounts with these companies and sell their products to the general public. If you ring the company they will put you in touch with a Decorator or furnishing shop who can supply you.

FABRIC SUPPLIERS

Colefax & Fowler (Trade and retail)
Showroom: 39 Brook Street, London W1Y 2JE
Tel 0181 874 6484 for nationwide stockists
Renowned for their exclusive chintzes, they now offer a wide variety of weaves and printed linens with an array of coordinating trimmings (see passementerie) as well as wallpaper ranges.

Designers Guild (Trade and retail)
Showroom: 267 -271 + 275-277 Kings Road, London SW3 5EW
3 Olaf Street, London W11 4BE
Tel for both: 0171 243 7300
Brilliantly coloured innovative fabrics including printed floral and geometrics, plains, checks and stripes, jacquards, tapestries, silks, velvets, children's collections, coordinating trimmings and wallpapers.

G P & J Baker (Trade and retail)
The Decorative Fabrics Gallery, 278-280 Brompton Road, London SW3 2AS
Tel 0171 589 4778
A large showroom full of classic ranges of prints, damasks, silks and velvets plus a range of passementerie.

Harlequin Fabrics and Wallcoverings (Trade and retail)
Cossington Road, Sileby, Leicestershire LE12 7RU
Tel 01509 816575
Fabrics and wallcoverings for both domestic and contract applications in a variety of traditional and contemporary styles, suitable for both curtains and upholstery.

Jane Churchill Fabrics and Wallpapers (Trade and retail)
Showroom: 151 Sloane Street, London SW1X 9BX
Tel 0181 874 6484 for nationwide stockists
The Jane Churchill Company offer a comprehensive range of young, innovative, easy-to-use designs at affordable prices.
The colourful trimming collections include fringes, fan edging and bobble trim.

Lelievre (UK) Ltd (Trade only, ring for stockists)
1/19 Chelsea Harbour Design Centre, London SW10 OXE
Tel 0171 352 4798
Specialists in weaving silks and damasks; they carry a large collection of jacquards and plains.

Osborne & Little (Trade and retail)
49 Temperley Road, London SW12 8QE
Tel 0181 675 2255
A very wide selection of designs, both classic and contemporary, including prints, wovens, chenilles, wool, silk and voile.

Pallu & Lake, Christian Fischbacher, Interior Selection and Charles Hammond Fabrics
Timney Fowler (Trade and retail)
388 Kings Road, London SW3 5UZ
Tel 0171 352 2263
An extensive range of fabrics suitable for all soft traditional and modern furnishings.

Romo Ltd (Trade only, ring for stockists)
Lowmoor Road, Kirkby in Ashfield, Nottinghamshire NG17 7DE
Tel 01623 750005
Romo continue to broaden their soft furnishing and wallpaper collections; a wide range of coordinating fabrics strengthens their reputation in home furnishing and interior design.

Sanderson (Retail)
112-120 Brompton Road, London SW3 1JJ
Tel 0171 584 3344
A wide range of prints and weaves including a selection of laces and voiles. The fabrics provide a choice of design, scale and colour and combine contemporary style with the comfort of tradition.

Today Interiors (Trade and retail)
Hollis Road, Grantham, Lincs NG31 7QH
Tel 01476 574401
Manufacturer of fabric from high quality 100% cottons, linens, and a range of weaves in a mixture of modacrylic and cotton. The fabrics are flame retardant to BS5867, and treated with a stain repellent.

Warner Fabrics plc (Trade only, ring for stockists)
Chelsea Habour Design Centre, Chelsea Harbour, Lots Road, London SW10 0XE
Tel 0171 376 7578
Using their extensive archive resources they produce traditional and original printed and woven fabrics for today.
They have complementary ranges of wallcoverings and can hand weave exquisite silks to order.

PASSEMENTERIE AND TRIMMING SUPPLIERS

A J Worthington (Leek) Ltd (Trade only, ring for stockists)
Portland Mills, Queen Street, Leek, Staffordshire ST13 6LW
Tel 01538 399600
An outstanding range of trimmings in luxurious colours, available from stock or custom-made.

Belinda Coote Tapestries (Trade and retail)
3/14 Chelsea Harbour Design Centre,
London SW10 OXE
Tel 0171 351 0404
Luxurious and versatile tapestry fabric and
borders. Use to liven up curtains or to add a
new dimension to plain fabrics. Mail order
available.

Colefax & Fowler (see Fabrics for address)
A large selection of wool, cotton and linen
trimmings from picot braids to generous bullion
fringes, ropes and fan edges.

Designers Guild (see Fabrics for address)
Brightly coloured trimmings to coordinate with
their fabric ranges.

G P & J Baker (see Fabrics for address)
A comprehensive range of trimmings in rich
colours.

Nottingham Braid Company (Trade only, ring for
stockists)
Gresham Rd, Osmaston Rd, Derby DE24 8AW
Tel 01332 331314
Manufacturers of made-to-order trimmings,
tie-backs and tassels. All colour matched
to coordinate with your fabrics in yarns of
your choice. Their designers can help with
design selection.

Osborne & Little (see Fabrics for address)
Comprehensive collections of unusual and
standard items: textures include cotton
and chenille in colourings that team with all
their fabrics.

Sanderson (see Fabrics for address)
Sanderson's collection of decorative
passementerie offers a wide range of designs
across a comprehensive colour palette.

DECORATIVE POLES
Artisan
4A Union Court, 20 Union Road London SW4
6JP
Tel 0171 498 6974
Standard and custom made forged and cast iron
curtain rails and accessories

The Bradley Collection (Trade and retail)
Lion Barn, Maitland Road, Needham Market
Suffolk IP6 8NS
Tel 01449 722724
Designers and manufacturers of poles, finials
and accessories in steel, wood and hand painted
decorative finishes.

Edward Harpley (Trade only)
Crownings, Buxhall Road, Brettenham, Ipswich,
Suffolk IP7 7PA
Tel 01449 737999
Edward Harpley make a wide range of

curtain poles and finials in a variety of
natural and decorated timbers to customers
own specifications.

McKinney & Co (Trade and retail)
Studio P, The Old Imperial Laundry
71 Warriner Gardens, Battersea,
London SW11 4XW
Tel 0171 627 5077
Suppliers of custom-made curtain poles in
numerous finishes with unusual and exquisite
finials plus decorative ombras, cornice boxes
and bed coronas.

CURTAIN AND WORKROOM SUPPLIERS
*These companies are trade only, ring for nearest
stockists*
A & C Valmic
9-10 Meadow View, Crendon Industrial Estate,
Long Crendon, Aylesbury, Bucks HP18 9EQ
Tel 01844 201610
Distributors of the Walton Everard range of
fabrics, tapes, tracks and poles and all soft
furnishing sundries.

Cope & Timmins Ltd
Angel Road Works, Advent Way, Edmonton,
London N18 3AY
Tel 0181 803 3333
Exclusive custom-made curtain poles,
soft furnishing accessories, workroom products,
a vast range of tapes and linings plus other
hardware.

Hallis Hudson
Bushell Street, Preston PR1 2SP
Tel 01772 202202
Distributors and manufacturers of window
furnishings with an extensive range of fabrics,
blinds, linings, tracks, poles and accessories.

Jones & Co (Nottingham) Ltd (Trade and retail)
Lortas Road, New Basford, Nottingham
NG5 1EH
Tel 0115 978 1263
Specialist suppliers of curtain tapes, lining,
interlinings, brassware accessories, curtain
tracks for contract and retail, wood poles, braids
and trimmings, fabrics, pipings, general
accessories.

F R Street Ltd
Frederick House, Wickford Business Park,
Wickford, Essex SS11 8YB
Tel 01268 766677
Established wholesalers of quality curtain
linings, interlinings and soft furnishings.
Exciting range of natural fibre, woven and
printed fabrics.

Porter Nicholson
Portland House
Norlington Road, London E10 6JX
Tel 0181 539 6895
Suppliers of linings and components to curtain
and upholstery workrooms.

Bancroft Soft Furnishing Products
Brook Mill, Parker Street, Macclesfield
Cheshire SK11 7BQ
Tel 01625 423828
Suppliers of sateen curtain lining, blackout and
thermal linings, bump and domett interlinings,
pelmet and tie-band buckram stiffenings, pinch
pleat heading buckram, pinch pleating tape
and curtain making sundries.

Rufflette Ltd
Sharston Road, Wythenshawe,
Manchester M22 4TH
Tel 0161 998 1811
Create beautiful interior window designs with
Rufflette tape and accessories, made to the
highest standards for quality. Available from
most soft furnishing outlets.

Selectus Ltd
The Uplands, Biddulph,
Stoke-on-Trent ST8 7RH
Tel 01782 522316
Sole UK manufacturers of VELCRO hook and
loop fasteners, including standard sewing, self
adhesive, and iron-on qualities. Available from
all good haberdashery and soft furnishing
shops.
Velcros is a Registered Trade Mark owned in
the UK and Ireland by Selectus Ltd.

CURTAIN TRACK MANUFACTURERS
Integra Products
Eastern Avenue, Litchfield,
Staffordshire WS13 7SB
Tel 01543 267100
Can advise on the type of track or pole to use
for various situations and suggest a retail
stockist.

Silent Gliss Ltd
Star Lane, Margate, Kemt CT9 4EF
Tel 01843 863571
A wide range of aluminium curtain and blind
tracks to suit every requirement, including
difficult or awkward shapes and sizes. Advice
and help available from the Sales Office.

DRESSING TABLES, SCREENS ETC.
Cover Up Designs Ltd (Trade and retail)
The Barn, Hannington Farm,
Hannington, Hants RG26 5TZ
Tel 01635297981/2/3
An extensive range of furniture including
dressing tables, TV tables and ottomans are
displayed in our showroom. A complete soft
furnishing service covering quilting, eider-
downs and upholstery is available.

EQUIPMENT
Morplan
56 Great Titchfield Street, London W1P 8DX
Freephone 0800 435333
Mail order service and shop in London's West
End supplying equipment for curtain making,
sewing, cutting and pattern making.

Staples Group
Lockwood Road, Huddersfield HD1 3QW
Tel 01484 513555
Specialist suppliers of equipment including
pattern paper and sewing accessories; mail
order.

FLAME RETARDANT FINISHING
FRS
3 Grange Farm Industrial Units, Grange Road,
Tiptree, Essex CO5 0QG
Tel 01621 818477
Flame retarding and Scotchguarding treat-
ments to fabrics, and dry cleaning, particularly
on site.

QUILTERS
Cliq Designs Ltd (Trade only, ring for suppliers)
460 Carr Place, Walton Summit, Bamber
Bridge, Preston PR5 8AU
Tel 01772 628141
Suppliers for interior designers with a full
range of quilting techniques from incredibly
detailed outline quilting to simple channels.

Premierechoice Ltd (Trade only, ring for
suppliers)
3 Algores Way, Weasenham Lane, Wisbech,
Cambridgeshire PE13 2TQ
Tel 01945 589558
Makers of bespoke tailored, quilted bedspreads including outline and raised Italian
quilting, using customer's own fabric.

SPECIALIST CLEANERS
Pilgrim Payne & Co Ltd
290-294 Latimer Road, London W10 6QU
Tel 0208 960 5656
Specialist cleaners of curtains, carpets, upholstery, fine rugs, and tapestries. Curtain makers
and re-upholsters, take down and re-installa-
tion service.

TRADE ASSOCIATIONS
The Registry of Master Blind and Curtain
Makers, 44-46 Bridge Road, Grays,
Essex RM17 6BU
Tel: 01375 379022 Contact: Peter Moody

The Association of Master Upholsterers
Francis Vaughan House, 102 Commercial
Street,
Newport, Gwent NP9 1LU
Tel 01633 215454 Contact: Mike Spencer

THE JOHN LEWIS PARTNERSHIP
23 Stores Nationwide (Retail)

For details of your nearest branch, phone 0171 828 1000

John Lewis are renowned for their home furnishings. They have an extensive range of quality fabrics and accessories. There are up to 1,800 different rolls of fabric on display, including Jonelle, a soft furnishing range exclusive to John Lewis, and many leading international designer brands.

They stock all your curtain making essentials – linings and interlinings, cottons and threads, heading tapes and tie-back buckrams, Velcro and cushion pads.

They also stock an impressive range of reasonably priced fabric trims – including fringes, ropes, ribbons, braids, and rope and tassel tie-backs. They offer a wide selection of tracks, poles, blinds and all the necessary fittings.

The John Lewis staff are there to help you, with friendly, expert advice. If required, John Lewis has a professional making up service, for curtains, large or small, pelmets, blinds and bedspreads. They also have a home measuring and fitting service, and can shape curtain tracks to fit even the most awkward window. They offer a full re-upholstery and loose cover service and will make up headboards in a fabric of your choice.

COURSES AND EDUCATION

Cambridge Fine Furnishings
Principal: Helen Metherell
Pelham House, 36 Grantchester Rd,
Cambridge CB3 9ED
Tel 01223 357456 Fax 01223 355437

One to four day structured courses in curtain making and complementary soft furnishings. Eleven day Curtain Making Certificate and twenty one day Soft Furnishings Diploma available. Recognised by the British Accreditation Council for Further and Higher Education as a provider of courses in soft furnishings and interior design.

KLC School of Interior Design
Principal: Jenny Gibbs
KLC House, Spring Vale Terrace,
London W14 0AE
Tel 0171 602 8592/3 Fax 0171 702 1964

KLC offers a comprehensive programme of courses ranging from one day workshops such as Soft Furnishings and Paint Effects to a 30 week Diploma Course for a career in Interior Design and Decoration. There is also a 10 week Certificate Course and two Home Study Courses. KLC Diploma Courses are accredited by the BAC and ODLQC and enjoy an international reputation.

National Design Academy
Principal: Pauline Riley
Rufford Hall, Trent Lane, Nottingham NG2 4DS
Tel 01159 419099 Fax 01159 123419

Short diploma courses for leisure or for starting a business: Interior Design, Soft Furnishings, Designer Curtain Making and Decorative Paint Finishes.

Rhodec International
Principal: Michael Dwyer
35 East Street, Brighton, East Sussex BN1 1HL
Tel 01273 327476 Fax 01273 821 668

Interior Design distance-learning courses: One year Associate Diploma course leading to credits towards full three year Diploma. Diplomates may submit a 10,000 word thesis to the American University in London to validate to Bachelor of Arts in Interior Design. Accredited by the Open and Distance Learning Quality Council; recognised by the Interior Decorators and Designers Association.

GLOSSARY

The fabric glossary, including linings, buckrams, weaves and patterns is on pp 76-91.

ALLOWANCE - A measurement which has to be added in order to turn in the fabric neatly at the seams, hems or headings.

ARCHITRAVE - The wooden surround to a door or window frame.

BATTEN - A narrow length of wood.

COLOURWAY - One of many combinations of colours in a print.

CONTRAST BINDING - Strips of contrasting fabric sewn onto the edges for decorative effect.

CORNICE AND COVING - Decorative or curved moulding where the wall meets the ceiling.

CORONA - A semicircular fitting used to hang curtains above a bed.

CUT DROP - The cut length of fabric. It is the finished length of the curtain or top with turning allowances added at the top and hem.

CUT DIAMETER - The cut size of a round table cloth. The finished size with a turning allowance added all round.

DROP PATTERN REPEAT- The measurement of a pattern which repeats itself diagonally across the width.

ESS HOOK - A figure of eight hook to extend the curtain length. It adds a link between the track eye and the curtain hook.

FABRIC COVERED LATH A narrow pelmet board with a fabric covered buckram fascia to conceal the curtain track.

FINIAL - A round or pointed shape, screwed into a curtain pole at both ends to contain the rings.

FINISHED LENGTH OF THE CURTAIN - The length of the curtain when ready to hang.

FULLNESS RATIO - The relationship between the track or pelmet board measurement and the width of the ungathered curtain or valance.

Fullness ratios range from 1.5 times fullness to 3 times fullness depending on the heading.

GRAIN LINE - The direction of threads on woven fabrics

HALF-TESTER - A rectangular pelmet board or curtain rail above a bed.

HEADING - The way the the top of a curtain, etc. is finished.

HOOK TO FLOOR/SILL - The measurement from the eye of the track or pole ring to the floor/sill.

HOOK TO HEM - The measurement from the top of the hook to the bottom of the curtain.

HOOK TO TOP - The measurement from the top of the hook to the top of the finished curtain.

LAMBREQUIN - A pelmet with deep sides which can extend to the floor.

LEADING EDGE - The edge of the curtain facing into the centre of the window as opposed to the outside edge.

LOOSE LINED CURTAIN- Has a detachable lining so that curtain and lining can be washed separately. Not often used.

OMBRA - A decorative round fitting with a stem to fix it to the wall; used to hold the curtains open.

ONE-WAY DESIGN - Has a directional pattern or weave going only one way.

OVERLAP ARMS - Extentions of corded tracks which let the curtains cross over at the centre.

OVERLAP ALLOWANCE - Extra width to allow curtains to cross over, avoiding draughty gaps.

OVERLONG - Extra length to allow curtains to lie on the floor. Also called 'puddling'.

PATTERN REPEAT - The length of the pattern before it repeats itself.

PELMET - A fabric covered band of buckram or plywood which is fixed onto the front edge of a pelmet board. It conceals the curtain track and heading.

PELMET BOARD - A piece of planed timber fixed to the wall like a shelf, used to support a curtain track, valance, etc.

PIN HOOKS - Small metal hooks that are stabbed into the back of hand sewn headings.

PIPING - Cord sandwiched inside a strip of fabric, often in a contrasting colour, and inserted into a seam.

RETURN - The space between the front of the window treatment and the wall. This is covered to give a neat finish.

CURTAIN RETURN - The outside edge which turns the corner from the face of the track to the wall.

PELMET BOARD RETURN - The measurement from the front of the board to the wall, covered by the pelmet or valance return.

SELVEDGE - The woven side edges of fabric.

SOFFIT - The underside of the top of the window.

SPACERS - Small wood or plastic rings inserted between the underside of pelmet boards and tracks to create a gap for brackets or to lower curtains.

STACK BACK - The wall area at the side of the window covered by the curtain. The curtain 'stacks back' or folds into this area when opened.

STIFFENING - Stiff fabric used inside flat pelmets and tie-backs.

TESTER - A full canopy over a four-poster bed.

TOLERANCE - An extra measurement added to the finished width of curtain for ease of movement.

TRACK - A metal or plastic rail from which the curtains are hung from gliders.

TRUE CROSS OF THE GRAIN - A line at 45° to the selvedge on fabric.

VALANCE - A gathered band of fabric hung from the front edge of a pelmet board or valance rail. It hides the track and curtain heading. A valance is the fabric equivalent of a pelmet and serves the same purpose.

WINDOW RECESS - The area inside the reveal of the window where blinds and sheer curtains can be fitted.

INDEX

ACKNOWLEDGEMENTS
Thanks to the following for their help and support:
David Chapman of Nottingham Braid Company; *passementerie*
Hallis Hudson; *roller blind kits and fabric information*
Cope and Timmins; *curtain poles and accessories*
Integra; *tracks*
Silent Gliss; *tracks*
Edward Harpley; *curtain poles and cornice boxes*
Jones & Co; *curtain and blind tapes*
Mike Spencer of The Association of Master Upholsterers
Coats Threads Ltd; *technical information*
Rufflette; *curtain and heading tapes*
Paul Battle of F R Streets; *technical information*
Slumbers Baltimore Co Cork; *shower curtains*
John Sellars & Co; *curtain workroom supplies*
Derek Stamper of The Scunthorpe Sewing Centre

For Fabric Glossary Acknowledgements for swatches and technical information:
Abbot & Boyd
GP & J Baker
Designers Guild
Turnell & Gigon
Zoffany